Third Edition

bju press®
Greenville, South Carolina

This textbook was written by members of the faculty and staff of Bob Jones University. Standing for the "old-time religion" and the absolute authority of the Bible since 1927, Bob Jones University is the world's leading fundamental Christian university. The staff of the University is devoted to educating Christian men and women to be servants of Jesus Christ in all walks of life.

Providing unparalleled academic excellence, Bob Jones University offers over 60 undergraduate programs with dozens of concentrations and over 30 graduate programs, while its fervent spiritual emphasis prepares the minds and hearts of students for service and devotion to the Lord Jesus Christ.

If you would like more information about the spiritual and academic opportunities available at Bob Jones University, please call ***1-800-BJ-AND-ME (1-800-252-6363). www.bju.edu***

Science 5
Third Edition

Coordinating Author
Joyce Garland

Authors
Peggy S. Alier
Janet E. Snow

Contributing Authors
Eileen M. Berry
Verne Biddle
Donald Jacobs
Jocelyn Loucks
Dawn L. Watkins

Project Editor
Naomi Viola

Design Coordinator
Aaron Dickey

Consultants
Brad R. Batdorf
R. Terrance Egolf
Thomas E. Porch
Sherri Vick

Compositor
Octavo Design and Production, Inc.

Project Manager
Dan Woodhull

Cover Design
John Bjerk
Elly Kalagayan

Photo Acquisition
Susan Perry

3-D Illustrators
Chris Davis
Nathan Freeman

Illustrators
Paula Cheadle
Courtney Godbey
Preston Gravely
Amber Cheadle Lindsey
Caroline G. Lott
Sarah Lyons
Kara Moore
Kathy Pflug
John Roberts
Dave Schuppert

Produced in cooperation with the Bob Jones University School of Education and Bob Jones Elementary School.

Photograph credits appear on pages 319–21.

Greenville, South Carolina 29614

ISBN 978-1-60682-184-8

15 14 13 12 11 10 9 8 7 6 5 4 3

CONGRATULATIONS

Your search for the very best educational materials available has been completely successful! You have a textbook that is the culmination of decades of research, experience, prayer, and creative energy.

The facts

Nothing overlooked. Revised and updated. Facts are used as a springboard to stimulate thoughtful questions and guide students to broader applications.

The foundation

Nothing to conflict with Truth and everything to support it. Truth is the pathway as well as the destination.

The fun

Nothing boring about this textbook! Student (and teacher) might even forget it's a textbook! Brimming with interesting extras and sparkling with color!

Table of Contents

UNIT 1 Out of the Earth 1

Chapter 1 — Minerals and Rocks 3

Chapter 2 — Fossils and Dinosaurs 29

UNIT 2 From the Beginning 53

Chapter 3 — Matter 55

Chapter 4 — Energy and Heat 83

UNIT 3 Because of the Climate 109

Chapter 5 — Weather 111

Chapter 6 — Biomes 139

UNIT 4 In Perfect Balance 167

Chapter 7 — Interactions in an Ecosystem 169

Chapter 8 — Changes in an Ecosystem 191

UNIT 5 By Waves of Energy 213

Chapter 9 — Sound 215

Chapter 10 — Light 235

UNIT 6 Inside the Body 259

Chapter 11 — Respiratory System 261

Chapter 12 — Circulatory System 281

Glossary 305

Index 314

Out of the Earth

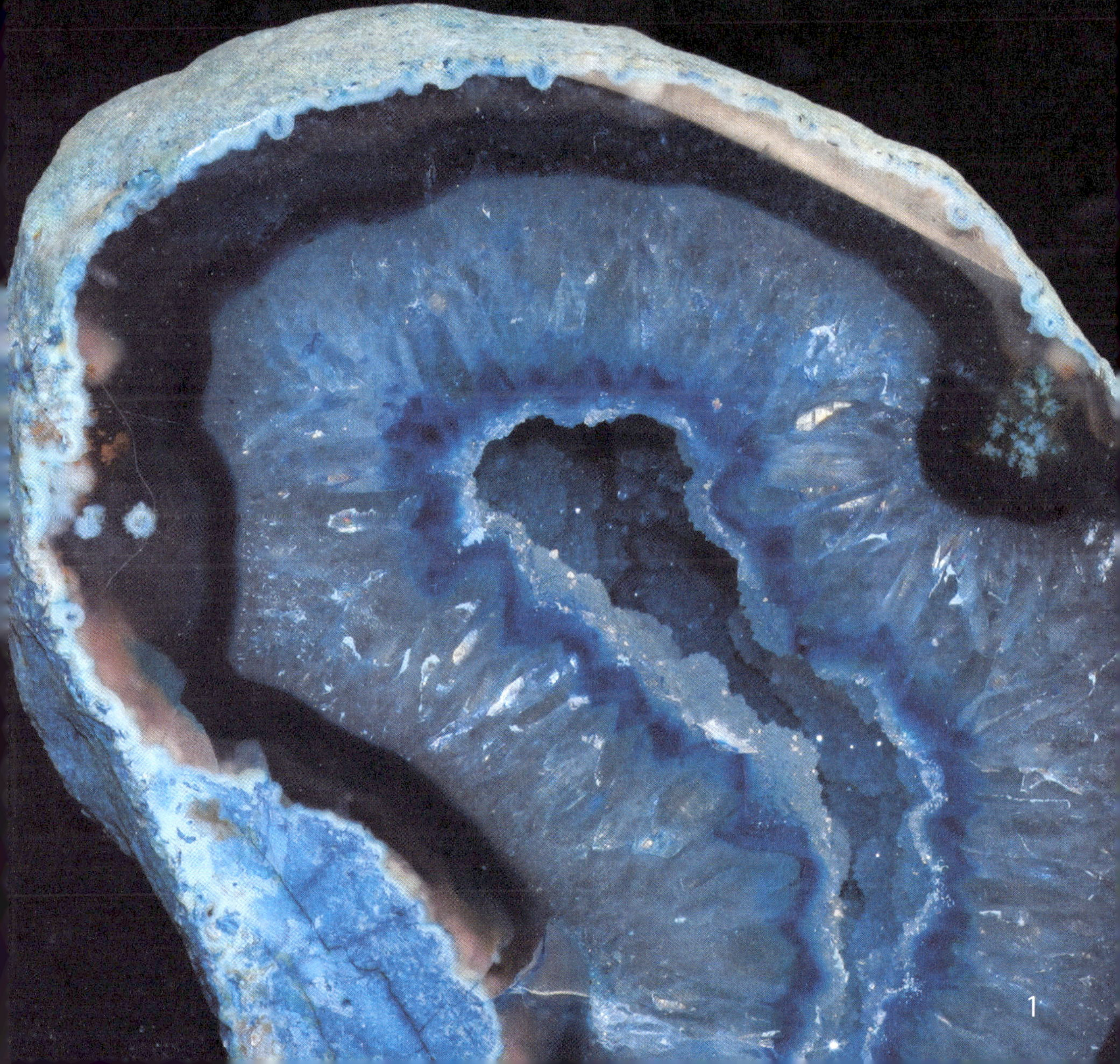

Flowers, vegetables, and trees all grow. Animals and people also grow. But not everything that "grows" is alive. In Chapter 1 find out about something that can "grow" quite large but is not alive.

History records many stories of dragons. The Bible also speaks of dragons. Chapter 2 tells what these unusual creatures may have been.

There are books for reading and books for writing. Find out in Chapter 1 about a "book" that can have pages so thin that you can see through them.

Minerals and Rocks

REMEMBER *now* thy CREATOR

Man's knowledge of science is constantly changing and expanding. As man studies God's creation, he learns more about the world. Man can then use this knowledge to design better forms of technology. Man cannot create as God can, though. Man's designs are only a reflection of the properties and principles that God established.

Many types of modern technology use computers. Computers, in turn, rely on the properties of certain minerals to function. Man applies his knowledge about these properties to design the computers. But God made the minerals and gave them the properties that make them useful. The Bible, in Ecclesiastes 12:1, says to "remember now thy Creator." God wants us to honor Him as the Creator. We should praise Him for His wisdom and His care for us in the design of our world.

Sometimes children try to dig holes that are deep enough to come out on the other side of the earth. But children are not the only ones who find this feat impossible. Even scientists with the most advanced equipment have not been able to dig through the earth. Much of what scientists think about the inside of the earth comes from their observations of events near the earth's surface. Events such as volcanoes and earthquakes give scientists a glimpse of what lies hidden beneath.

Layers of the Earth

Geologists (jee OL uh jists), scientists who study the nonliving parts of the earth, divide the earth into layers. Each layer has characteristics that are different from the other layers. The three main layers of the earth are the core, the mantle, and the crust.

The **core** is the center of the earth. Scientists believe that the core is very hot and under extreme pressure. They think that the inner part of the core is a solid, dense sphere made mostly of iron. Scientists also believe that there is an outer part of the core that is liquid.

The middle layer of the earth is called the **mantle**. This large area surrounds the core and makes up most of the earth's mass. The mantle is

Layers of the Earth

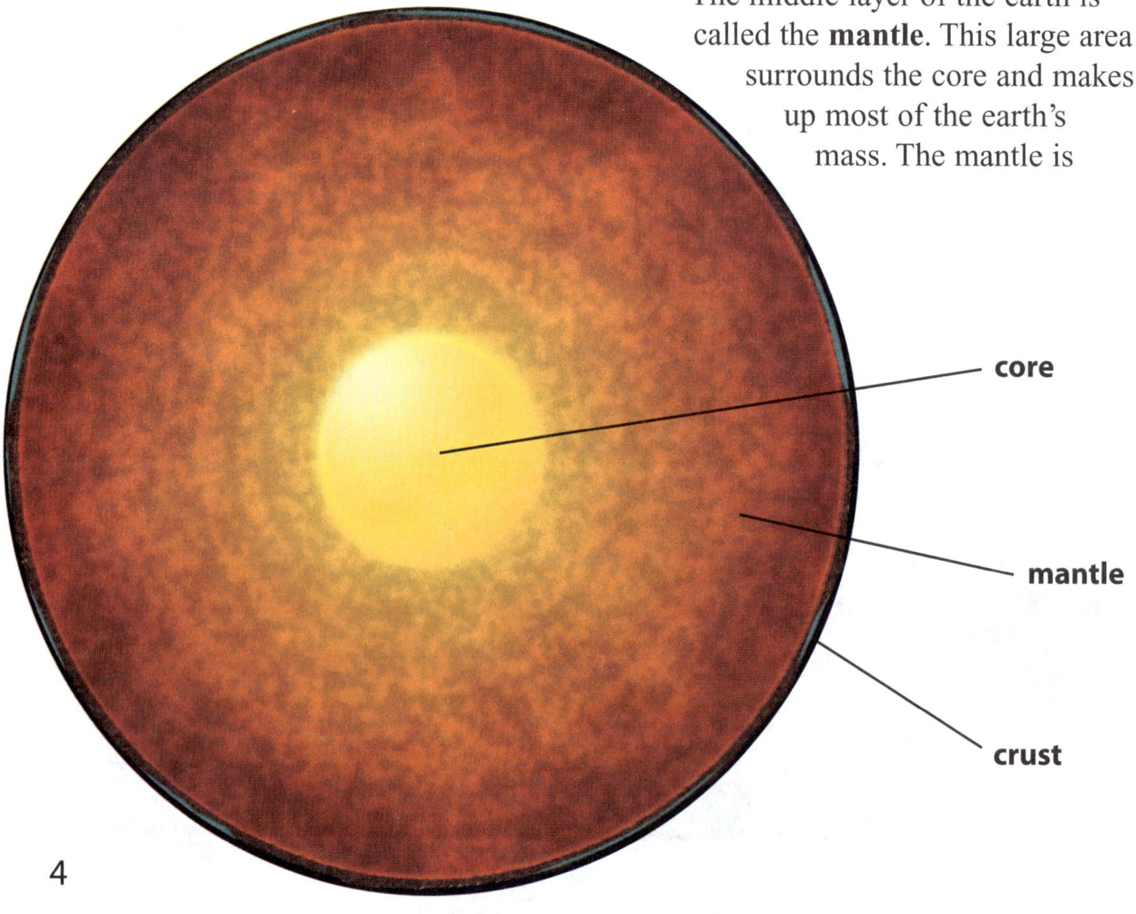

core

mantle

crust

made of hot, melted rock known as **magma**. Movements under the surface of the earth sometimes push the magma toward the surface. The places where magma comes through cracks in the earth's surface are called *volcanoes*. The magma that reaches the surface is known as *lava*.

The outer layer of the earth is called the **crust**. This thin layer is only about 7 to 45 km (4 to 28 mi) thick. The crust under the oceans is thinner than the crust under the continents is.

Some scientists believe that the earth's crust is not one solid sheet of rock. Instead, they believe that the crust is made of many pieces. These pieces, called plates, rest on the mantle. Changes in the liquid magma of the mantle may cause areas of the crust to move. Volcanoes and earthquakes sometimes result from these movements.

Meet the SCIENTIST BENO GUTENBERG

Beno Gutenberg (GOOT in BURG) was born in Germany in 1889 to Jewish parents. His father wanted him to work in the soap factory that the family owned. But Gutenberg was more interested in seismology, the study of earthquakes.

As a young man, Gutenberg worked as a scientist in Germany. After World War I, he worked many different jobs. Even with several jobs, though, he could not earn enough money to live on. Finally, in 1930, he was offered a job in California. There, he was at last able to experience the earthquakes he had spent years studying. During World War II, he helped Jewish scientists escape from Germany.

Gutenberg is famous for the methods he used to measure distances and substances inside the earth. In fact, he is known for being the first to determine the size of the earth's core. He also worked with Charles Richter to develop the scale used to measure earthquakes. Gutenberg died in 1960.

Surface of the Earth

God spoke and the earth was created. Genesis 1:9–10 tells us that God gathered the waters together to form dry land. This land includes the rocks, minerals, and soil.

Since the Fall of man, the earth has been aging and the crust has been wearing away. This wearing away of the earth is called *weathering*. Weathering produces **sediment** (SED uh mint), or small bits of weathered rock. This sediment does not usually stay in one place, though. Wind and water often pick up the sediment and move it. The movement of sediment from one place to another is known as *erosion* (eh RO zhuhn). Sometimes the sediment settles at the bottom of bodies of water. In time the sediment may form new rock.

The Flood that happened in Noah's time caused the crust of the earth to change a lot. Some of the rocks and mountains were quickly worn away by the moving water. This weathering and erosion caused many landforms such as canyons, mesas, and caverns to form.

Today, weathering and erosion continue to wear away the surface of the earth. However, there is no danger of the earth wearing completely away. Pressures within the earth continue to expose new rock. The new rock is pushed upward by earthquakes and volcanoes.

San Juan River, Utah

Monument Valley, Utah

Cheddar Gorge, Somerset, England

God planned for the land to supply the food and shelter needed by plants, animals, and people. Part of God's plan for supplying these needs is the continuing formation of soil. **Soil** is the loose material on the surface of the earth. Soil is made of bits of weathered rock and other materials. Some particles in soil are **organic** (or GAN ik), meaning these particles were once part of a living thing. Organic particles in the soil are called *humus* (HYOO muhs). Humus forms from decayed plants and animals.

Soil forms in layers, much like the layers of the earth itself. Plants usually grow in the top layer of soil, called *topsoil*. The moisture and humus in this fertile layer supply the nutrients that many plants need. The particles in each soil layer are larger as they get farther from the surface. The lower layers of soil are made mostly of pieces of rock.

God has given us the job of caring for the earth. Part of this job is to use the soil wisely. We must be careful not to cause conditions in which soil and rocks erode too quickly. By being careful, we wisely use and manage the resources that God provides for us.

✓ QUICK CHECK

1. Name the three main layers of the earth.
2. What is sediment?
3. What is soil?

Minerals in the Earth

Each layer of the earth contains minerals. A **mineral** (MIN uhr ul) is an inorganic substance found naturally in the earth. An **inorganic** substance is made of things that have never been alive. Most minerals that make up the earth's crust are solid parts of rock.

Minerals are not just found in the earth. They are also found in you! When God created man, He formed Adam's body from the dust of the ground (Genesis 2:7). God designed your body to use minerals to grow and function properly. The minerals in your body and in the food that you eat are the same as the minerals in the ground.

Characteristics of Minerals

The earth contains thousands of minerals. Many look very similar to one another. Scientists who study minerals are called *mineralogists* (MIN uhr OL uh jists). They work with mineral pieces called *samples*. Mineralogists identify mineral samples by their unique characteristics. Some of the characteristics of minerals are crystal structure, color, luster, hardness, and cleavage.

Crystal structure

All minerals have a crystal structure. Heat and pressure cause substances within the earth to combine. When this happens, crystals often form. A **crystal** (KRIS tull) results from the orderly arrangement of the particles that make up the mineral. Some crystals, such as those of diamonds, are very beautiful.

Most mineral crystals have straight sides and sharp corners or edges. However, some crystals, such as the desert rose, form in rounded shapes that resemble a flower. The sizes of crystals vary. Because a mineral hardens as it connects to the parts of a crystal that have already formed, the crystal seems to "grow."

desert rose

The largest crystals often result from minerals that harden slowly. Pockets of softer materials or air provide the space needed for large crystals to form. A mineral that forms and hardens quickly usually has small, tightly packed crystals. If a mineral hardens very quickly, it may not have time to develop any crystals.

The substance that forms a crystal determines the number and shape of the sides of a crystal. This means that each mineral has its own crystal structure. God has made our world a very orderly place. This order allows man to use these predictable structures to identify minerals.

All minerals have a crystal structure, but not all crystals are minerals. Other substances can also form crystals. For example, the sugar that you eat is not a mineral. Sugar is made from plants. Yet if you look carefully at a piece of sugar, you can see its crystals.

When you study mineral crystals, you are studying geology. However, you are also studying geometry. The flat sides, or faces, of crystals, are geometric shapes. Different crystals have faces in different geometric shapes. Diamonds, for instance, have faces that are all square in shape. These square faces give the crystal a cube shape. Other faces of crystals vary in shape. A quartz crystal, for example, looks like a column. It has two faces that are hexagons. The other six faces are rectangles that connect the two hexagons.

A mineral crystal keeps adding molecules in its same geometric pattern unless something keeps it from growing in that pattern. Often, crystals grow into each other. The mineral may look like a jumble of crystals. But if you look at a single crystal, you can see the geometric pattern. The crystals are an example of God's order and design in the earth.

amethyst

smoky quartz

rose quartz

Color and streak

A mineral may be identified by its color. The **color** of a mineral is the color that you see. Impurities, such as dirt or other particles, can cause a wide range of colors in minerals. For instance, amethyst, smoky quartz (KWORTS), and rose quartz are all types of quartz, but each is a different color.

Some minerals look the same and are hard to tell apart. For example, gold and pyrite (PIE right) are about the same color. In fact, they look so much alike that pyrite is called fool's gold. When minerals look alike, mineralogists may use *streak tests*.

The **streak** is the color of the mark that is made when a sample is rubbed on a harder surface. The hard surface causes small bits or powder from the mineral to rub off. A piece of white porcelain or ceramic tile is often used to test the streak color of minerals.

The color of the streak left by a sample may help identify a mineral. Some minerals leave a streak that is a different color from the color of the mineral. Gold and pyrite are similar in color, but their streak tests are quite different. Gold leaves a yellow-gold streak. Pyrite, on the other hand, leaves a greenish-black streak.

The mineral *hematite* (HEE muh TITE) has a black color but a red streak.

Luster

The **luster** of a mineral is the way that it reflects light. A variety of terms are used to describe the luster of minerals. The mineral cinnabar (SIN uh bar) has a *dull* luster. Very little light reflects from the mineral's surface.

cinnabar

Both gold and pyrite have a *metallic* luster. A metallic luster is shiny, almost like a piece of aluminum foil.

pyrite

An opal has a *pearly* luster. This means that the mineral looks similar to the inside of some shells. Colors of light often reflect from the surface of a mineral with a pearly luster.

opal

A diamond has a *brilliant* luster. Light and colors appear to bounce on the outside and the inside of a carefully cut diamond. The light and colors cause the diamond to sparkle. Minerals that can be cut and polished to a brilliant, or high, luster are often used in jewelry.

diamond

Hardness

The **hardness** of a mineral refers to how easily it resists scratching. Soft minerals may be easily scratched with a fingernail. But some minerals are so hard that they cannot be cut with steel. They must be cut by tools made from even harder materials.

In the early 1800s, a German mineralogist by the name of Friedrich Mohs (MOHZ) developed a scale to compare the hardness of minerals. The Mohs scale is still used today. The scale ranks minerals by how hard they are.

A scratch test may be done to determine how hard a mineral is. In a scratch test, the mineral sample is scratched with a substance shown on the Mohs scale. The sample's hardness is decided by which substance can scratch the sample. For example, a sample of iron may be tested with feldspar and then with fluorite (FLOOR ite). The feldspar scratches the iron, but the fluorite does not. This means that iron has a hardness of about 5 on the Mohs scale.

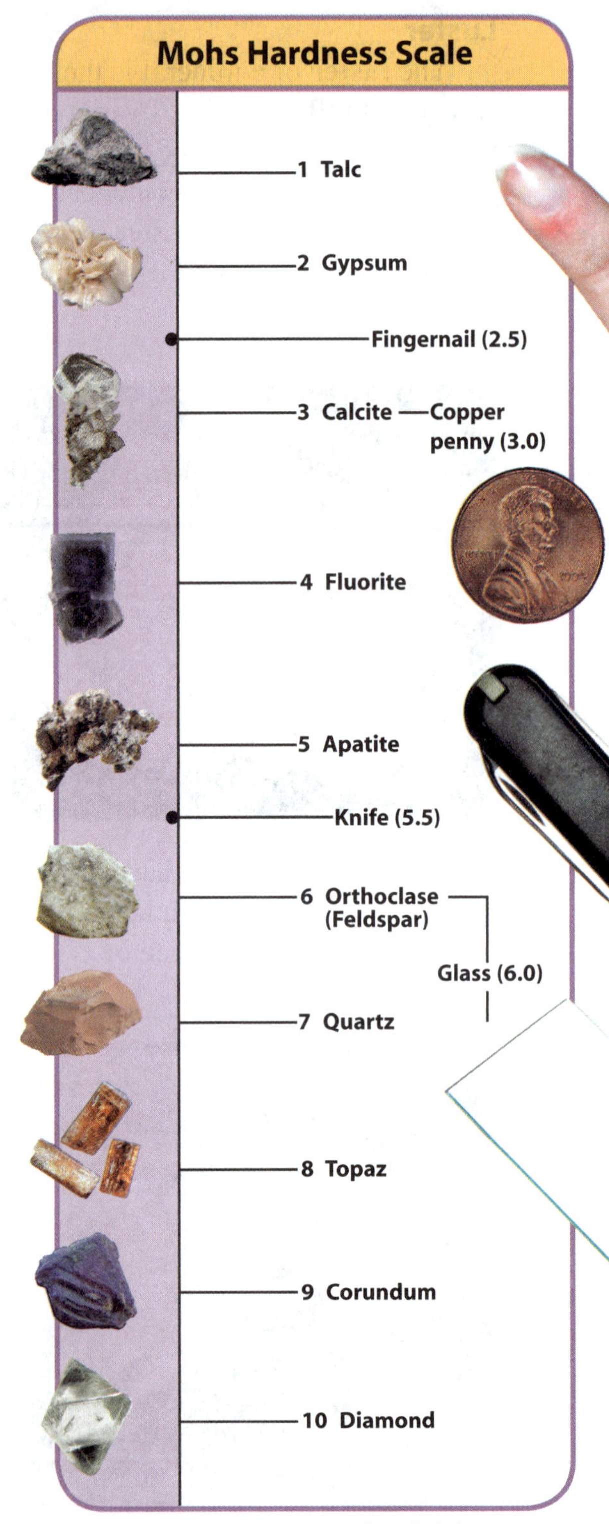

The Mohs scale shows minerals from the softest (1) to the hardest (10). In a scratch test, a harder substance scratches a softer one.

corundum (ruby): Image by Alain Darbellay courtesy of GGGems.com

This arrangement of sheets of mica is called a book.

Cleavage and fracture

Different minerals break in different ways. One way that some minerals break is called cleavage. **Cleavage** (KLEE vij) is the breaking of a mineral along smooth, straight lines or into flat sheets. Many of the minerals used in jewelry have cleavage. People use this characteristic to cut the minerals into beautiful shapes.

Some minerals with cleavage will break into geometric shapes. The smaller, broken pieces of some of these minerals are shaped like the original piece. For example, the crystals of halite, or rock salt, are shaped like cubes. When broken, halite cleaves into smaller cubes that look like the original.

Halite cleaves into small cubes.

Mica (MY kuh) has a different type of cleavage. It does not break into cubes or other geometric shapes. Instead, this mineral peels easily into thin layers, or sheets. Some of the sheets are so thin that you can see through them.

Not all minerals have cleavage, however. Some minerals, such as quartz, do not break along straight lines. Quartz breaks unevenly in many directions. This type of breaking is called *fracture*. The fracture of some minerals is rough and jagged. Other minerals break along curved lines. Some minerals have fractures that look fuzzy or like thin threads.

The mineral asbestos has thin, fiberlike crystals.

1. What is a mineral?
2. What are five characteristics that mineralogists can use to identify minerals?
3. Scratching a sample with other minerals or substances is a test for which characteristic?

ACTIVITY

Salty Crystals

Some minerals form into beautiful, large crystals. Others have clusters of tiny crystals or no crystals at all. Some crystals form slowly; others form quickly. Temperature and time are some factors, or conditions, that can affect how crystals form.

In this activity, you will observe how crystals form under different conditions.

Process skills
- Measuring
- Experimenting
- Observing
- Identifying and controlling variables
- Collecting, recording, and interpreting data

Problem

How do temperature and light affect the size of crystals?

Procedure

Materials:
- 100 mL water
- metric measuring cups
- saucepan
- food coloring
- 200 mL Epsom salts
- large spoon
- hot plate
- potholder
- 2 sturdy bowls
- 600 g pebbles
- balance (mass scale)
- Activity Manual

1. Complete the sentence in your Activity Manual that tells how you think the Problem will be answered.
2. Measure 100 mL of water and pour it into the saucepan. Add several drops of food coloring.
3. Measure 200 mL of Epsom salts. Stir the salt into the water.
4. Place the saucepan on the hot plate. Heat and stir until you cannot see the salt. The water does not have to boil. Remove the saucepan from the heat.
5. Label one bowl with the number *1* and the other bowl with the number *2*. Measure and pile 300 g of pebbles in the center of each bowl.

6. Choose a cool, dark location to place bowl 1. Record this location in your Activity Manual.
7. Choose a warm, bright location to place bowl 2. Record this location in your Activity Manual.

8. Stir the salt water. Measure 100 mL of the salt water into each bowl. Try to wet the pebbles with the water as you pour. Make sure that some wet pebbles remain above the level of the water.
9. Place the bowls in the locations that you chose.
10. Observe and record the appearance of the salt water for seven days.

Conclusions

- Did crystals form? If so, which bowl had the larger crystals?
- What characteristics in the different environments do you think affected the formation of the crystals?

Follow-up

- Compare the crystal formation of salt water placed in other locations such as outside or near a fan, an air vent, or an open window.
- Compare the crystal formation of other minerals such as alum or table salt.

Uses of Minerals

Man has found many uses for the minerals that God placed on and in the earth. Some minerals, such as those used in jewelry, provide beauty and pleasure. The minerals used in glass and building materials help provide shelter. Many minerals, such as those used in lasers and other machinery, help make our lives easier. The minerals in food strengthen our bodies.

Gemstones

Some minerals form beautifully colored crystals that reflect light. A mineral that can be cut and polished for use is called a **gemstone**. Once it is cut and polished, it is called a gem. Gems are often used in jewelry.

Some gemstones are rare, or hard to find. A rare one is worth more money than common ones are. A *precious stone* is a gemstone that is beautiful and rare. Some examples of precious stones are diamonds, rubies, sapphires, and emeralds. Large precious stones that do not have impurities are extremely valuable. In fact, many of the larger precious stones are too valuable to wear. These gems are usually placed on display in museums. There they are safe, and people can enjoy their beauty.

Semiprecious stones are more common, or easier to find, than precious stones are. Though not worth as much money, semiprecious stones are still very beautiful. Some kinds of semiprecious stones are amethysts (AM uh thists), garnets, opals, turquoise (TUR KWOIZ), and jade. These stones are often used in jewelry.

For centuries, people have carved stones such as turquoise and jade. These stones have been used in sculptures, ornaments, and even the handles of weapons. Turquoise can be found in the western part of the United States. Turquoise is usually a beautiful blue-green color. Green is the most common color of jade. However, the stone is also found in a variety of other colors. Jade is mostly found in the Orient in places such as China.

jade figures

Science and the BIBLE

God created minerals, such as precious stones and gold, for our enjoyment and use. These minerals are of great value. But no amount of gold, silver, or precious stones could purchase the salvation of a single soul. In 1 Peter 1:18–19 the Bible tells us that man is "not redeemed with corruptible things, as silver and gold . . . But with the precious blood of Christ." Only Christ's blood and sacrifice could pay the penalty for man's sin and redeem him to God.

Real gemstones form naturally in the earth. But scientists have developed ways to copy this formation in a laboratory. As a result, many gems have a **synthetic** (sin THET ik), or man-made, version. Synthetic gems may look very much like the real gems but are not as valuable. Cubic zirconia is a synthetic gem. It looks like a diamond and is sometimes used in jewelry in place of the more expensive diamond.

Gemstones are used in more than just jewelry and art, though. Some gemstones are not only beautiful but are also very strong. Diamonds and rubies are the strongest and hardest minerals and can cut many other substances. Chips of these gemstones are added to the drill bits or saw blades of some tools. These kinds of tools are used to cut very hard materials, such as other gemstones and rocks. Diamonds and rubies are also used inside some watches. The gemstones help the gears of the watches move smoothly and last longer.

diamond

cubic zirconia

Rhinestones are used in jewelry and in decorating clothing. In the past, these clear, sparkling stones were cut from rock crystal, a type of clear quartz. Today, most rhinestones are made from glass, a synthetic material.

Metals

Some minerals are also metals. Metals are usually found in rocks called *ores*. Sometimes, to remove the metal from the ore, the ore is crushed and then heated. The extreme heat causes the metal to melt and separate from the other rock materials. This process is called *smelting*.

Metals have several properties that make them very useful to man. Most metals are strong but are still easy to shape or bend. Some soft metals such as gold, silver, and copper are used to make jewelry and sculptures. Most metals also conduct electricity. One metal that conducts electricity especially well is copper. In fact, the wires in your house are probably made of copper.

copper wire

Titanium (ti TAY nee uhm) and aluminum (uh LOO mi nuhm) are two metals that are strong but do not weigh much. Most airplanes and spacecrafts have parts made of titanium. Aluminum is very common. It is often used to make containers, such as those used for canned drinks.

Melted metals can be poured into molds. Early settlers used molds to form musket balls and cannonballs. Even now, many items are formed in this way. Parts of many pots, pans, cars, nails, and tools are made from molded metals.

Sometimes metals are combined to increase their strength or change other properties. Steel is an example of a mixture of metals. Iron is melted with other metals to form different kinds of steel. The different metals determine what kind of properties the steel has. Different kinds of steel are used in things such as buildings and cars.

Many metals can be hammered or flattened into thin sheets. These thin sheets are then used in items such as file cabinets, shelves, and toys.

Since Bible times, craftsmen have skillfully hammered gold into thin sheets. These sheets, known today as gold leaf, can be used to cover wood, stone, or other metals. In 2 Chronicles 3 the Bible tells of how gold covered many wooden parts of the temple.

Other minerals

Gemstones and metals are just some of the minerals we use. Each day, we also use many other minerals. Common minerals such as calcite and sulfur are sometimes added to fertilizers. Gypsum (JIP suhm) is used in making dry wall. Dry wall sheets form the inside walls of most houses. Fluorite is used in both toothpaste and pottery. Mica has many common uses. It is added to paint and is used as an insulator for electronics. Mica also gives the shine and sparkle to some cosmetics. Quartz is an important part of electronic devices such as cell phones and televisions.

Many plastics, fabrics, and other substances that you use each day contain minerals. Glass is a blend of several minerals. Some foods, drinks, and medicines have minerals added to them. Even some daily vitamin pills include minerals.

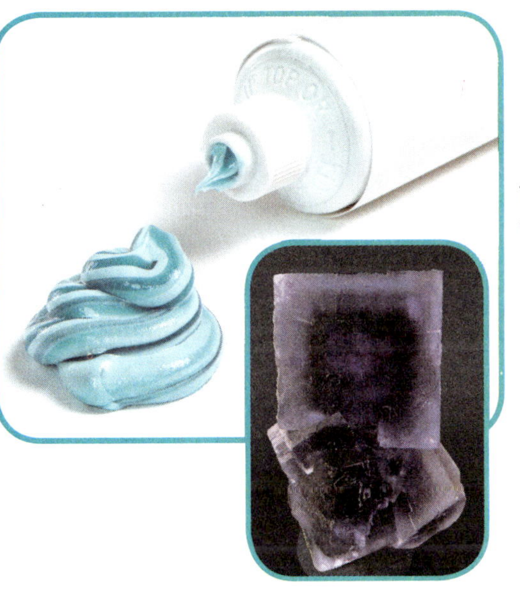

Toothpaste may contain the mineral fluorite.

fluorite

calcite

Fertilizer may contain the minerals calcite and sulfur.

sulfur

lapidary at work

Finding Minerals

Some minerals are found on the surface of the earth. Most minerals, however, are buried in the earth's crust. The mining industry digs to find and remove minerals and other usable materials from the earth.

The crust of the earth is made up of layers of soil and rock. In these layers mineral veins can form. A *vein* is a pocket or strip of a mineral within the earth. Some minerals also form in vertical cracks through the layers. A vertical vein that forms in the shaft of a volcano is called a *pipe*. Pipes often contain diamonds or other minerals that form deep in the layers of the earth's crust. Magma moving toward the surface pushes the diamonds upward through cracks in the earth's crust.

Most minerals cannot be used when they are first mined from the earth. They must be removed from any surrounding rock and ores. Then the minerals go through special processes to clean and sort them.

Even most gemstones do not sparkle and shine when they are first removed from the earth. Most look like ordinary, dull rocks. Gemstones must be handled with extra care. They are carefully cut by a person called a *lapidary* (LAP ih DARE ee). These skilled craftsmen know the best way to cut each type of gemstone to reveal the beauty hidden inside.

QUICK CHECK

1. What is a gemstone?
2. What term is used to identify a man-made gem?
3. What is a pocket or strip of a mineral inside other rock layers called?

Explorations Munching Minerals

God designed our bodies to use minerals. Our bodies get these minerals from the things that we eat and drink. Look at the label on a food package. Minerals are often listed on the nutrition label. Nutritionists (new TRISH uh nists) study the nutrients in foods and how these nutrients affect our bodies.

In this exploration, you are a nutritionist in training. Choose a mineral that has nutritional value. Research to find food and beverage sources of your mineral. Then research the ways that the mineral is beneficial to our bodies. Be prepared to discuss your findings with other nutritionists in training.

What to do

1. Choose a mineral from the list.
2. Research the mineral that you chose. Your report should include some foods and beverages in which your mineral is found. Also include the ways that God designed our bodies to use this mineral.
3. Display samples of foods or the labels of products that contain your mineral.
4. Prepare a one- to two-minute presentation of your findings.

calcium	**phosphorus**
chromium	**potassium**
copper	**selenium**
iron	**sodium**
magnesium	**sulfur**
manganese	**zinc**

Rocks

When you think of a rock, you probably think of something that is hard and not easy to break. Many rocks are also large and cannot be moved. Large rock formations do not seem to ever change.

The Bible uses rocks as examples of strength and reliability. In many verses in the Psalms, the writer calls God his Rock. Psalm 62:6 says, "He only is my rock and my salvation: he is my defence; I shall not be moved." Like a rock, God is strong and reliable. He is faithful to keep His Word.

A **rock** is a hard, natural substance made of one or more minerals. Rocks may also contain organic materials. Most rocks are found in the top 17 km (10 mi) of the earth's crust. Since rocks are usually a mixture of several minerals, many types of rocks exist. This makes classifying rocks only by mineral content or appearance very difficult. There would be almost as many categories as there are rocks. So geologists classify rocks according to how they form.

Igneous Rock

Igneous (IG nee us) rock forms from volcanic magma or lava. Magma is the very hot, melted rock under the surface of the earth. *Granite* forms from magma. The minerals in granite are quartz, feldspar, mica, and hornblende. The arrangement and color of the mineral crystals in the granite determines how it looks. Granite is very hard rock and can be polished to a smooth shine. Many statues and monuments are carved from granite.

granite

Lava is magma that comes out of the earth. Some lava looks like hot foam as it flows along the ground. As the foam cools, it hardens into a rock called *pumice* (PUM iss). The gases that were in the foam leave holes in the hardened rock. These holes make some pumice rocks so light that they can float on water! Some pumice rocks are the "stones" used to produce stone-washed denim. Pumice can also be used in landscaping or a gas grill.

pumice

Obsidian (ob SID ee uhn) is another type of rock that forms from lava. These rocks cool quickly. This gives little time for crystals to form. As a result the rock looks like shiny, black glass. Obsidian breaks into curved pieces with very sharp edges. For years Native Americans used obsidian to make arrowheads and other tools. Today some surgical instruments are made from sharp pieces of obsidian.

obsidian

Basalt columns can be clearly seen at the Giant's Causeway in Northern Ireland.

Most igneous rocks are very hard. One of the hardest kinds of igneous rock is *basalt* (buh SOLT). It often forms large, wide columns. These columns are tightly packed and usually have six sides. Basalt is often used for construction. Many of the old stone buildings and cobblestone streets in Europe are made from basalt rocks. Even after hundreds of years, they show very few signs of weathering.

Science and HISTORY

Ballast is any material used to balance the weight in ships. For hundreds of years, heavy rocks were added or removed from ships to make them heavier or lighter. Ballast rocks left at port cities were often used by the town as building materials. In fact, many of the cobblestone streets in port cities were made from discarded ballast rocks. Today water in special tanks is used as ballast in ships.

layers in sedimentary rock at Twelve Apostles, Australia

Sedimentary Rock

Sedimentary (SED uh MEN tuh ree) rock forms when layers of sediment and organic material harden. As water or wind move the particles, some of them settle into layers at the bottom of bodies of water. The layers of sediment are then pressed and cemented into rock. Most sedimentary rocks are not as strong as igneous rocks are.

Sandstone is a common sedimentary rock. The sediments that form it are usually similar in size. Some sedimentary rocks look like pebbles that have been cemented together. This type of rock is called a *conglomerate* (kuhn GLOM uh RATE).

conglomerate

Organic material can also settle and compress into the rock. *Coal* forms from decayed plant matter. Animal bones and shells are sources of the mineral *calcite*. Some rocks, such as *limestone* and *chalk*, are made almost completely of calcite. Calcite mixes easily with water. As a result, limestone and chalk weather easily.

Weathering and erosion has caused large pieces of rock to separate from the chalk cliffs at Dover, England.

Metamorphic Rock

Scientists believe that some igneous and sedimentary rocks change form while deep below the earth's surface. The changed rocks are called metamorphic rocks. **Metamorphic (MET uh MOR fik) rock** forms by heat and pressure deep below the earth's crust. The amount of heat or pressure affects the way the rocks change.

Some metamorphic rocks are *foliated* (FOE lee ATE ed). These rocks can split into flat sheets that easily break apart. Tremendous pressure squeezes the rocks to form the sheets. One type of foliated metamorphic rock is slate. *Slate* forms from a sedimentary rock called shale. When shale is exposed to additional heat and pressure, it changes to slate. This hard rock easily breaks apart into thin sheets. In the past slate was commonly used for chalkboards.

shale
slate

marble

Non-foliated metamorphic rocks do not break into thin sheets. Most of the time, these rocks have tightly packed crystals. An example of this type of rock is *marble*. Heat and pressure form marble from the sedimentary rock limestone. Marble often contains tiny crystals of various minerals. Sometimes these minerals form thin veins or swirled patterns in the rock. Marble is often used as a building material and for sculptures.

God created many kinds of rocks and minerals. Each can be used in many ways. Man is still learning about these rocks and minerals, though. As man studies them, he often finds even more ways to use these treasures buried in the earth.

1. What is a rock?
2. List the three main groups that geologists use to classify rocks.
3. What term is used to describe metamorphic rocks that can break apart into flat sheets?

Rock Hounding

ACTIVITY

No matter where you live, you will find rocks. Rocks are in yards. Rocks are in flower beds and gardens. Rocks are at the edges of roads. Rocks are in parks and at the bottoms of streams. A person who enjoys finding and collecting rocks is called a *rock hound*. A rock hound usually labels his rocks and records information about where each was found. The types of rocks are also identified when possible.

In this activity, you are the rock hound who finds, labels, and groups his rocks.

Process skills
- Observing
- Classifying
- Communicating
- Defining operationally

Materials:
- 10 different rocks
- correction fluid
- fine-tipped marker
- magnifying glass
- rock and mineral field guide (optional)
- Activity Manual

Purpose

Classify rocks.

Procedure—Part 1

1. Use correction fluid to make a white dot about the size of a pencil eraser on each rock. Number the rocks by writing on the dots with a fine-tipped marker.
2. Record in your Activity Manual the place where each rock was found.
3. Record the appearance of each rock. Describe its color(s) and features such as layers or stripes of color.
4. Record the texture of each rock.

. 5. Record any other features of the rock such as how the rock breaks.

Procedure—Part 2

. 6. Sort the rocks into two groups. Each group should share a similar characteristic. Write the characteristic of each group on the chart. List the numbers of the rocks that you placed in each group.

. 7. Choose the rocks in one of the two groups. Follow the same procedure as in Step 6.

Conclusions

- Did some rocks fit into more than one category? How did you choose where to place them?
- What other characteristics may be used to sort the ten rocks?
- How can you further divide one of the groups of rocks?

Follow-up

- Try to identify the minerals in each rock. Use pages 8–13 of your Student Text or the field guide.

Answer the Questions

1. A mineral is an inorganic substance found naturally in the earth. How is a mineral different from a rock?

2. Minerals are usually found under the surface of the earth. How could weathering and erosion help people find minerals?

3. Why would it be useful for a saw blade used for cutting gemstones to have diamonds on it?

Solve the Problem

Your friend shows you a small, shiny piece of yellowish rock that he found in a stream. He is sure that he has found gold. You, however, suspect that he has a piece of pyrite. What test could you do to determine whether the rock is gold or pyrite?

Fossils and Dinosaurs

2

REMEMBER now thy CREATOR

Technology built for one purpose is often used in other ways. For example, CT scanners produce 3-D images of the inside of the human body. But they also have a new use. CT scanners are now also being used to find and research fossils. The scanner can reveal the position of fossilized bones, even through layers of rock. This visual map helps the scientists see how best to remove the fossils.

Scientists also use a CT scanner to look inside fossils. The scanner makes a 3-D image of the inside of the fossil. A computer then allows that image to be viewed, measured, moved around, and evaluated. All this can be done without damaging the valuable fossil. Scientists are finding out many new things about fossils through these images. Tools like these help man find out even more about the amazing things that God created for His world.

Suppose that you are walking along the foot of a cliff one day, and you find some large animal bones lying on the ground. You pick up a bone and study it carefully. It is brown and hard—as hard as rock—and appears to be very old.

Several questions might come to your mind as you think about these bones. To what kind of animal did they belong? How did they become so hard and stony? What can they tell you about life on the earth? These are some of the same questions that scientists seek to answer when they study fossils.

Fossil Formation

A **fossil** (FOS uhl) is any part or trace of a living organism that is naturally preserved after it dies. Most fossils are found in sedimentary rock. These types of fossils form when organisms, or living things, are buried quickly beneath sediment. The softest parts of an organism usually **decompose**, or rot away, first. The harder parts are sometimes preserved as fossils. If not buried quickly, the organism would decompose completely.

The Bible tells us that, in the days of Noah, God judged the earth with a great Flood. The waters of the Flood would have caused great erosion. Huge amounts of sediment would have been formed in a short time. The sediment would have buried all creatures that were not safe in the ark. The fossils that we see today are clear evidence of this worldwide Flood.

petrified fossils

Fossils Preserved in Sediment

Many fossils are preserved parts of an animal or a plant. These fossils are usually the hardest parts of an animal, such as its bones, teeth, claws, shells, or tusks. Sometimes, as an animal's bone or the wood of a tree decays, it is slowly replaced by minerals. The minerals harden over time and form rock. Such fossils are called **petrified (PET ruh fide) fossils**.

Other fossils also show how an organism used to look, even though the organism has decomposed. This happens when an organism is pressed into the rock. As the organism decomposes, it leaves an empty space in the rock. This imprint of the organism in the rock is called a **mold**. If sediment fills in the empty space in the mold, a **cast** is formed. A cast is a copy of the shape of the organism.

Sometimes plants decay under the weight of sediment and leave an image of themselves in the rock. This dark image forms when parts of the plant turn to carbon. This kind of fossil is called a **carbon film**.

carbon film fossil

Fossils are not always part of a plant or animal itself. **Trace fossils** form from something that an organism left behind—such as a footprint, a hole where an animal lived, or its droppings. Trace fossils sometimes give scientists clues about how an organism lived. For example, fossilized footprints might show whether an animal walked upright on two feet or walked on all four feet. Fossils of droppings might reveal to scientists what an animal ate.

cast fossil

trace fossil

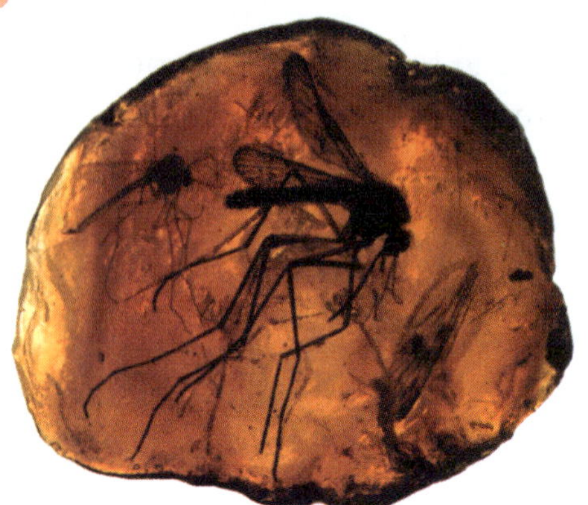

insect preserved in amber

Fossils Preserved in Other Materials

Not all plant and animal fossils are preserved in sediment. Sometimes plants or animals have been found preserved in amber. *Amber* is sap from a plant that has hardened into a yellow, gemlike substance. Insects are often fossilized in this way.

Fossils have also been found frozen in ice. In the far North, arctic animals have been found almost fully preserved. The woolly mammoth was a large, hairy animal that looked like an elephant. Woolly mammoths died many years ago. Within the last fifty years, however, scientists have dug mammoth fossils, complete with hair, out of glacier ice.

Tar can also preserve fossils. In some places thick crude oil oozes out of the earth and forms tar pits. Living things get trapped in the sticky tar and die. The tar then preserves them. Fossils of plants, insects, birds, and mammals have all been recovered from the Rancho La Brea Tar Pits in California. These tar pits even contained many fossils of animals such as the ground sloth, the ancient bison, and the saber-toothed cat.

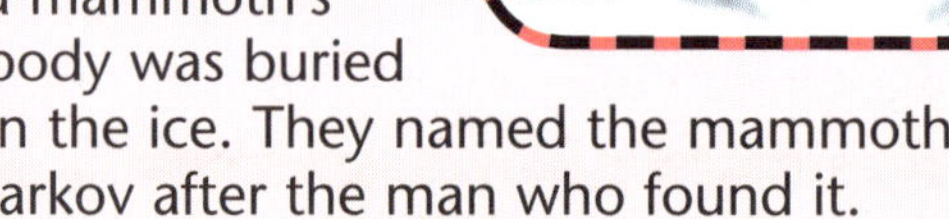

In 1997, a reindeer herder in Siberia noticed a tusk sticking out of the snowy tundra. Scientists explored the area and guessed that a mammoth's body was buried in the ice. They named the mammoth Jarkov after the man who found it.

In 1999, a helicopter airlifted the huge block of ice containing Jarkov to a cave. Scientists thawed the ice slowly with hair dryers to avoid damaging the mammoth. Although the mammoth's body was not as complete as they had hoped, it has continued to provide new information about the animal.

✓ QUICK CHECK

1. How did fossils found in sedimentary rock form?
2. What is formed when sediment fills in a mold?
3. What materials, other than sediment, have preserved plants and animals as fossils?

Two Ways of Looking at Fossils

Science is based on man's observations. But no one observed how fossils formed. People can look at the same fossils and have very different theories about how the fossils came to be. These theories are based on what the people believe about how the earth began.

Evolution

Most evolutionists (EV uh LOO shuhn ists) believe that the earth came into being by chance. They also claim that life on earth **evolved**, or developed gradually, over millions of years. They say that rock layers represent *geologic ages*, or long time periods. Books about fossils often use the names Jurassic, Cretaceous, and Triassic for these ages. According to the theory of evolution, the layer of rock in which a fossil is found reveals how old the fossil is.

Evolutionists say that early forms of life slowly changed into the life forms we see today. They try to support their theory by relating modern plants and animals to their "ancestors" in the fossil record.

Creation

Creationists (kree AY shuh nists) believe that God's Word in Genesis 1 explains the true origin of the earth. Genesis says that God created the earth and all forms of life in six days by His spoken word. Adam was created during this time. And if we trace life back to Adam, the earth could be only thousands of years old, not millions.

Creationists also accept what the Bible says in Genesis 6–8 about the Flood. They believe that it accounts for most of the fossils we find today. And as scientists continue to study the fossil record, it provides a wealth of evidence that God's Word is true.

1. What determines how a person looks at the fossil record?
2. What event accounts for the formation of most fossils, according to Creationists?

Fact or Theory?

Man makes judgments about the evidence of fossils based on his beliefs. A man who believes God's record of Creation and history will look at fossils in one way. A man who believes in evolution will view fossils in a different way.

When men write about fossils, especially fossils of dinosaurs, they usually will say things that show what they believe. Understanding what view a writer has is important. The Bible says that Christians should be discerning. That means that Christians should understand what is right and wrong.

In this activity, you will be given several books or articles to read. You must evaluate whether the writer is writing from an evolutionist viewpoint or Creationist viewpoint. Use the following chart to help you.

Process skills
- Inferring
- Collecting and interpreting data
- Communicating
- Defining operationally

Materials:
5 books or articles about fossils or dinosaurs
Activity Manual

Creationist Viewpoint	Evolutionist Viewpoint
God created the heavens and the earth.	Earth and space are a result of a sudden explosion.
The earth is thousands of years old.	The earth is millions of years old.
Fossils are probably a result of the great Flood recorded in the Bible.	Fossils show the great geologic ages of the earth.
God created all the kinds of animals in the beginning.	Different kinds of life have gradually evolved over long periods of time.
Man is God's special creation. He is different from the animals because he is created in God's image.	Man is the highest level of animal.

Purpose

Evaluate viewpoints in books or articles.

Procedure

 1. Choose one of the books or articles. Record the title in the chart in your Activity Manual.

 2. Skim through the book or article. Look for examples of the author's viewpoint. Record one of these examples in the chart.

 3. Repeat steps 1–2 for four more books or articles.

Conclusions

- Which viewpoint did you find more often?
- From which viewpoint is your *Science 5* Student Text written?

Follow-up

- Whenever you read a science book or article, keep a record of examples of the writer's viewpoint.

Molds and Casts

Process skills
- Making and using models
- Observing
- Inferring

There are many different types of fossils. One type of fossil looks like an imprint pressed into rock. Another type looks like actual bones or plant parts that have hardened and turned into stone. Details found in and on these and other fossil types can help scientists determine what life may have been like in the past.

In this activity, you will make two types of "fossils." Then you will examine them for information.

Purpose

Model fossils.

Procedure—Part 1

1. Draw a line around one cup about 5 cm from the top. Cut along the line. Set the bottom part of the cup aside for use in step 6.
2. Place the ring part of the cup on the foam plate. Press a 2 cm layer of clay into the ring. Press the clay tightly against the sides of the ring. Smooth the surface as much as possible.
3. Choose an object. Press the object into the clay and carefully remove it. Wipe any clay from the object.
4. Measure 200 mL of plaster powder and pour it into the other cup.
5. Measure 100 mL of water. Stir the water into the plaster powder. Mix so that there are no lumps. It should be thick like pudding. Pour about half of the plaster into a 2 cm layer over the clay.

Materials:
- 2 foam cups, 16 oz
- centimeter ruler
- scissors
- foam plate
- modeling clay
- assorted hard objects such as seashells, split wood, nuts, pinecones, or plastic dinosaurs or bugs
- 200 mL plaster of Paris
- 100 mL water
- metric measuring cups
- spoon
- magnifying glass
- Activity Manual

6. Pour the remaining plaster into the bottom part of the first cup. Smooth the surface with the spoon.
7. Wait five minutes and press the object into the wet plaster in the cup bottom. Wait another five minutes and remove the object. The plaster should keep the shape of the object. If the plaster is too soft, press the object back into the plaster and wait one minute more. Make sure the object is removed before the plaster becomes too hard.
8. Let the plaster set overnight.

Procedure—Part 2

9. Peel away the cups and clay from the plaster pieces. Wipe away any clay. The plaster pieces are your fossils.
10. Examine your fossils using the magnifying glass. Identify each as a cast or a mold. Record characteristics and details about each in your Activity Manual.

Conclusions

- How are the fossils alike? How are they different?
- Which fossil provides you with more information about the original object?

Follow-up

- Try making mold or cast fossils with other materials such as mud or wet sand. Compare the features of these fossils with those made with plaster.
- Make trace fossils of animal footprints.

Learning from Fossils

The scientific study of fossils is called **paleontology** (PAY lee uhn TOL uh jee). People who study fossils are called *paleontologists* (PAY lee uhn TOL uh jists). They do not just study fossils, though. There are many jobs that paleontologists may do. They may find fossils and take them to a place where they can be studied. Or they may clean the fossils and prepare them for display.

Excavating Fossils

Sedimentary rock usually erodes more easily than other types of rocks do. When sedimentary rock erodes, it may reveal buried objects such as fossils. Cliffs, beaches, and deserts are good places to look for fossils. Paleontologists search for fossils in these areas.

excavation site in East Turkana, Kenya

It is common to find many fossils buried with each other in one place. This place is called a site. When paleontologists find a site, they first take photos of it and then make a detailed map of it. The location where a fossil was found will be helpful to know later when studying the fossil.

After mapping its location, the fossil is dug out. Removing a fossil from the rock around it is called **excavation** (EK skuh VAY shuhn). This process must be done carefully and may take a very long time. Small fossils can be excavated with simple tools such as hammers and spades. Larger fossils may require cranes and bulldozers, though.

When a fossil is found, paleontologists usually remove some of the surrounding rock along with the fossil. This extra rock helps to protect the fossil. Scientists number each fossil and then wrap it in foam to keep it from breaking on its way to the laboratory. Very fragile fossils are also painted with a protective coating.

Preparing Fossils

When fossils arrive at a laboratory, they need to be cleaned. All the dirt and rock around them must be removed. Paleontologists who clean fossils are called *preparators* (prih PAR uh ters). They must work very carefully so the fossils are not damaged. Most fossil preparation is done with small tools and brushes.

Maybe you know someone who had an x-ray taken. The x-rays gave doctors a picture of the inside of the person. Scientists can use the same technology on fossils. The x-rays allow scientists to look inside the fossils and learn more about them.

Reconstructing Fossils

Sometimes bones from one animal's skeleton are all found in one place. When this happens, scientists try to put the bones back together to re-create the animal's skeleton. Sometimes all the bones are not available, and scientists must guess about the bones that are missing. Even an almost-complete skeleton, however, cannot show what the animal's muscles or outward appearance was like. So scientists guess. They base their guesses on how modern animals look.

If you visit a natural-history museum, you may see models of animals such as dinosaurs on display. These models were usually made by artists. The artists based the models on scientific data. But they also used their own ideas about what the animals might have looked like.

Dating Fossils

Most evolutionists do not believe that there was one great Flood. So they look for other ways to explain how fossils were formed.

Evolutionists think that the different layers of rock contain fossils from different periods of time. They believe a fossil is as old as the rock layer that it is buried in. The farther down in the rock layers that a fossil is found, the older it is.

A polystrate fossil is buried in more than one layer of rock.

Evolution teaches that life on the earth began with simple organisms. Over millions of years these organisms gradually evolved into new, complex forms of life. If this were true, simple life forms would all be buried in the lowest layer of rock.

Fossils do not always follow the pattern that evolutionists expect. For example, complex and simple fossils are sometimes found in the same rock layer. And some fossils are turned sideways so they are buried in more than one layer.

It appears that most fossils were buried during a sudden catastrophe like the Flood. In this case, the rock layer a fossil is found in would not reveal its age. The rock layer may show, however, that an organism was able to move. Animals that could swim or float would survive longer in the water. Other animals may have been able to move to higher ground. The animals that lived longer were buried in the top layers of the rock.

Paleontologists use several methods to try to test how old fossils of plants and animals are. One of these dating methods, called **carbon dating**, measures the amount of a substance called *carbon 14* in the fossil. All living things contain carbon. When an organism dies,

Creation CORNER

In 1990, one of the most complete fossils of a *Tyrannosaurus rex* (tih-RAN-uh-SAWR-us REKS) was found in the Black Hills of South Dakota. Nicknamed Sue after the woman who found it, this dinosaur is now on display at the Field Museum of Chicago. It is the largest of its kind ever found. When Sue was found, its head and hips were close together. The position of the bones suggested that Sue was buried by a quickly moving flood. During the Genesis Flood only the people and animals in the ark were saved from God's destruction on man's wickedness. The moving water during the Flood would have been quick and powerful. Even an animal as large as Sue would have been swept away and rapidly buried under the sediment carried by the moving water. When we look at science with a Creationist viewpoint, even dinosaur bones support God's Word.

Sue

it no longer takes in carbon. The carbon 14 inside it slowly breaks down until there is none left. By measuring how much carbon 14 is still in the fossil, scientists can guess how old the fossil is.

Carbon dating is not exact, though. It can only estimate how many thousands of years old the fossil is. So scientists have to guess in order to find a date. These guesses are based on how things are today. But scientists do not know that things have always been the same. And if even just one guess is wrong, the date will also be wrong.

Many dating methods assume that evolution is true and that life on earth began millions of years ago. Creationists believe the earth is much younger. When we are told that fossils are millions of years old, we know it cannot be true. These ages do not agree with the biblical account of God's Creation.

QUICK CHECK

1. What is a person who studies fossils called?
2. How do paleontologists guess how to reconstruct the fossil of an animal?
3. What is carbon dating?

Explorations Fossil Dig

When paleontologists are digging for fossils, they divide the site into small sections. The sections are then labeled to match sections on a map or drawing of the dig site. As fossils are found, the locations are marked on the map. Paleontologists also record other helpful information about each fossil and its location. This additional information about the fossil may include the depth and position at which it was found, its condition, its color, and the type of soil or rock in which it was found. Accurate records and drawings will help the scientists as they later analyze their notes.

You have been given an area of a site to excavate for "fossils." You and your team of workers are responsible to divide and label your area. As you excavate the site, draw and record information about your findings on a site map.

What to do

Materials:
- fossil pan
- 2 pieces of string, 30 cm long
- *Site Map* page
- spoon
- toothpick
- watercolor paintbrush
- *Fossil Description* page

1. Decide the types of information you will record about each fossil.
2. Set the fossil pan carefully in your workspace so that the dirt and buried fossils do not move.
3. Use string to divide the fossil pan into four sections. Label each section to match the *Site Map* page.

4. Use a spoon to lift some of the soil from one section. Excavate, or dig, slowly and carefully to avoid damaging any buried objects. When you find a fossil, lay the spoon aside and use a toothpick to uncover the fossil. Assign the fossil a number. Before removing the fossil from the soil, draw a picture of the fossil in the matching location on the *Site Map* page.

5. Carefully lift the fossil out of the pan. If it is broken, be sure that the picture on the map shows the broken part. Use the paintbrush to clean any remaining dirt from the fossil.
6. Examine your fossil. On the *Fossil Description* page, record any additional information about the fossil's location and a description of the fossil's characteristics.
7. Continue excavating each section of your fossil pan. Remember to clean, map, and describe each fossil.
8. Display your fossils and the information about them.

Dinosaurs

Some people wonder whether dinosaurs (DIE nuh SORS) really lived on the earth. Fossils prove that they did. And God's Word describes large land and sea creatures that may have been dinosaurs.

Sir Richard Owen, a British scientist, studied the fossils of these large animals. In 1841, he gave the animals the name *dinosaurs*, which comes from words meaning "terrible lizards." At the time, the dinosaur bones that had been found seemed to be a larger version of lizards. But as more bones were found, scientists decided that dinosaurs were not lizards. In fact, scientists cannot definitely classify dinosaurs as reptiles. Reptiles are cold-blooded, but scientists are not certain that all dinosaurs were.

Dinosaurs might still exist somewhere on the earth, but scientists do not know of any that are still alive today. Whatever is learned about them has to come from the fossils they left behind.

The *Brachiosaurus* was a type of *Sauropod. Sauropods* were a group of large dinosaurs.

What Their Fossils Teach Us

At one time, there were many different kinds of dinosaurs on the earth. Paleontologists have found fossils of dinosaur bones all over the world. The fossils tell us certain things about the dinosaurs. Some of them were very large, while others were as small as a chicken. Some of them appear to have been able to fly, and others were equipped to swim. Many of them lived on land.

Appearance

Scientists cannot know exactly what any dinosaur looked like. Paleontologists can look at its skeleton for clues, though. These clues may tell such things as how big the dinosaur was or what its body shape was. From these clues, scientists make guesses.

Some dinosaurs had unusual features. The *Stegosaurus* (STEG uh SAWR us) had platelike "armor" down its back. Another type of dinosaur, the *Spinosaur* (SPINE uh SAWR), had bony spikes on its body. The *Tyrannosaurus rex* had very small arms in comparison to the rest of its body. Scientists are not sure how the dinosaurs used these body parts. But we know that God had a perfect design for each of His creatures.

One kind of dinosaur, the *Sauropod* (SOR uh POD), was the largest creature ever known to walk the earth. Fossils of *Sauropods* indicate that they were close to 70 ft long from head to tail. If a *Brachiosaurus* (BRACK ee uh SAWR us), a type of *Sauropod*, had stood erect with its neck straight, it would have been about 43 ft tall. A male giraffe is only about half this height.

Paleontologists have also found examples of dinosaurs that had wings. A dinosaur called the *Pteranodon* (tuh RAN uh dahn) was a large flying creature that had a thin, bony crest on top of its head. Some scientists believe that this crest was used to provide balance during flight.

Meet the SCIENTIST — MARY ANNING

Mary Anning (1799–1847) grew up in the coastal town of Lyme Regis, England. Her father taught her how to hunt for fossils along the cliffs by the sea. After her father's death she provided for her family by finding and selling fossils. She is credited with discovering two marine dinosaurs: the *Ichthyosaur* (IK thee uh SAWR) and the *Plesiosaur* (PLEE see uh SOR). Anning did not have any formal education. She just read and studied the scientific writings of her day. But she became an expert at identifying the fossils that she found. Her work was recognized by well-known paleontologists, displayed in museums, and discussed in scientific papers.

Diet and behavior

Fossils can also give clues about what dinosaurs ate. Genesis 1:30 tells us that before sin entered the world all animals were plant eaters. Only later did some animals become meat eaters.

Dinosaurs with blunt teeth are usually assumed to have eaten only plants. But some dinosaur fossils have very sharp teeth. God could have designed sharp teeth for tearing bark from trees or cutting open fruit with tough rinds. However, after man sinned, some dinosaurs may have become meat eaters.

The best way to tell what a dinosaur ate is to find food remains inside of the dinosaur. For example, the *Pteranodon* had a long pouch under its jaw. Fossilized fish bones have been found in this pouch. So scientists believe that the dinosaur held fish in its pouch, much as a pelican does.

Paleontologists can learn many things about a creature's behavior from looking at fossils. Tracks often show how it walked and whether it traveled in herds. You have probably seen models of a dinosaur called the *Tyrannosaurus rex*. Its name means "tyrant lizard king." By studying trace fossils, scientists have changed their minds about the way it walked. At one time they thought that it walked upright with its tail dragging the ground. But then trace fossils of the *Tyrannosaurus rex*'s tracks were found. These tracks showed footprints but no tail markings. Most scientists now think that the *Tyrannosaurus rex* kept its body level and extended its tail as it walked.

Pteranodon

Oviraptor

Some fossils give us clues about the family life of dinosaurs. We know that some dinosaurs laid eggs, because fossilized eggs have been found. One type of dinosaur, called the *Oviraptor* (o vih RAP tor), was discovered in the Gobi Desert of Mongolia. The dinosaur's bones were found lying on top of a nest of eggs. At first scientists thought that these eggs belonged to another kind of dinosaur. They thought that the *Oviraptor* had died in the act of stealing the eggs and so gave this dinosaur a name that means "egg stealer."

But later other fossils of *Oviraptor*s were found on nests as well. Then a fossil of a baby *Oviraptor* was found—inside one of the eggs! These nests held the *Oviraptor*'s own eggs. The dinosaur was not stealing eggs. It was protecting its own eggs.

Evolutionists would like to find a fossil of an animal that is a cross between a dinosaur and a bird. They think that this would prove that birds evolved from dinosaurs. Even if such a fossil were found, it would not prove evolution to be true. It would only show that God used similar designs in some of His creatures.

In Genesis 1:24–25, the Bible tells us that animals "bring forth . . . after their kind." Babies look like their parents. God planned it this way.

an *Oviraptor* nest with eggs

QUICK CHECK

1. What kinds of clues can scientists gain from observing a dinosaur's skeleton?
2. How could the fossil of a dinosaur give clues about its diet?
3. What characteristics of dinosaur behavior might scientists guess from fossils?

What the Bible Teaches Us

Dinosaurs were "discovered" in the early 1600s by an English scientist named Robert Plot. He found the bones of an animal that had clearly been huge. But long before Plot found these bones, the Bible talked about unusual animals that were very likely dinosaurs.

Evolutionists believe that dinosaurs and man never lived on the earth at the same time. But the Bible says that God created all the land and sea animals during the fifth and sixth days of Creation. And He created man on the sixth day of Creation. So dinosaurs and man would have lived at the same time. God's Word is always accurate. We can trust it to be true even in areas of science.

We also know that God spared some of the dinosaurs during the Flood. Genesis 7:15 says that "two of all flesh, wherein is the breath of life" went into the ark. So after the Flood, some dinosaurs must have survived for a time.

In Job 40:15–19, the Lord talks about an animal that He called Behemoth (bih HEE muth). This large, grass-eating animal had a "tail like a cedar." The animal also had

Kronosaurus

bones that were as strong as brass and iron, and it drank great quantities of water. The Bible calls Behemoth "the chief of the ways of God." All of these descriptions lead us to think of an animal such as a *Sauropod*. Fossils of *Sauropods* show animals with long necks and long tails. They were plant eaters, and some of them grew to be very large.

In the next chapter of Job, the Lord describes another animal. This one He calls Leviathan (luh VIE uh thun). This large sea creature had very strong scales. Job 41:14 says, "Who can open the doors of his face? his teeth are terrible round about." We do not know exactly what kind of animal this was. Some believe it may have been a type of large marine animal known as a *Plesiosaur*. This kind of dinosaur also had powerful, interlocking teeth. Fossils of one type of *Plesiosaur*, called a *Kronosaurus* (KRON uh SAWR uhs), have been found with 10 ft long skulls!

The book of Job seems to be describing dinosaurs. This means that dinosaurs might have been on the earth during Job's time. Other books of the Bible, such as Psalms and Isaiah, mention dragons and flying serpents. The descriptions of these animals seem to match other kinds of dinosaur fossils that scientists have found.

History has also recorded many stories about dragons. The history of England tells the story of a man named Saint George who killed a dragon. Chinese history includes legends of families who bred and raised dragons. These dragons might have been dinosaurs.

Scientists will probably never be able to tell us exactly what dinosaurs looked like and how they lived. We can be certain, however, that God created these animals. They fit into His perfect plan and fulfilled His purpose.

Science and the BIBLE

The book of Psalms mentions sea creatures that it calls "dragons" (Psalms 74:13; 148:7). We think of dragons as creatures only from myths and legends. But dragons may have been alive even in Bible times. Over the years, their looks and habits have probably been fictionalized. Now the fossils of dinosaurs may be all that is left of these long-ago creatures.

Extinction of Dinosaurs

We know that dinosaurs were alive on the earth at one time. Their fossils clearly tell us so. There may in fact still be dinosaurs on the earth. If so, they are very rare, though, and live in places so remote that no one has found them.

Extinction (ik STINGK shun) is when the last of a certain plant or animal dies. Extinction can be caused by many things. Disease, lack of food, and weather changes are just a few of the reasons why some kinds of animals are now extinct.

The fossil record points to a time when many animals, including dinosaurs, died all at once. Genesis 7:21–22 tells what happened to the animals that were not in the ark during the Flood: "And all flesh died

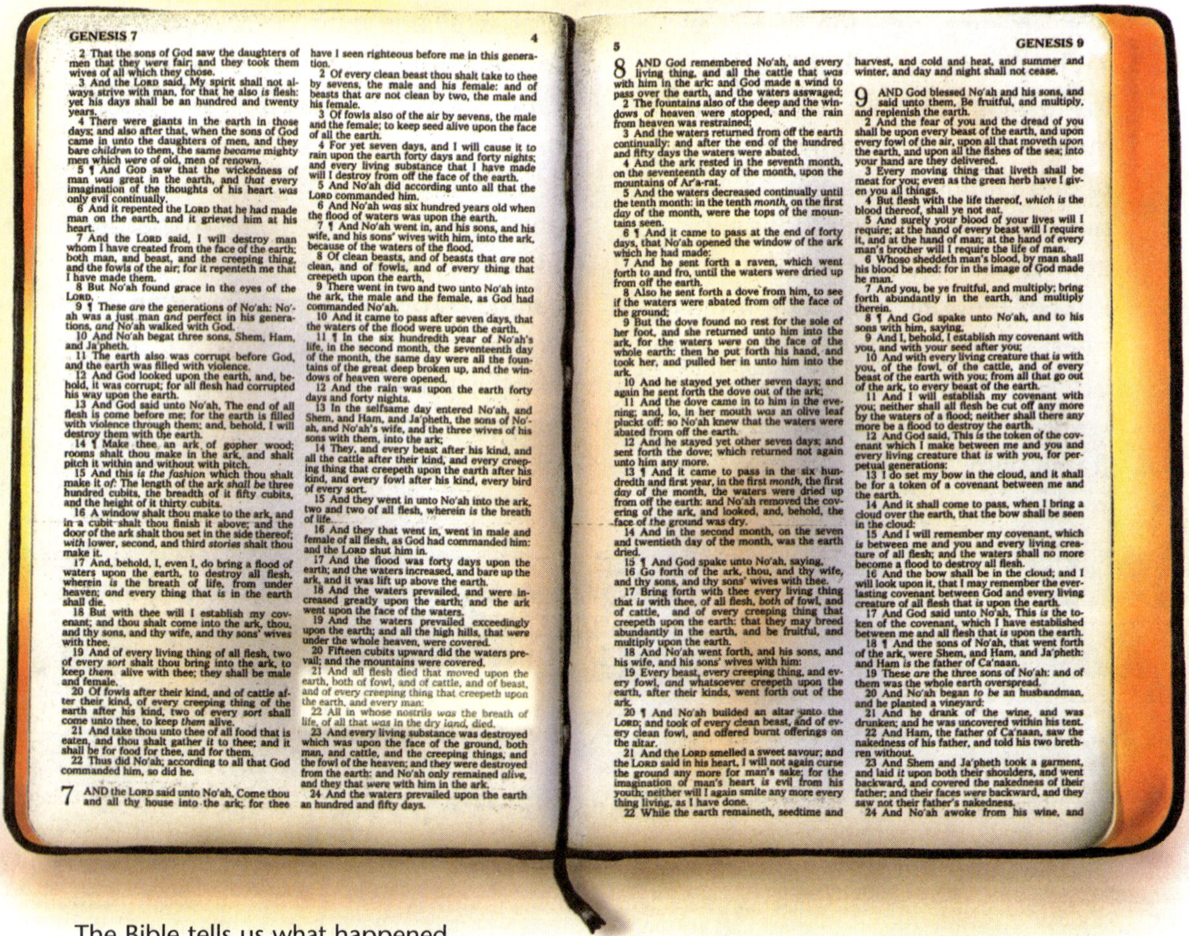

The Bible tells us what happened to all living flesh during the Flood.

that moved upon the earth, both of fowl, and of cattle, and of beast, and of every creeping thing that creepeth upon the earth, and every man: all in whose nostrils was the breath of life, of all that was in the dry land, died." Not all dinosaurs died in the Flood, though. Two of each land dinosaur would have been safe in the ark. Also, some marine dinosaurs would have lived.

Evolutionists have formed several theories about how dinosaurs became extinct. One theory says that a meteorite hit the earth and caused major climate changes. The dinosaurs then died from the sudden heat or cold. Another theory says that volcanoes killed the dinosaurs. Less popular theories say that all the dinosaurs died from changes in the air or from diseases. These are unlikely events that people try to use to explain the extinction of dinosaurs without taking the Flood into account.

The Flood brought many changes to the earth. The Bible is not clear about what the earth's pre-Flood climate was like, but we know it was not like it is now. Genesis 2:6 tells us that a mist went up from the earth and watered the land. Some Creationists believe that the earth's pre-Flood climate was very mild, with no extreme temperatures. After the Flood the earth's climate was probably very different from what it was before the Flood. It may have been much closer to what we have today. Some plants and animals, including dinosaurs, may not have been able to adjust to the change.

Dinosaurs may have also had to change their diet. Plants that they had eaten before the Flood may not have been able to grow well in the changed climate. With limited food, different types of animals would have had to compete for survival. God also commanded humans to begin killing animals for food after the Flood (Genesis 9:2–3). The dinosaurs may have been a major source of food.

No one can prove what happened to the dinosaurs, just as no one can prove how dinosaurs, or any other creature, came to be. No one was there at the beginning to see it—no one, that is, except the most faithful Witness there ever could be, the Creator Himself. We can choose to believe His Word. Or we can choose to search for truth apart from Him.

QUICK CHECK

1. What animals mentioned in the Bible and in history records may have been dinosaurs?
2. What is extinction?
3. What are some reasons that Creationists give for the extinction of dinosaurs after the Flood?

Answer the Questions

1. How does a person make judgments about the fossil record?

___

___

___

2. What evidence of a worldwide flood does the fossil record show?

___

___

___

3. What kinds of information can paleontologists gather from trace fossils that they cannot get from fossilized bones?

___

___

___

Solve the Problem

You are watching a program about the Grand Canyon. The narrator says that the layers seen in the canyon were formed over millions of years and show geologic ages. Even though the program was not about Creation or evolution, what do you know about the people who wrote the program? How should that knowledge affect how you listen to the rest of the program? Why?

___

___

___

___

___

___

UNIT 2
From the Beginning

Melted chocolate chips can freeze without being in the freezer. Find out in Chapter 3 how this happens.

God designed a very efficient and portable cooling system for us. Chapter 4 tells us what this system is and why it is so important to each of us.

Thunderstorms, molten rock under the earth's surface, and a pot of boiling water all have something in common. Chapter 4 explains about a characteristic these very different things share.

Matter

3

REMEMBER *now* thy CREATOR

Man sometimes looks at his scientific advancement and forgets the God Who allows man to have dominion over the earth. Even some everyday situations of life would change greatly without God's perfect plan. Suppose all kinds of matter melted at the same temperature. You would not be able to melt chocolate in a pot on the stove. The pot and chocolate would both melt at the same time. Ice in a glass of water would melt, but so would the glass that holds the water. These things may sound silly, but they are examples of how God created properties of matter to work in useful ways. Man can learn about science and can design technology only because of God's faithful maintaining of His creation.

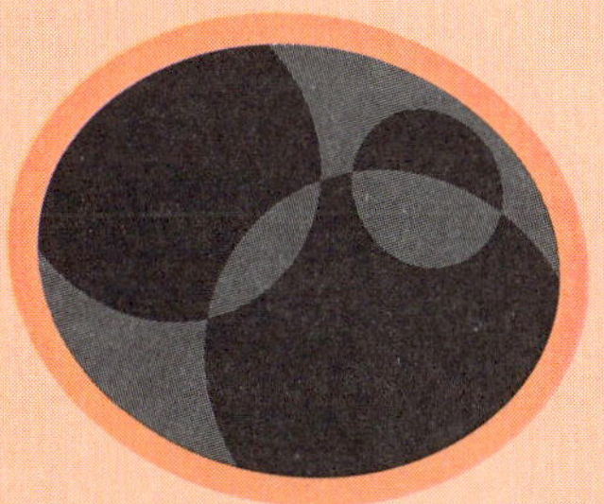

Measuring Matter

Look around you. You probably see many objects. These may include things such as books, pencils, paper, and carpet. These items are different in many ways, but they are all alike in at least one way. Each is made of matter. **Matter** is anything that has volume and has mass. Volume and mass are characteristics of matter that we can often measure. Sometimes we use the term *substance* to refer to matter.

Volume of a Liquid

The **volume** of a substance is the amount of space that it takes up. The standard unit of metric measurement for volume is the liter (L). Many soft drinks come in two-liter bottles. A smaller unit for volume is the milliliter (mL). Liquid medicine often uses this unit. A teaspoon of medicine is about 5 mL.

We measure the volume of a liquid by using a graduated (GRAJ oo ATE ed) container. *Graduated* means that the container is divided into equally marked parts. A graduated container has the units of measurement marked on its side. A liquid is poured into the container. The level of the liquid is then compared with the numbers on the side of the container. The numbers show the volume of the liquid. Scientists use containers called graduated cylinders, but even the measuring cups in a kitchen are a type of graduated container.

graduated cylinder

Science and the BIBLE

In 2 Kings 4 the Bible tells us about a widow who owed money. Her sons were going to be taken as slaves unless she could pay her debts. All that the widow had was a pot of oil. The pot held a small volume of oil. The prophet Elisha told the widow to borrow vessels, or large containers, from her neighbors. She started pouring her little bit of oil into the vessels and kept pouring until all of the vessels were filled. Elisha told her to sell the oil to pay her debts. God caused the small volume of oil to increase to fill many large pots. In this way, He miraculously provided for the widow's needs.

Volume of a Solid

There are two ways to measure the volume of solid objects. To measure the volume of regular shapes, such as cubes and rectangular solids, multiply the measurements of the length, width, and height of the object. The volume is written as a cubic measurement. An object that is 15 centimeters (cm) long, 10 cm wide, and 10 cm high has a volume of 1,500 cubic centimeters. A cubic centimeter is written as *cm³* or *cc*.

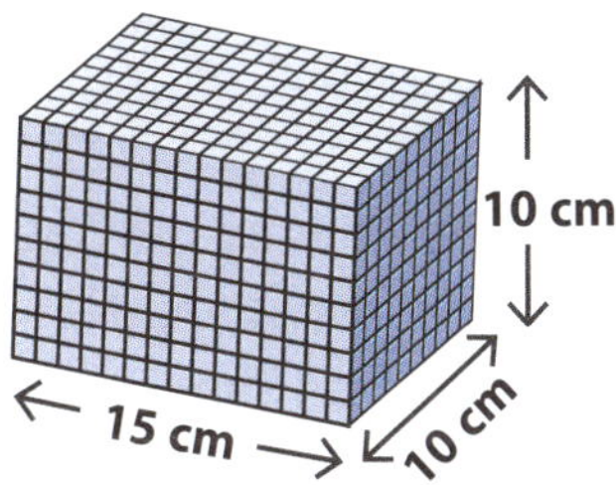

length × width × height = volume
15 cm × 10 cm × 10 cm = 1500 cm^3

You can see water displacement when you add marbles to the water in a fishbowl. The volume of the marbles is the difference between the beginning level of the water and the level after the marbles were added. The volume can be written in milliliters or liters. For example, suppose a fishbowl contains 1,000 mL of water. After the marbles are added, the level of the water is at 1,250 mL. The volume of the marbles is 250 mL.

1250 mL – 1000 mL = 250 mL

In the metric system one cubic centimeter is equal to one milliliter. Scientists usually use milliliters to describe the volume of a liquid. They use cubic centimeters to describe the volume of a solid. So the volume of the marbles in the example is also equal to 250 cm^3.

However, we cannot always measure a solid object by using its length, width, and height. For instance, it would be difficult to measure a rock or a marble in this way. The volume of irregularly shaped objects can be measured using a method called *water displacement*.

Mass and Weight

Mass is another way that matter is measured. **Mass** is the amount of material in a substance. It is measured by comparing an unknown mass with a known mass. For example, a student with an unknown mass can sit on one end of a seesaw. A substance with a known mass, such as a sack of sand, can be placed on the other end of the seesaw. If the seesaw balances, we know that the mass of the student is the same as the mass of the sand.

We usually measure mass with an instrument called a balance. The substance to be measured is placed on the instrument. Standard masses, objects of known masses, are used to balance the unknown mass of the substance. The mass of the substance to be measured is equal to the sum of the standard masses.

Some metric units of mass are the gram (g) and the kilogram (kg). The mass of a paper clip is about 1 g. A one-liter bottle of water has a mass of about 1 kg.

It is usually easy to determine which of two objects has the greater mass. A large dog has more matter than a small cat does and, therefore, has more mass. The dog probably also weighs more than the cat does. But the dog's mass and the dog's weight are not actually the same.

Mass and weight are related, but they measure different things. Mass measures the amount of matter. **Weight** measures the amount of force gravity places on the matter. If we measure two items at the same location, the object with greater mass weighs more.

Mass can change only as the amount of matter changes, but weight can vary based on the gravity at a location. A student whose mass is 40 kg would weigh 88 pounds (lb) on the earth. But that student would weigh about 220 lb on Jupiter and only 15 lb on the moon. The difference occurs because the gravity of the moon and the gravity of Jupiter are different from the gravity of the earth.

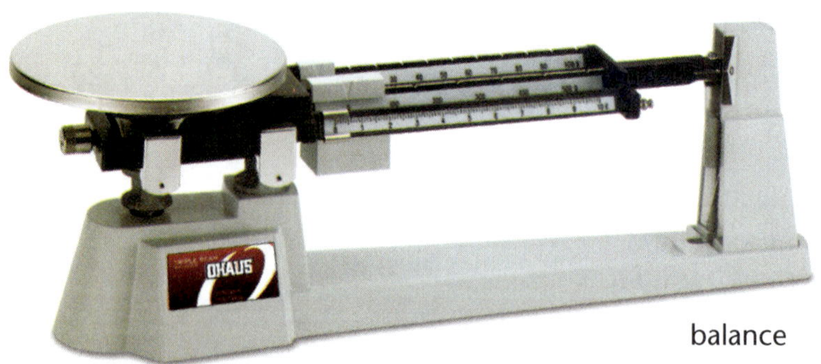

balance

Density

Density (DEN sih tee) is the amount of matter in a certain space. Suppose you are given the task of carrying one of two boxes in a race. The two boxes are the same size and look the same on the outside. However, one box is filled with cotton. The other box is filled with rocks. You would probably choose the box with the cotton inside. The two boxes have the same volume, but the box with cotton has less mass than the box with rocks has. This difference in mass makes the box of cotton less dense than the box of rocks is.

Creation CORNER

Most substances have a greater density in a solid form than in a liquid form. One exception is water. During the winter ice floats on top of lakes and rivers instead of sinking. If the ice sank, it would continue to displace the water. The water on top would freeze and sink. All the living things in the water would die. However, God designed ice to be less dense than water. In this way, He provided a top layer that keeps the water below from freezing.

DENSITIES OF OBJECTS

Object	Density
gold	19.3 g/mL
lead	11.4 g/mL
silver	10.5 g/mL
water	1.0 g/mL
ice	0.92 g/mL
wood (pine)	0.7 g/mL
wood (oak)	0.4 g/mL
cork	0.2 g/mL

The density of an object is calculated by dividing its mass by its volume. The formula is mass ÷ volume = density. An object that has 12 g of mass and takes up 3 mL of volume has a density of 4 grams per milliliter. Notice this density is measured in grams per milliliter. It is written as *g/mL*.

mass ÷ volume = density
12 g ÷ 3 mL = 4 g/mL

1. What is matter?
2. How is mass different from weight?
3. What is density?

Physical Properties

Man cannot create or destroy matter. Only God can. In John 1:3 the Bible says, "All things were made by him; and without him was not any thing made that was made."

When God created matter, He gave it many characteristics. Some of these are called physical properties. A **physical property** is a characteristic of a substance that can be observed without changing the identity of the substance. Some physical properties are easy for us to observe with our senses. The color, texture, and smell of a substance can usually be readily observed. Other properties can be hard to observe. These properties include things like a substance's density or its ability to conduct electricity. Whether easy or hard to observe, these characteristics are all important. They help us distinguish one substance from another.

rose

spruce

States of Matter

One physical property of matter is whether it is a solid, liquid, or gas. These properties are called the **states of matter**. Almost all matter on the earth is in one of these states.

All matter is composed of tiny particles that are always in motion. These particles attract each other. This attraction tends to hold the particles together. The motion of the tiny particles and the strength of their attraction determine a substance's state of matter.

Solid

A desk, a pencil, and a book are all solids. **Solid** is the state of matter in which a substance has a definite volume and shape. If you put a pencil in a glass, the pencil stays in its own shape. It does not take on the shape of the glass. The particles that make up a solid do vibrate, but they do not move very much. They have a strong attraction to each other. This strong attraction keeps the particles close together and allows solids to keep their shape.

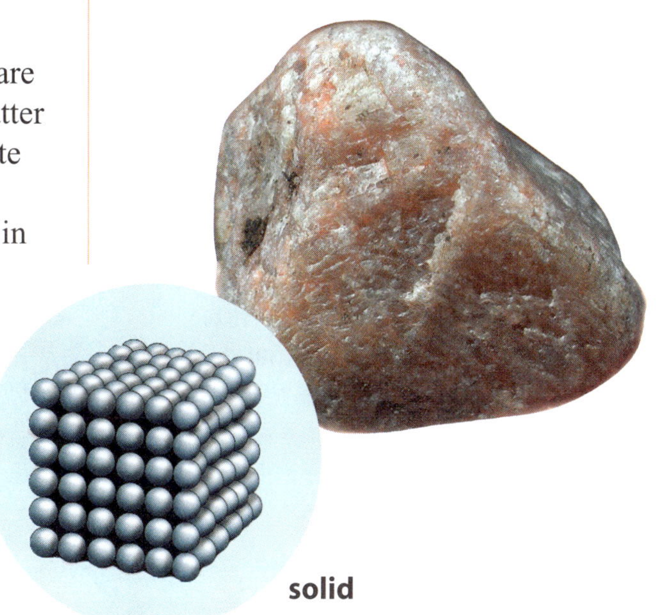

solid

Liquid

Water, juice, and soft drinks are all liquids. **Liquid** is the state of matter in which a substance has a definite volume but not a definite shape. A liquid takes the shape of the container that it is in. The same amount of liquid can be poured from a tall, thin container into a short, wide container. The liquid's volume stays the same, even though the shape of the liquid changes. The particles in liquids move more than the particles in solids do. Yet the attraction between the particles is still strong enough to keep the matter from completely spreading apart.

liquid

Gas

Air in a tire and helium in a balloon are examples of gases. **Gas** is the state of matter in which a substance does not have a definite shape or a definite volume. Like liquids, gases take the shape of their containers. But unlike solids or liquids, gases can also expand to fill the volume of their containers.

Gases are also different in that they can be compressed. Perhaps you have seen a balloon being filled from a tank of helium gas. The gas in the tank is compressed. Only a small amount of helium gas is released into each balloon, but the gas expands to fill and inflate the balloon.

The particles in gases are very active. They have only a weak attraction to each other. Because of this, gas particles spread apart until they meet a barrier that contains them.

gas

Fantastic FACTS

We often talk about the "three states of matter," but most of the matter in the universe is made up of a fourth type called plasma. Plasma occurs only at very high temperatures such as those found on the sun. On the earth plasma naturally occurs in a lightning bolt. Man-made plasma causes a fluorescent light to shine. Some scientists think plasma may have great potential as a future energy source.

STATES OF MATTER

State	Shape	Volume
Solid	definite shape	definite volume
Liquid	no definite shape	definite volume
Gas	no definite shape	no definite volume

Changing States of Matter

Although man cannot create or destroy matter, he can change it from one form to another. Matter does not always stay the same. If you use a hammer to break a rock into smaller pieces, the rock will change in size, but the pieces are still rock. The rock has had a physical change. A **physical change** is a change in matter that does not form a new substance.

A physical change also occurs when matter changes from one state to another. You have probably observed this. Ice cream is usually a solid. It has a definite shape and a definite volume. But if you leave it out of the freezer for a while, it will change to a liquid. It has the same volume, but it will take the shape of whatever container you put it in. The ice cream has not changed into another substance, nor has it lost or gained matter. The ice cream just changed its form, or state of matter.

The temperature at which a substance changes from one state of matter to another is one of its physical properties. This physical property can help us describe and identify different kinds of matter.

An ice cube is the solid state of water. An ice cube has its own shape and volume. If you take the ice cube out of the freezer, though, the ice starts to change to a liquid. This process of a solid changing to a liquid is called **melting**. The temperature at which a solid changes to a liquid is called its melting point. Different solid substances melt at different temperatures. Ice melts at 0°C (32°F), but lead melts at about 328°C (622°F). Most metals have very high melting points.

Plumbers can use a metal substance called solder (SAH der) to connect copper pipes because solder melts at a much lower temperature than the copper does.

Matter can also change from a liquid to a solid. If you put an ice cube tray of water into the freezer, the water freezes into solid ice cubes. The process of a liquid changing to a solid is called **freezing**.

We usually think of freezing as meaning something is cold. But in science a substance does not have to be cold to be frozen. Any substance that is changing from a liquid to a solid is freezing. Another word that we could use to describe this is *solidifying* (suh LID uh FIE ing). Think about a piece of solid chocolate. The chocolate can be melted to use for cooking. But if melted chocolate is left at a cool room temperature it will change back to a solid. It does not have to be in a freezer to freeze, or solidify. The temperature at which a substance changes to a solid is its *freezing point.* The melting point and the freezing point of a substance are the same temperature.

Another way matter can change is from a liquid to a gas. This can be harder for us to see, but it happens all around us. The process of a liquid changing into a gas is called **vaporization** (VAY puh rih ZAY shun). A liquid is boiling when vaporization is occurring throughout the liquid and bubbles of gas rise and break away from the liquid's surface. The temperature at which this occurs is called the *boiling point*. Different substances have different boiling points, just as they have different melting points. Water boils at 100°C (212°F).

Boiling water is an example of vaporization.

Water vapor in the air condenses on the outside of a cold glass.

Evaporation (ih VAP uh RAY shun) is another form of vaporization. A substance evaporates when it changes from a liquid to a gas at a temperature below its boiling point. Evaporation occurs only at the surface of a substance. You may have noticed a puddle of water that gradually dried up during the day. The water did not boil, but it did change to a gas through evaporation.

A substance can also change from a gas to a liquid. This process is called **condensation** (KON den SAY shun). Perhaps you have set a cold glass of liquid on a table. After a little while, you saw drops of water on the outside of the glass. Water vapor in the air had cooled and changed back to a liquid. The *condensation point* is the temperature at which a gas turns to a liquid.

We often see water changing states. But in certain conditions almost all matter changes states. Even iron can get hot enough to change to a vapor. The condition at which a substance changes states is a physical property that helps scientists identify the substance.

QUICK CHECK

1. What two things determine a substance's state of matter?
2. Do particles move faster in a liquid or in a gas?
3. What is freezing?
4. What is vaporization?

Classifying Matter

Atoms and Molecules

All matter is made up of small particles called **atoms**. These atoms are much too small for you to see. Most matter contains more than one kind of atom. The paper used to make this page is made of different kinds of atoms. Your chair is made from a variety of atoms. You are even made of dozens of kinds of atoms.

Some matter contains only one kind of atom. Matter that is made up of only one kind of atom is called an **element** (EL uh ment). Gold, silver, and oxygen are all elements. Scientists have named more than 100 different elements.

Atoms may join with other atoms to form particles called **molecules** (MOL ih KYOOLS). Air contains molecules of oxygen and molecules of water. Each molecule of oxygen contains only the element oxygen. However, each molecule of water contains two elements: hydrogen and oxygen. Substances such as water are called compounds. A **compound** is formed by combining atoms of different elements.

O_2 is a molecule made up of 2 oxygen atoms.

A compound is a new substance. It is different from the elements that formed it. Water is different from either hydrogen or oxygen. Both hydrogen and oxygen are usually found as gases. Hydrogen is an explosive gas that burns easily. Oxygen is needed to help many other things to burn. But water does not burn. It can be used to put out fires.

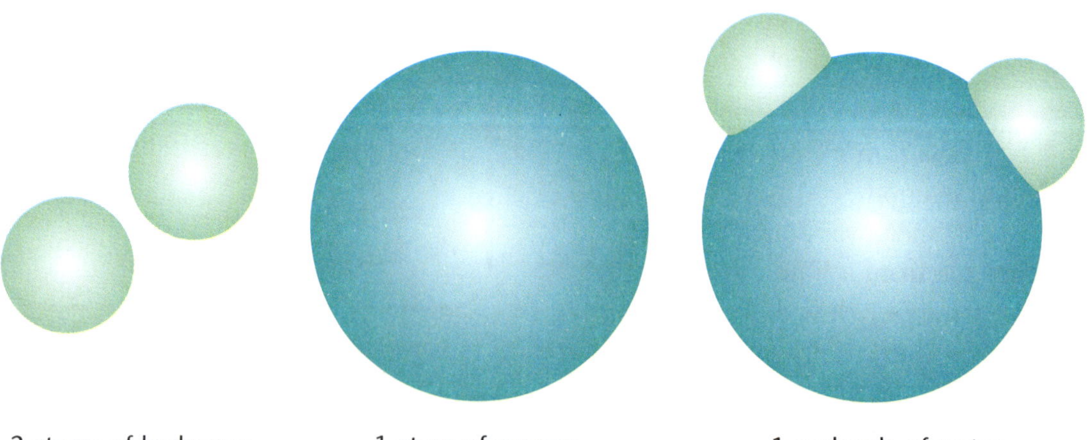
2 atoms of hydrogen

1 atom of oxygen

1 molecule of water

Every molecule of a compound is identical. For example, every molecule of water is the same. Each molecule of water always has two atoms of hydrogen and one atom of oxygen.

Compounds form through a chemical change. A **chemical change** is the process of two or more elements or compounds combining to form a new substance. Unlike a physical change, a chemical change causes the elements or compounds to lose their individual properties and take on new ones. For example, the elements sodium and chlorine are both poisonous to people. When the atoms in these elements join, however, they form the compound known as table salt.

You can often observe the effects of chemical changes. Rust can form on a garden tool as the result of a chemical change. This change happens when the oxygen in water and iron in the tool combine. They form a new substance that we call rust. Chemical changes can also occur in the kitchen. A cake is the result of chemical change. The properties of the flour, eggs, and other ingredients change into a tasty substance—cake.

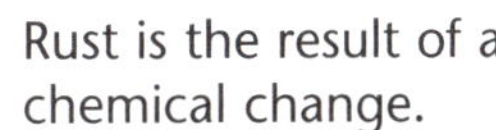
Rust is the result of a chemical change.

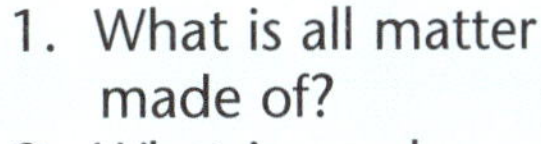
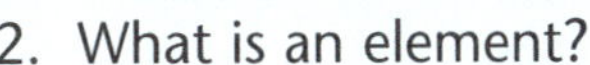

1. What is all matter made of?
2. What is an element?
3. What is a chemical change?

ACTIVITY

Separating a Mixture

Process skills
- Predicting
- Experimenting
- Observing
- Inferring
- Communicating

Matter has many properties. Size, shape, and mass are some physical properties that we can observe and measure. The ability of matter to dissolve in water or to be attracted to a magnet is also a physical property. By using these properties and others, you can separate a mixture into its individual parts.

In this activity, you will be given a mixture of four items. Your task is to separate each type of item from the mixture. You may need to use a different method for each item. You may also need to use more than one method to isolate a specific item. Plan your procedure carefully. One method of separation may affect another.

Materials:
- mixture of iron filings, rice, sand, and sugar
- 4 containers
- paper plate
- cheesecloth
- funnel
- magnet
- spoons
- strainer or sieve
- tweezers
- water
- Activity Manual

Problem

How do you separate a mixture into its individual parts?

Procedure

1. Get your mixture from your teacher.
2. Plan the order in which you will separate each item. You may use any of the materials included in the materials list. Record your plan in your Activity Manual.
3. Choose the material that you will use to separate the first item. Record the name of the item, the method that you will use to separate it, and the property of matter that the method uses.
4. Test your method for the first item. Record the results. If needed, try other methods until most of the item is removed.
5. According to your plan, repeat steps 3–4 for the other items. Remember to record your information at each step.

Conclusions

- Did your plan work?
- Was there a better method or order that you could have used?

Follow-up

- Use other materials or methods to separate the items.
- Separate a mixture containing other items.

Mixtures

Sometimes different substances combine without going through chemical changes. A **mixture** consists of two or more substances that are physically combined. Unlike the molecules in a compound, each particle in a mixture keeps its identity. Think of a snack mix. A snack mix is a mixture that can include pretzels, peanuts, and raisins. The pretzels, peanuts, and raisins did not change to other substances when they were added to the mixture. They each kept their own identities and properties.

The amount of each substance in a mixture may vary. If your family likes lots of raisins, you can add more raisins to the snack mix. You also could add other substances such as crackers and candy pieces.

Each substance in a mixture can be separated from the mixture. Since each substance keeps its properties, it may be identified and removed. You may like to pick all the peanuts from the snack mix and eat them first. The peanuts look and taste different from the pretzels and the raisins.

The matter in a mixture may sometimes undergo a physical change. Physical changes include changes of physical properties such as the state of matter, color, texture, or taste. Strawberries and ice cream go through a physical change when they are blended to form a milkshake. Combining the strawberries and the ice cream does not form a new substance, though. You can still taste both the strawberries and the ice cream.

In some mixtures the individual substances are not spread evenly throughout the mixture. An example of this kind of mixture is granite. If you look closely at a piece of granite, you will see that several kinds of minerals have "mixed" to form it. However, the minerals are not mixed evenly throughout the granite. Each piece of granite may have a different mixture of minerals in it.

A snack mix is an example of a mixture.

granite

It is easy to identify some mixtures as being evenly mixed or not. You can easily see that vegetable soup is not evenly mixed. Likewise, if you look at the sand on a beach, you can see a variety of rocks and shells in it. No two handfuls of sand have exactly the same substances in them.

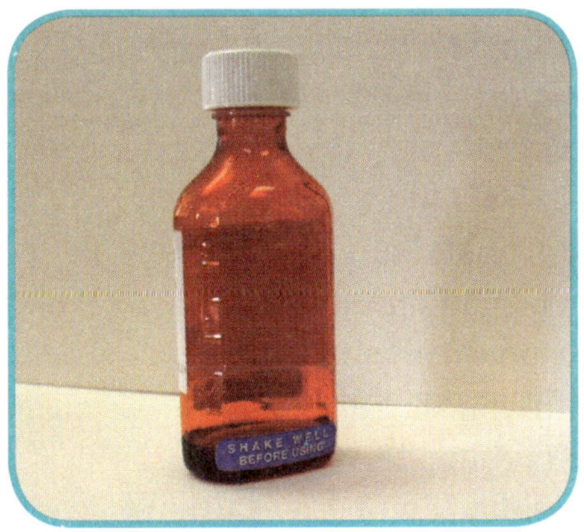

Some mixtures separate and must be mixed again by shaking.

Some mixtures separate if they sit for a while. Orange juice, some liquid medicines, and paint are mixtures that separate. These mixtures may have labels that say "Shake well before using." Shaking these mixtures mixes the substances back together.

The shaving cream that many men use each morning is also a type of mixture that is not evenly mixed. Shaving cream mixes a gas with a liquid to form a mixture called foam. An aerosol (AIR uh SAWL) is also a mixture of liquid in a gas. In some aerosols, you may even be able to see the droplets of liquid. Some hair sprays come as aerosols.

foam

aerosol

before shaking

after shaking

Separating substances in mixtures

Substances in mixtures are not held together chemically. They can be separated using their physical properties. Some mixtures are easy to separate based on how the parts look. You could look at a snack mix and easily remove each ingredient. You could take out all the pretzels and put them in one pile. Another pile could then be made of all the peanuts, and so on for each food item.

Suppose you had a jar full of coins. You could separate them by how they look. But if you had a coin sorter, you could separate the coins more quickly. The coin sorter separates the coins based on each coin's size.

Sometimes you can separate dry items by gently shaking them. The smaller items fill in the gaps at the bottom of the container. The larger items are pushed to the top. The items often settle into layers because of their sizes.

When each of the liquids in a mixture has a different density, the mixture may separate into layers. The order of the layers depends on how dense each liquid is. The densest liquid will be at the bottom. The least dense liquid will be at the top. Oil-and-vinegar salad dressing separates in this way. Oil is not as dense as vinegar and goes to the top. Until you shake the mixture, the two liquids will stay in different layers. If you are careful, you can separate the mixture by pouring off most of the oil.

Science and HISTORY

One method of separating mixtures had a great impact on the history of the United States. This method is gold panning. It was once used to separate gold from the mixture it was in. In 1848, James Marshall found gold in California in a river while building a sawmill for John Sutter. This began the great California gold rush.

Many men rushed to try their hand at panning for gold. To pan for gold, a man would put a small amount of dirt, gravel, and water from a stream into a shallow pan. He would then slowly shake the pan. Shaking the pan caused the materials to separate based on how dense each material was. Gold has a high density and would sink to the bottom. Much of the other material could be carefully poured off with the water. Gold and some other dense rocks would remain at the bottom of the pan. The shiny gold would then be picked out of the pan.

Solids may also separate based on density. Perhaps you have seen how sediment in a stream forms. The densest substances settle out first. Then other substances settle out according to how dense they each are.

Not all mixtures separate easily, though. Suppose you had a mixture of salt and sand. The pieces of salt and the pieces of sand would be nearly impossible to separate from each other. However, you could use some of the physical properties of salt and sand to make them easier to separate. One of the substances dissolves in water and one does not. If you added water to the mixture of salt and sand, the salt would dissolve in the water. The sand would settle to the bottom of the water. After pouring out the salt water, the sand would be separated through its physical properties.

However, the mixture would not yet be completely separated. The salt would still be combined with the water. A way to separate the salt and water would be to boil the salt water. Boiling causes the water to change from a liquid to a gas. The salt would remain in the container.

QUICK CHECK

1. What is a mixture?
2. How is granite an example of a mixture that is not evenly mixed?
3. What are three ways that you might separate a mixture?

Solutions

Salt and sand do not mix evenly. But water added to the mixture does mix evenly with the salt. Salt and water form a solution (suh LOO shun). A **solution** is a mixture in which all the substances are spread evenly throughout. The salt dissolves in the water and seems to disappear. *Dissolving* is the process in which the particles separate and spread evenly throughout the mixture.

Other substances can dissolve and form solutions as well. Suppose you mix sugar into iced tea. You cannot observe the grains of sugar in the tea because some physical properties of the sugar have changed. However, if you taste the tea, you know that the sugar is there. The sugar has undergone a physical change to form a solution, but it has not become another substance.

Scientists have special terms they use to describe the parts of a solution. A **solute** (SOL yoot) is the substance that is dissolved. A **solvent** (SOL vent) is the substance that dissolves the other substance. In salt water the salt is the solute, and the water is the solvent.

Water is the most common solvent on the earth. It is often called the "universal solvent" because so many things dissolve in it. Water's ability to dissolve many substances is very important to life on the earth.

solute solvent solution

A soft drink is a solution of a gas mixed in a liquid. The gas is the solute, and the liquid is the solvent.

You might think that all solutions are formed from a solid being dissolved in a liquid. That is not the case, however. Actually the solute and the solvent of a solution can be a solid, liquid, or gas. This means that there are different types of solutions. Air is a solution of gases. The oxygen you breathe and the carbon dioxide plants need are two of the most common gases in the air solution.

A soft drink is a solution of a gas in a liquid. The bubbles you see are from the carbon dioxide gas that has dissolved in the liquid. The carbon dioxide in the soft drink is the solute, and the liquid is the solvent.

You use many metal products that are formed from a mixture of two solids. These mixtures of two or more metals are called alloys. A nickel coin is actually an alloy of the solid metals nickel and copper. Even fourteen-carat gold jewelry is gold that has had silver added to it.

A nickel is made from a type of solution called an alloy.

Concentration and saturation

The **concentration** (KON sun TRAY shun) of a solution is the amount of solute that is dissolved in the solvent. Suppose you mix a powdered fruit-drink mix with water. The powder contains flavoring and sweetener. When you mix the powder with water, the powder is the solute, and the water is the solvent. By altering the amount of solute, the concentration of the fruit drink can be changed to suit your taste.

If you put a lot of the powdered mix into the water, the solution will taste strong. It will be concentrated. *Concentrated* means that the solvent is holding more than a normal amount of solute.

concentrated

If you put just a little of the powdered fruit mix into the water, the solution will taste weak. It will be diluted. A solution is *diluted* when there is less than a normal amount of solute in the solvent.

diluted

Sometimes the concentration of a solution can be adjusted to make the solution more useful. Often a cleaner is mixed with water to form a cleaning solution. To wipe counters and sinks, you might use a diluted solution with only a weak concentration of cleaner. To clean a very dirty floor, though, you would use a more concentrated solution.

If you continue to add more and more solute into a solvent, the solution will become *saturated* (SACH uh RAY tid). This means that the solvent is holding all of the solute that it can dissolve.

Rate of dissolving

Sometimes a solute can take a long time to completely dissolve in a solvent. There are ways to speed up the process, however. One way is to increase the surface area of the solute. This can be done by crushing, crumbling, or cutting it into small pieces. The more solute that touches the solvent, the faster the solute dissolves. That is why rock salt dissolves more slowly than a teaspoon of salt does.

Another way to speed up the rate of dissolving is to stir the solution. Stirring helps spread the solute in the solvent. Perhaps you have seen someone sweeten coffee with sugar. Usually he does not just put the sugar in the coffee. He also stirs the coffee. This causes the sugar to dissolve more quickly.

Temperature also affects how fast a solute can dissolve. This is because heat increases solubility. **Solubility** (SOL yuh BIL ih tee) is the ability of a solvent to dissolve a certain amount of a solute. The particles in a heated solvent are farther apart. This leaves more room for the particles of the added solute to dissolve.

Suppose that you want to add sugar to tea. The sugar will dissolve more quickly if the tea is hot. The sugar does not dissolve as easily in cold tea. Instead the sugar tends to settle to the bottom of the glass.

A substance with greater surface area will dissolve more quickly than one with less surface area.

God's Care

God provides all things for us. Yet we often fail to see the many ways that He takes care of our needs. Even the way matter combines and mixes is an example of God's care for us.

1. What is a solution?
2. In a solution of salt water, what is the solvent and what is the solute?
3. What are three ways to speed up the rate at which a solute dissolves in a solution?

A Disappearing Act

ACTIVITY

When a chef needs melted chocolate for a recipe, he could melt an entire block of chocolate whole, but he usually does not. Instead, he cuts the chocolate into small pieces before he melts it. If he needs a large amount of melted butter, he probably cuts the butter into smaller pieces, too. Why would he do that? Does the surface area of the substance make a difference?

In this activity, you will use peppermints to find out how the surface area of a solute affects its ability to dissolve.

Process skills
- Hypothesizing
- Experimenting
- Observing
- Inferring
- Defining operationally

Problem

Which will dissolve first—a whole peppermint or a crushed peppermint?

Materials:
- 2 clear plastic cups, 9 oz
- 100 mL hot water
- metric measuring cups
- 1 whole peppermint
- 1 crushed peppermint
- stopwatch
- 2 spoons
- Activity Manual

Procedure

1. Complete the hypothesis in your Activity Manual.
2. Label one cup *whole* and the other *crushed*.
3. Pour 50 mL of hot water into each cup.
4. Add a peppermint to each cup at the same time. Be sure that the label of the cup and the type of peppermint that you add match.
5. Begin timing the peppermints as they dissolve. Stir each cup until a peppermint is dissolved. Stop timing when one of the peppermints has completely dissolved.
6. Record your observations.

Conclusions

- Was your hypothesis correct?
- Which peppermint dissolved first?
- How did the surface area of a peppermint affect its ability to dissolve?

Follow-up

- Use a different type of candy. Compare the results.
- Use a larger amount of water. Compare the results.

Explorations Float a Boat

Buoyancy

If you were to build a ship, what materials would you use? Perhaps you would use wood to make a ship like those used by the early explorers. Most modern ships are huge vessels made of thousands of tons of steel. During World Wars I and II, supplies of steel were limited, so some ships were made of concrete!

The ability of an object to float is called its *buoyancy* (BOY un see). Wood is known for its buoyancy. Until it becomes saturated with water, wood naturally floats. Steel and concrete, however, are not known for their buoyancy. These substances are usually expected to sink. Yet huge floating vessels are made of these materials. How do the vessels stay afloat?

Whether an object floats or sinks is based on its volume and mass. An object placed on water pushes down on the water because of gravity. The water also pushes back on the object, though. This push against the object is known as *buoyant force*.

When an object pushes down, it displaces, or moves, the water. You can use this displaced water to measure a submerged object's volume. But you can also use this displaced water to measure a floating object's weight. For an object to float, it must displace an amount of water that is equal to its own weight. So the displaced water is equal in weight to the weight of the floating object.

An object's ability to float also has to do with its density. Ice is less dense than water is, so ice floats on the top of water. An object such as an iron anchor is very dense, so it will sink.

You may wonder how a huge ship can float. Although the ship's hull is very heavy, the open spaces within its hull are filled with air. The air helps make the overall density of the ship less than the density of the water so that the ship will float.

A contest

You have been invited to take part in a boat-building contest. Using only the given materials, you will build a boat. The goal is to make the boat that will hold the most pennies while floating.

Materials:

- 100 g modeling clay
- large dishpan or similar container
- water
- pennies
- Activity Manual

What to do

1. Plan the design of your boat. Sketch the design in your Activity Manual.
2. Use the clay to build a boat.
3. Test your boat in the dishpan of water to make sure that it floats. Make adjustments as necessary before the contest.

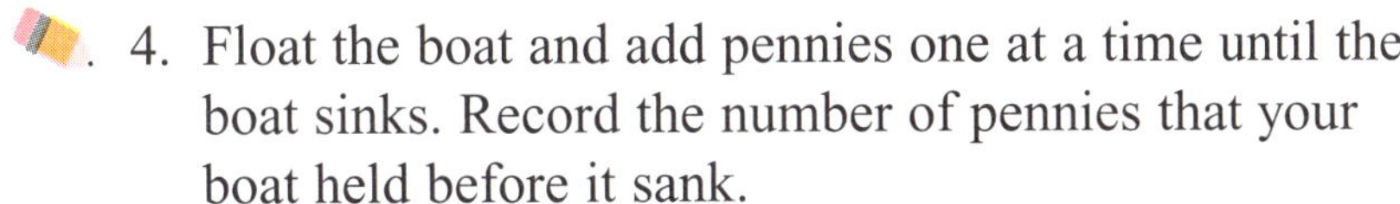

4. Float the boat and add pennies one at a time until the boat sinks. Record the number of pennies that your boat held before it sank.

Answer the Questions

1. What is the difference between mass and weight?

2. How are evaporation and boiling alike? How are they different?

3. Making jelly requires that a lot of sugar be dissolved in fruit juices. Why do you think that most jelly recipes instruct you to boil the juices before adding the sugar?

Solve the Problem

You are trying to decide whether your cup of hot chocolate is a solution or a mixture that is unevenly mixed. You stir the hot chocolate to combine the ingredients. After you drink the hot chocolate, though, you notice that some of the chocolate has settled in the bottom of the cup. Is the hot chocolate a solution or a mixture that is unevenly mixed? How do you know?

Energy and Heat

4

In God's world there are certain natural laws that are always the same. Man often uses these laws to design useful technology. One natural law is that heat always flows from a warmer substance to a cooler substance. A refrigerator is designed using this principle. Pipes inside a refrigerator contain a substance that is cooler than the inside of the refrigerator is. Heat from inside the refrigerator moves to the substance in the pipes. The pipes then carry the heated substance to pipes on the outside of the refrigerator. Once outside, the substance is warmer than the outside air. So the heat flows to the outside air, leaving the substance cool again. In this way, man's design depends on the principles God established.

Energy

Think about some of the things that you do each day. Maybe an electric alarm woke you this morning. You may have turned on a light. Hopefully you ate a good breakfast. Perhaps a car or bus took you to school. Someone adjusted the temperature in your classroom to make you comfortable. All of these activities required energy.

Energy is the ability to do work. Some forms of energy are light, sound, and electricity. Machines, such as cars, use a type of energy known as mechanical energy. Thermal energy causes your room to be the temperature it is. Even the food that you eat is a form of energy. The food provides chemical energy for your body's needs.

You can see that energy comes in many forms. But energy would not be very useful if it could not change from one form to another. A flashlight works because of converted energy. The chemical energy in the batteries changes to electrical energy. This energy then causes the bulb to burn and produce light energy.

A flashlight changes energy from one form to another.

Scientists sometimes classify energy as potential energy or as kinetic energy. **Potential (puh TEN shul) energy**, or stored energy, is the energy that an object or substance has because of its position or condition. A roller coaster at the top of the track has potential energy. As the roller coaster starts down the track, some of its potential energy changes into kinetic energy. **Kinetic (kuh NET ik) energy** is the energy that an object or substance has because of its motion. A flying jet and flowing water both have kinetic energy. They are both moving.

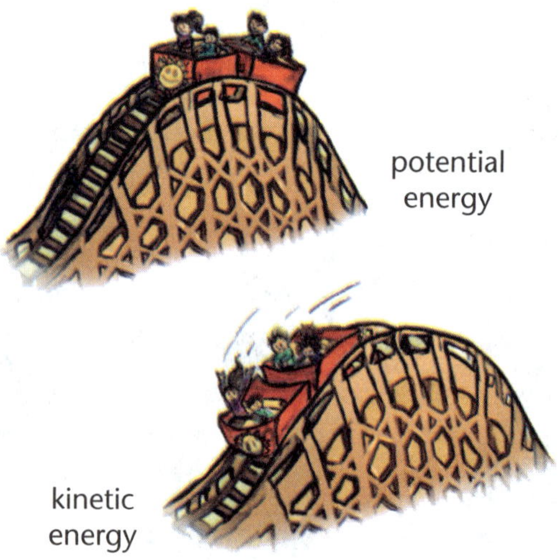

God is the Creator of all matter and energy. Man can at times change energy from one form to another. He can also use matter to produce energy. But man cannot create energy from nothing. Only God can do that as He did at Creation.

Thermal Energy

All matter is made up of tiny particles called atoms and molecules. They are always in motion. This means they have kinetic energy. One kind of kinetic energy is thermal energy. **Thermal energy** is the total kinetic energy of the particles in a substance.

The thermal energy of a substance depends on the temperature and mass of that substance. As the temperature of a substance increases, the particles move faster. The faster the particles move, the more thermal energy the substance has. For example, the particles in a cup of hot water move faster than the particles in a cup of cold water do. Therefore, hot water has more thermal energy than the same amount of cold water does.

The mass of a substance also affects the thermal energy of that substance. If two substances are at the same temperature, the substance with the greater mass will have more thermal energy. More mass means that more particles are present and moving. The more particles that are moving, the more thermal energy a substance has. For example, a large pitcher of water at room temperature has more thermal energy than a small glass of water at room temperature does.

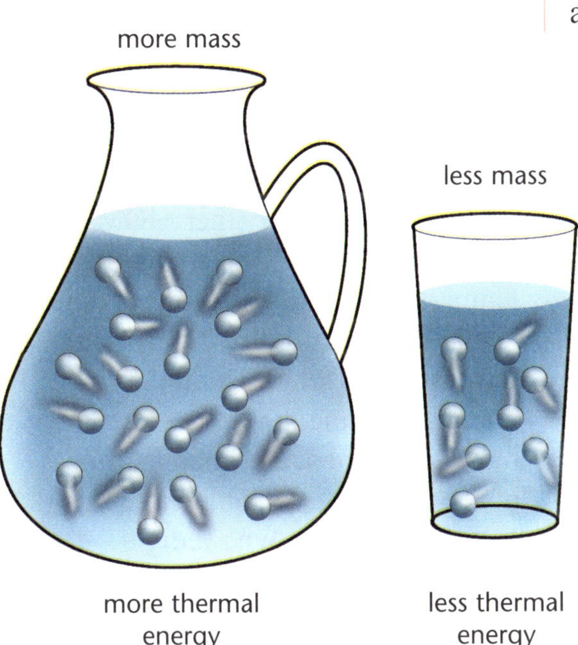

Temperature

When we talk about temperature, we usually mean how hot or cold something feels to us. On a summer day you may feel hot. On a winter day you may feel cold. Sometimes, even in the same conditions, one person may feel comfortable, another may feel cold, and still another may feel warm. *Hot* and *cold* are words that we use to describe how we feel, but they are not very accurate or useful for science experiments. Scientists need terms that have more exact meanings.

One word scientists use in an exact way is *temperature* (TEM per uh CHUR). **Temperature** is the measure of the *average* kinetic energy of the particles in a substance. Particles are always moving. However, not all the particles in a substance move at the same speed. Some particles move faster than average. Others move slower. So, finding the average speed is much more exact than saying how hot or cold the substance feels to us.

Temperature is not the same as thermal energy. A substance with great mass has a lot of thermal energy. However, the average speed of its particles may be slow. The substance may still feel cold. In this case, it has a lot of thermal energy but a low temperature.

How can temperature be measured exactly, though? God designed your body to adjust to different temperatures. For this reason, you cannot measure temperature by how something "feels." If you go swimming in a pool, the water may feel cold at first. But after a while, the water no longer feels cold to you. The water has not gotten warmer. Your body has adjusted to it. So, to get an accurate measurement of temperature, an instrument that does not adapt to its surroundings must be used.

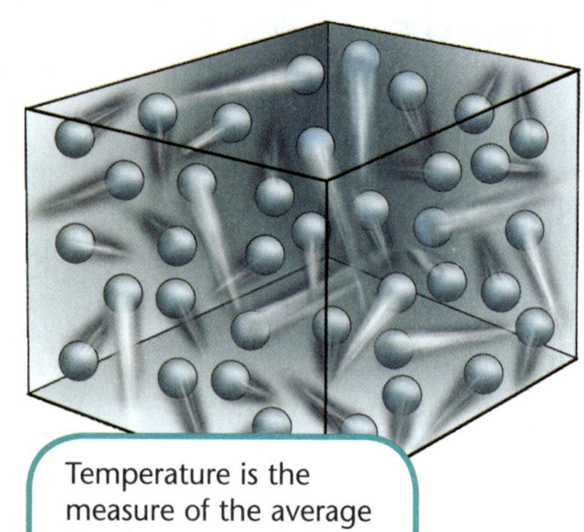

Temperature is the measure of the average kinetic energy of all the particles in a substance.

A **thermometer** (ther MOM ih tur) is an instrument that measures temperature. One type of thermometer is made of a glass tube containing red-colored alcohol. Numbered markings on the tube allow you to measure temperature in units of degrees. You have probably had your temperature taken with a digital thermometer. The temperature shows as a number on a small screen.

Temperature is usually measured in degrees Fahrenheit (FAIR un HEIGHT) or degrees Celsius (SELL see us). Some people use the Fahrenheit scale. The nurse probably takes your temperature using the Fahrenheit scale. The weatherman usually tells the temperature outside using this scale. On the Fahrenheit scale water freezes at 32°F and boils at 212°F.

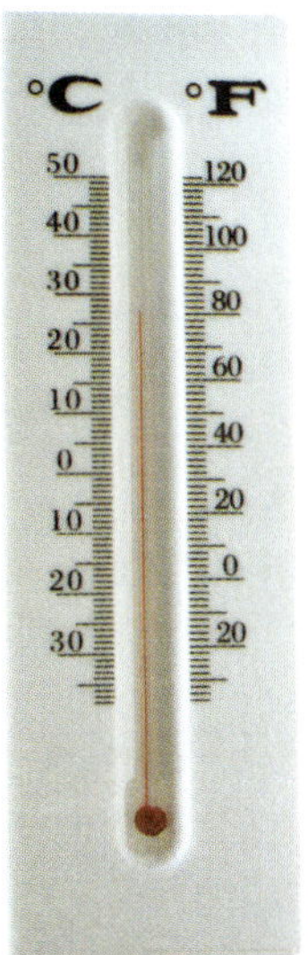

thermometer

Scientists, however, usually use the Celsius scale to measure temperature. The Celsius scale is based on the freezing point and boiling point of water. On the Celsius scale water freezes at 0°C and boils at 100°C.

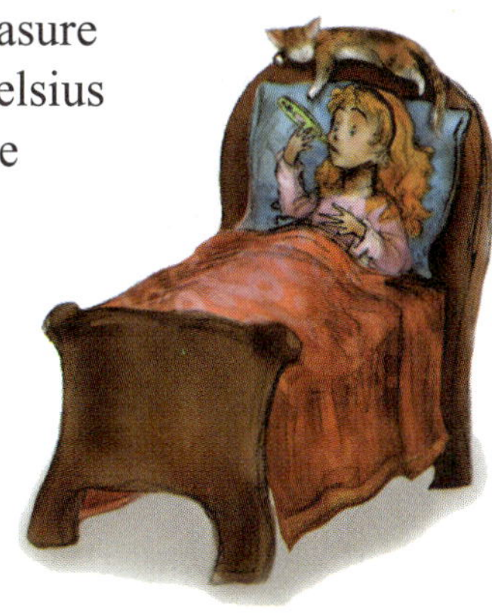

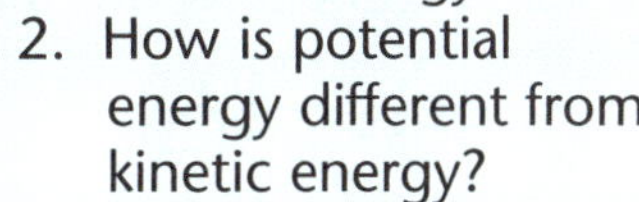

1. What is energy?
2. How is potential energy different from kinetic energy?
3. How is thermal energy different from temperature?

Meet the SCIENTIST LORD KELVIN

Fahrenheit and Celsius are not the only scales used to measure temperature. The Kelvin scale was developed by William Thomson. Born in 1824 in Belfast, Ireland, Thomson studied thermodynamics, the science of heat and energy. His temperature scale is based on the movement of molecules. He placed zero at the point where he believed molecules no longer move or have kinetic energy. Absolute zero, 0°K, on his scale is equal to about –273°C.

Thomson also had a great impact on communication technology. His inventions allowed the first telegraph cable to be laid across the Atlantic. In 1866 he was knighted by Queen Victoria of England. Later, his title became Lord Kelvin.

Although Lord Kelvin was a highly honored scientist, he was also a humble Christian. He said, "If you think strongly enough you will be forced by science to the belief in God." He studied science until his death in 1907.

Rock Heaters

In times past, houses usually did not have heat in the bedrooms. In cold weather people would often heat a brick by placing it in or close to the main fireplace. At bedtime they would cover the brick with cloth and place it at the foot of the bed. The warmth from the brick would help keep the bed warm.

Do you think that the size of the brick affected how long it stayed warm? In this activity, you will use rocks to test how the mass of a substance affects its thermal energy.

Process skills
- Hypothesizing
- Measuring and using numbers
- Collecting and recording data
- Defining operationally

Problem

How does the mass of a substance affect the amount of thermal energy the substance transfers to water?

Procedure

1. Place a piece of cheesecloth on a balance and measure 50 g of aquarium rocks. Remove the cheesecloth and place the other piece on the balance. Measure 100 g of aquarium rocks.
2. Gather the corners of each piece of cheesecloth together so that it forms a bag with the rocks inside. Tie a string around the gathered top of each bag to hold it shut.
3. Predict which mass of aquarium rocks will transfer more thermal energy to the water. Complete the hypothesis in your Activity Manual.
4. Add water to the saucepan and place it on the hot plate. Put the bags of rocks into the saucepan. Heat the water until boiling. Boil the rocks for 10 minutes.

Materials
- 2 squares of cheesecloth
- 150 g aquarium rocks
- balance (mass scale)
- 2 pieces of string
- hot plate
- saucepan
- water
- tongs
- 2 containers
- metric measuring cups
- 2 thermometers
- Activity Manual

5. Label one container *50 g* and the other container *100 g*. Pour 150 mL of room-temperature water into each container.
6. Measure the temperature of the water in the containers. Record the temperatures.
7. Place each bag of heated rocks into the appropriate container.
8. Measure the temperature of the water again after 5 minutes. Record the temperatures.

Conclusions

- Was your hypothesis correct?
- How did the mass of the rocks affect the temperature of the water?

Follow-up

- Use two different substances that have the same mass.
- Make the bags identical in both substance and mass but use different amounts of water.

Matter and Thermal Energy

You already know of ways that thermal energy affects you and the things around you. If you wait too long to eat hot food, it cools off. If you do not eat your ice cream quickly enough, it melts. A fire burning in a fireplace warms the air in the room. All of these situations involve the flow of thermal energy.

As a substance is heated, it gains thermal energy. This additional energy causes the particles to move faster and to attract each other less. A solid may become a liquid, or a liquid may become a gas.

If a substance is cooled, the opposite occurs. It loses thermal energy and may change to a state of matter in which the particles move less and are attracted to each other more.

State Changes

The moving particles in matter attract each other much as magnets attract each other. The amount of attraction can vary, though. It depends on the speed at which the particles move. As the temperature of a substance increases, the speed of its particles increases. As the particles move faster, there is less attraction between them.

Particles in a solid do not move very much. They just vibrate back and forth. Because they move so little, the attraction between the particles is great. In a liquid the particles move a little faster and there is less attraction. Particles in a gas move rapidly and cover great distances. There is little attraction between the particles.

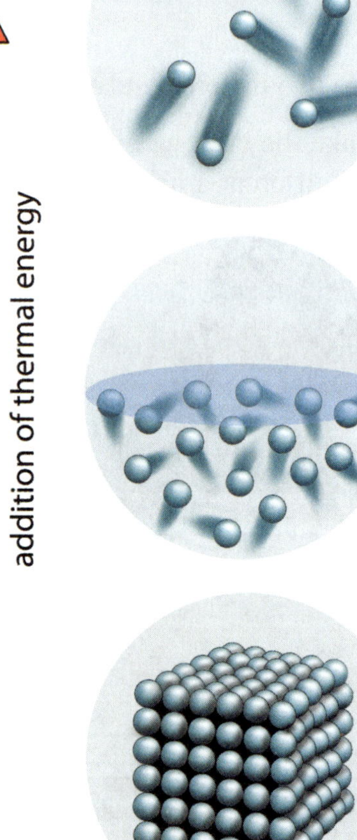

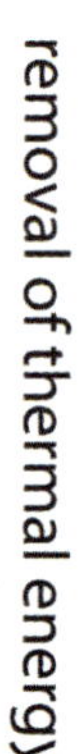

Spaces between sections of a bridge allow the sections to expand and contract.

Thermal Expansion

Sometimes, when the temperature change is not very great, a substance does not change its state. The substance's particles may only move faster and occupy a larger space. This property is known as **thermal expansion**.

A liquid thermometer uses thermal expansion to measure temperatures. When thermal energy is added to the liquid in the thermometer, it increases the energy of the liquid's particles. The liquid in the thermometer expands and takes up more space. This increased volume causes the liquid to show an increased temperature on the thermometer's scale.

The reverse is also true. When a substance is cooled, the particles move less rapidly and occupy less space. In this case, the substance shrinks, or contracts. Almost every substance expands when it is heated and contracts when it is cooled.

When the temperature of most substances changes only a little, they expand or contract only a small amount. However, even a small amount can cause great problems. Engineers must allow room for these small changes in size as they plan structures. If you look at a bridge, sidewalk, or highway, you may see spaces between the sections. These spaces allow the structures to expand and contract without buckling or cracking.

You can observe how thermal expansion works. Blow up two balloons about halfway. Place one balloon in the refrigerator or freezer. As the thermal energy is removed from the balloon, the balloon shrinks. Place the other balloon in a very warm place. Observe what happens. The increased thermal energy causes the gas in the balloon to expand and take up more space.

Measuring Thermal Energy

Since thermal energy and temperature are not the same, they are not measured in the same way. One of the units used for measuring thermal energy is the calorie (KAL uh ree). A **calorie** (cal) is the amount of thermal energy needed to raise the temperature of 1 g of water 1°C.

Raising the temperature of 10 g of water 1°C takes 10 calories of thermal energy. It also takes 10 cal to raise 1 g of water 10°C. The amount of thermal energy required depends on both the mass of the substance and its change in temperature.

Stored Thermal Energy

Some substances heat or cool more easily than others do. This means that the substances have different abilities to store thermal energy. Perhaps you have noticed that the metal parts of a bicycle get hotter than the plastic parts do. Metals can store a lot of thermal energy. Even just a little heat will make them warm up. Plastics do not store as much. It takes a lot of heat to warm them up.

QUICK CHECK

1. What happens to particles of a substance as it is heated?
2. Why do engineers put spaces between the sections of a bridge?
3. What is one unit of measurement used to measure thermal energy?

The metal parts of a bicycle will get hotter than the plastic parts will.

Explorations

Energy for Your Body

You may have heard someone say, "That food has a lot of calories in it." He was probably thinking about his possible weight gain. But calories in food are actually a measure of the energy available from that food. A food calorie is 1,000 times bigger than the calorie a scientist uses. A food calorie is labeled as a *kcal* (kilocalorie) or *Cal*. However, it is usually written simply as *calorie*.

Your body converts the calories from the food that you eat into energy for doing work. If the amount of calories that a person eats is the same as the energy that he uses, his weight stays about the same. If he eats more calories than he uses, he tends to gain weight. If he eats less, he loses weight. Other things, such as growth or illness, can also affect how many calories a body needs.

Most of the calories that the body uses are for basic functions such as breathing and maintaining body temperature. The energy needed for these functions is called the resting metabolic rate (RMR). A person's RMR is dependent on factors such as age, weight, height, and gender. This rate can be adjusted, based on average daily activity, to show about how many calories a person needs each day.

What to do

 1. Calculate your resting metabolic rate (RMR) and adjust it based on your average daily activity.

 2. For three days record everything that you eat and drink.

 3. Research to find an estimate of the number of calories in each of the foods and drinks that you consumed. Add the results to find a total calorie count for each day. Average the totals to find an average daily amount.

4. Compare your average daily calories with your adjusted RMR.

Heat

Thermal energy is the total kinetic energy in a substance. But thermal energy does not stay in one place. It moves, or transfers. **Heat** is the transfer of thermal energy from one substance to another.

Heat always flows from a warmer substance to a cooler one. When this happens, we say the cooler substance has been heated. The cooler substance has gained thermal energy. The warmer substance has lost thermal energy, or cooled. Heat can flow in several ways: conduction, convection, or radiation.

Conduction

Conduction (kun DUCK shun) is heat that occurs when particles bump into each other but do not change location. Solids are usually heated by conduction. The particles in a solid are tightly packed together. Being tightly packed together allows heat to flow easily between the particles.

When part of a solid is heated, the increased thermal energy of the heated particles causes them to vibrate faster.

As the particles vibrate faster, they cause the particles around them to vibrate faster as well. These particles then cause even more particles to vibrate faster. Eventually all the particles of the solid are vibrating faster. This makes the whole solid warmer.

Conduction does not just occur within a substance. It can also occur between substances. For example, a metal spoon in a cup of hot chocolate heats up through conduction. At first, the hot chocolate has more heat, or thermal energy, than the spoon does. This means that the hot chocolate's particles move faster than the spoon's particles do. As the faster hot chocolate particles bump into the slower spoon particles, the spoon is heated. The hot chocolate particles lose some energy and get cooler. The spoon particles gain some energy and get warmer. In time, the thermal energy will become equal, and the two substances will have the same temperature.

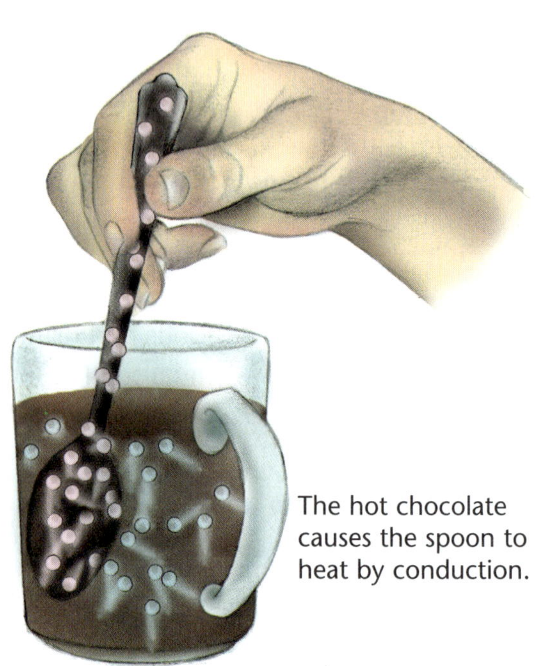

The hot chocolate causes the spoon to heat by conduction.

Most cooking on a stove top uses conduction. A stove burner heats a pan. The pan heats the food. You would also feel the results of conduction if you touched the hot pan. Your hand would be cooler than the hot pan, and the pan would quickly heat your hand. The quick transfer of energy would cause pain and might burn your hand.

Conductors are substances that allow heat to move through them easily. The best conductors are metals. For this reason metals such as silver, copper, and aluminum often are used when rapid heating is desired. Many kinds of cookware are made of copper or aluminum.

Insulators (IN suh LAY turs) are substances that do not allow heat to move through them easily. Wood, brick, glass, and plastic are good insulators. Cookware may have a wooden or plastic handle that acts as an insulator so your hands do not get burned.

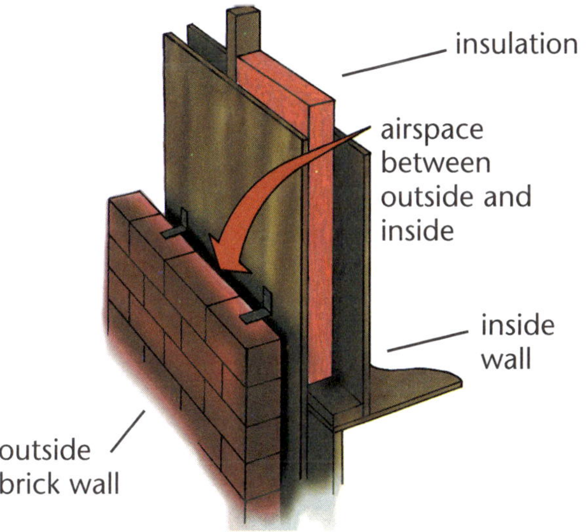

A bird fluffs out its feathers to help insulate itself from the cold.

You might be surprised to learn that air is also a good insulator. Birds fluff out their feathers on cold days to keep warm. Air between a bird's feathers and its body helps insulate the bird from the cold. You use the same principle when you wear several layers of clothing to help keep warm in the winter.

Air also helps insulate buildings. Double-paned windows trap air between the glass panes. This helps to keep buildings warmer in the winter and cooler in the summer. The trapped air does not easily transfer thermal energy by conduction. In a similar way, the insulation used in the ceilings and walls of buildings often use many pockets of air to reduce heat loss.

Convection

In conduction, the particles transfer energy but do not move from one place to another. But not all heat moves this way. **Convection** (kun VECK shun) is heat that occurs when particles carry thermal energy as they move from one place to another.

Convection usually occurs in liquids and gases. For example, as you heat water, only some of the water particles touch the bottom of the pan. These particles are heated by conduction. As they get hotter, they move faster and spread out. This spreading out makes the water at the bottom become less dense. The particles in the hotter water are pushed up as the particles in the cooler, denser water above sink. The new, cool particles at the bottom are then heated, and the whole process starts again. This process is continuously repeated. This movement of particles is called a *convection current*. The current moves particles that carry thermal energy from one place to another.

You have probably seen the convection currents in a pan of boiling water. There are also other kinds of convection currents. Huge thunderstorm clouds are caused by convection currents in the air. Most geologists think that the magma under the earth's crust flows in this type of current as well.

convection currents

Radiation

Radiation (RAY dee AY shun) is heat that occurs when there are no particles to carry the energy. Both conduction and convection need matter for heating. Radiation, however, happens without particles directly touching or particles moving. The transfer of thermal energy is indirect. Radiation can occur even through empty space.

Solar radiation, or energy from the sun, is an important source of both heat and light for the earth. The sun heats the earth even though a great distance separates them. There is no matter that can be used to transfer the energy of the sun to the earth. Yet energy from the sun still reaches the earth by radiation. Much of this solar radiation is absorbed by the earth and converted to thermal energy.

Not all substances absorb the same amount of radiation. The amount depends on the type of surface the substance has. Dark colors absorb radiation better than light colors do. This is why you feel warmer in the sunshine when you wear dark clothing than when you wear light-colored clothing. Likewise, an asphalt parking lot will feel much hotter on a sunny day than a light-colored sidewalk nearby will.

The sun is not the only source of radiation, though. The glowing coils of a toaster use radiation to brown your bread. You also can feel the warmth of radiation from a glowing light bulb.

toaster coils

All three forms of heat can be observed at a campfire. *Conduction* heats the air particles that directly touch the fire. As the thermal energy of the particles increases, their temperature also increases. The particles become less dense. They rise, and cooler air particles sink and replace them. This causes *convection* currents and heats the air above the fire. Several feet to the side of the fire, you can sense the heat mostly by *radiation* from the flames.

QUICK CHECK

1. Which type of heating requires particles to touch each other?
2. What is the difference between an insulator and a conductor?
3. In which type of heating does matter move from one place to another?
4. Which type of heating transfers energy without using particles?

Keeping Warm

Process skills
- Hypothesizing
- Predicting
- Inferring
- Collecting and recording data
- Communicating

Sometimes insulation keeps something from getting hot. Many cooking pots have insulated handles. The handles stay cool and keep you from burning your hand.

Insulation can also keep hot things warm, though. For example, an insulated thermos can keep cold foods cool or keep hot foods warm. Many animals, such as polar bears, have air-filled spaces in their fur. The air helps the animals keep warm during the winter. Likewise, insulation in the ceilings or walls of buildings keeps heat inside during cold weather.

In this activity, you will test several kinds of insulation to determine which is the most effective.

Materials
- 5 plastic cups, 3 oz
- cotton batting
- rubber bands
- craft foam
- bubble wrap
- aluminum foil
- 250 mL hot water
- metric measuring cups
- 5 thermometers
- plastic wrap
- Activity Manual

Problem

Which kind of insulation will keep hot water warm the best?

Procedure

1. Wrap cotton batting around one of the cups. Be sure to cover the bottom and the sides of the cup. Use a rubber band to secure the cotton batting against the cup.
2. Prepare three more cups: one wrapped with craft foam, one with bubble wrap, and one with a double thickness of aluminum foil. Use rubber bands to secure each material. Do not wrap anything around the fifth cup.
3. Predict which cup will best keep the hot water warm. Complete the hypothesis in your Activity Manual.
4. Pour 50 mL of hot water into each cup. Place a thermometer in each cup.

5. Cover the top of the cup with plastic wrap. Do not cover the thermometer with plastic wrap. You should be able to read the temperature without removing the plastic wrap.
6. Measure and record the starting temperature for each cup.
7. Leave the cups undisturbed for five minutes. Then measure and record the water temperature in each cup. Measure and record the temperatures again after another five minutes.
8. Calculate the difference between the starting and ending temperatures for each cup.

Conclusions

- Was your hypothesis correct?
- Which cup had the greatest change in temperature?
- Which type of insulated cup would you choose to hold hot chocolate? Why?

Follow-up

- Test other materials as insulation.
- Use ice cubes instead of hot water. Determine which insulation is the best for keeping ice cubes from melting.

Heat at Work

If you tried to burn a piece of granite, you would find it very difficult. It would take a tremendous amount of heat to do so. You also would have to use much more energy than you could gain from the hot rock. Some kinds of matter can be easily converted into energy, though. These kinds of matter are often called fuels.

crude oil

Fuel Sources

A **fuel** is any substance that releases energy when it burns. Some common fuels are wood, oil, gasoline, and natural gas. Each contains matter that can be changed into energy by a chemical change. As the fuel burns, some of it changes into thermal energy.

Some of the fuels that we use are known as fossil fuels. **Fossil fuels** were formed when the remains of plants and animals were buried quickly during the Genesis Flood. Fossil fuels include coal, crude oil, and natural gas. The worldwide Flood of Noah's day, recorded in Genesis 7–8, can account for the abundance of fossil fuels that we find in the world today.

There are still large quantities of fossil fuels around the world. But these fuels are often described as *nonrenewable*. A nonrenewable resource is one that is being used faster than it is forming.

Another form of fuel is wood. This fuel has been used throughout history. Today many people use fossil fuels instead of wood. However, there are still places in the world where wood is the only available fuel. Unlike fossil fuels, wood is a *renewable* resource. That means it can be replaced. New trees can grow naturally, or man can plant new ones.

natural gas

coal

firewood

Fuel Uses

Releasing thermal energy is usually the purpose for burning a fuel. Many people burn fuel to keep warm in cold weather. As fuels burn, they can heat homes and other buildings. Natural gas, heating oil, coal, and wood are all common fuels used for heating.

However, fuels are not just used to heat homes. Some people use natural gas to cook food, dry clothes, or heat water. Sometimes wood is used to cook food as well.

Power plants use fuel to produce electricity. The burning fuel gives off thermal energy. This energy heats water and produces steam. The steam is used to turn a propeller-like device called a turbine. The turbine then turns a generator to produce the electricity.

Many other industries also burn fuels. Without heat from fuels, many products could not be made. For example, iron ore, a rock-like mineral used to make steel, must be melted to remove any impurities. However, the melting point of iron is very high, about 1,535°C. Fossil fuels produce the very high temperatures needed for this process.

steel plant

Fuel is important to transportation.

Once the impurities are removed from the liquid iron, it is mixed with other substances and poured into molds. As the metal cools and solidifies, it forms many of the steel products that you use.

Most forms of transportation involve the burning of fuels made from crude oil. Almost all cars burn gasoline made from crude oil. Large trucks use diesel fuel, which is also made from crude oil. Even jet fuel is a product of crude oil.

God used a burning bush to speak to Moses. A bush burning in the desert would not have been unusual. A bush that was on fire but did not burn up was miraculous, though. Moses says in Exodus 3:3, "I will now turn aside and see this great sight, why the bush is not burnt." His curiosity at God's miracle caused him to come closer to the bush. From that burning bush, God spoke to Moses and sent him to deliver the children of Israel from the slavery of Egypt.

Unwanted Heat

Often when energy changes from one form to another, thermal energy is also produced. Sometimes the heat is the desired result. At other times, though, the heat is not wanted. In these cases, it is a waste product, or *byproduct*. The heat from a light bulb is an example of this. The electrical energy in the light bulb produces light. Light is the desired form of energy, but the light bulb also gets very hot. The energy that produces the light also creates heat. This heat is a byproduct.

Unwanted heat can sometimes damage equipment. For example, when a car engine burns fuel, the engine produces mechanical energy. This energy moves the car, but it also produces heat. Some of this heat is a byproduct. If not removed, it will cause the engine to get too hot. To prevent that, a car radiator uses fluid to transport heat away from the engine. A fan near the engine also helps move away extra heat.

Other machines also use fans and moving air to remove unwanted heat. A computer produces a lot of heat as electricity moves through its parts.

A fan moves air through a computer to help remove unwanted heat.

This heat could damage sensitive parts of the computer. So a fan moves heat away from these parts.

Even your body has its own type of cooling system. God designed the human body to maintain a certain temperature range. When you exercise, though, your body converts energy from one form to another. This produces extra heat. The fluid in your body carries this heat to your skin's surface and produces sweat. The sweat evaporates on your skin and helps cool your body. Because of this loss of fluid, though, you should drink plenty of fluids when you exercise. Replacing the fluids helps maintain your body's cooling system.

Sweating helps the body remove extra heat.

1. How were fossil fuels formed?
2. What are three uses of fuels?
3. Give an example of how thermal energy affects everyday life.

Heat in Space

Man has designed many kinds of technology to control heat. Sometimes the purpose is to make equipment run better. Other times it is to make people more comfortable. During space travel, though, controlling heat is not just a matter of efficiency or comfort. It is a matter of survival. The lives of the space crew depend on it.

the bottom of a space capsule

Space Capsules

Rubbing your hands together produces friction. The friction causes heat that you can feel. In a similar way, a space vehicle produces friction when it moves through the air. However, a space vehicle is much larger than your hands and moves much faster. It creates a lot of friction and a lot of heat. The temperature on the exterior of a spacecraft can reach hundreds of degrees Celsius during liftoff.

The temperature during liftoff is very high. But the temperature of the space vehicle is even greater as it returns to the earth. A spacecraft's exterior can reach more than a 1,000°C (1,832°F) as the spacecraft moves through the earth's atmosphere.

At the beginning of the space program, rockets designed for manned space travel had a capsule at the top of the rocket. Only the space capsule, with the astronauts inside, returned to the earth. This capsule had a flat bottom. While entering the earth's atmosphere, the flat bottom faced toward the earth. This design slowed the capsule down.

Although the design slowed the capsule down, the flat bottom also produced a lot of friction. The heat from this friction caused the capsule to get very hot. No one inside the capsule would have been able to live through it. So scientists and engineers had to find a way to remove some of the heat.

To solve the problem, scientists used an idea similar to how sweat cools your skin. They put a material on the capsule's outside that melted and vaporized as the capsule heated up. As the material vaporized, it cooled the capsule. Sweat keeps us cool in much the same way.

The tiles on the bottom of a shuttle are made to withstand very high temperatures.

Space Shuttles

Exterior heat

As scientists and engineers developed new spacecraft, new problems had to be solved. The cooling method used on a space capsule would not work on a space shuttle. Space shuttles were meant to be used again. They could not use material that would melt and vaporize.

A space shuttle is also larger than a space capsule was. More size means more surface area to cause friction. It also means that more surface area gets hot. As a shuttle returns to the earth, the shuttle's exterior may reach 1,650°C (3,000°F). This would cause the shuttle's aluminum frame to melt if not protected.

To protect the shuttle and its crew, several kinds of insulation are used. One kind is like a heavy blanket. It is made with waterproof glass cloth and is quilted. This kind of insulation protects areas of the shuttle that do not get the hottest.

A shuttle also uses ceramic tiles as insulation. A shuttle returning to the earth glides like an airplane. In doing this, the bottom of the space shuttle produces most of the friction that slows the shuttle down. However, the friction also causes the bottom of the shuttle to heat up more than any other part of the shuttle does. For this reason, special tiles designed to protect against very high temperatures cover the bottom of the shuttle.

Faulty tiles can create serious problems. Scientists believe that tile damage caused the explosion of the space shuttle *Columbia*. The tiles may have been broken or damaged during liftoff. When the shuttle returned to the earth, the tiles could not protect the shuttle from the intense heat. The shuttle exploded as it flew back into the earth's atmosphere.

The ceramic tiles on space shuttles are carefully checked.

Interior heat

The insulation on a shuttle keeps heat outside the shuttle—but also keeps heat inside. Computers and other electronic equipment generate a lot of heat as they work. Just imagine how much heat is produced by all the equipment on a space shuttle!

a space shuttle with its cargo-bay doors open

Shuttles do not get hot only from computers, though. One of the greatest sources of heat in space is the sun. Space is a very cold place, but the sun's radiation causes objects in space to heat up. The earth is protected by the atmosphere. Without the protective layer of the earth's atmosphere, objects in space get very hot if not cooled in some way.

You may have seen a picture of a shuttle in orbit. Most likely, the shuttle had its huge cargo-bay doors open. Even if no work was being done outside the shuttle, the doors were open for a reason. Because space is so cold, opening the doors helps cool off the shuttle.

The shuttle also has a system, similar to a refrigerator, that cools the inside of the shuttle. Pipes transfer some of the heat from the shuttle's interior to an area inside the cargo bay. When the cargo-bay doors are open, the area is exposed to the outside. The heat flows from the warmer pipes to the coldness of space. This removes some of the unwanted heat from the inside of the space shuttle.

Through the space program, we have learned many things about our universe. All our knowledge could not have been gained, however, if we were not able to control heat in a spacecraft.

We seldom think about how thermal energy impacts us. Each day, we are affected by it, though. We dress in clothing that is appropriate for how warm or cool the day is. We put ice cream in the freezer so that it will not melt. We use a wooden or plastic spoon, instead of a metal one, to stir boiling liquids. Each of these decisions is based on our knowledge of how thermal energy and heat affect us.

God designed His creation to be consistent and predictable. The things we make and use rely on this natural order. Without it, we would not be able to use the energy God created. The consistency of nature reflects God's mercy toward us. As the psalmist said, "Bless the Lord. . . . Who laid the foundations of the earth, that it should not be removed for ever" (Psalm 104:1, 5).

QUICK CHECK

1. Why is controlling heat while in space so important?
2. What causes the heat that occurs when space vehicles take off or land?
3. What technology causes a lot of heat inside the space shuttle?

Explorations Moon Station

The earth's atmosphere traps heat from the sun. This helps keep the earth from experiencing extreme changes in temperature. But the earth's moon has no atmosphere. The moon's daytime temperature can reach around 120°C (250°F). At night the temperature can drop to −173°C (−279.4°F). The length of time from one sunrise to another is also longer than that on the earth. It takes over twenty-seven Earth days for the moon to complete one rotation, or day.

Imagine that scientists have asked you to help design equipment for a station on the moon. You will need to consider the extreme temperature changes on the moon as you design your equipment. You will also need to keep in mind that the extreme temperatures last for many Earth days.

What to do

1. Decide what your equipment will do. Will it be used for clothing, housing, communication, transportation, or something else?
2. Fill in your Activity Manual and draw a sketch of your piece of equipment.
3. Be able to explain how your invention is designed to withstand the temperatures on the moon.

Answer the Questions

1. Give examples of how conduction, convection, and radiation are used for cooking.

____

____

2. Why does a set of doors with space between them help keep a building cool in summer and warm in winter?

____

____

3. Some houses in very warm locations have high ceilings. Why would having a high ceiling help keep a house cooler in hot weather?

____

____

____

Solve the Problem

Your family is camping at a national park in the desert in late spring. Although it is dusk your family decides to go on a short hike. The day has been very warm, but the night air is quickly turning cool. The park ranger says to watch out for snakes on large rocks. He says that snakes are cold-blooded and are trying to stay warm in the cooler evening temperatures. Why would a large rock still be warm after the sun had gone down and the air had cooled off?

____

____

____

____

____

UNIT 3

Because of the Climate

The hot Sahara Desert and parts of the cold Antarctica seem very different. But Chapter 6 explains how these land areas have something in common.

You probably would not expect ice to fall during warm weather. However, Chapter 5 tells about ice that not only falls during warm weather but can be bigger than a grapefruit.

God designed your body to carry thousands of pounds of weight around every day. In Chapter 5 find out what the weight is and why it does not flatten you.

Weather

REMEMBER *now* thy CREATOR

What do airplanes and roofs have in common? Both of these objects are affected by the way air flows around them. One of the principles of air flow is called the Bernoulli principle. Scientists use this principle to design airplane wings that give the lift needed for airplanes to fly.

In recent years scientists have found that severe winds during hurricanes may cause roofs to act similar to airplane wings. As the winds flow over a roof, the roof tends to lift up. To design better roofs, scientists often use a wind tunnel to duplicate the hurricane winds. They experiment with different roof designs to see which are better able to withstand the severe winds. Although man cannot control the weather, God's creation stays consistent. This consistency allows man to design ways to improve his surroundings.

God created the earth with all the conditions necessary to maintain life. He knew what conditions man needs. And He planned for these needs to be met. Part of this plan is a protective layer that surrounds the earth.

Atmosphere

The earth has a special covering that protects its surface. This thin blanket of gases and dust particles that surrounds the earth is called the **atmosphere** (AT muh SFEAR). If the earth were the size of an apple, the atmosphere would be thinner than the apple's skin. This very thin covering is very important to us, though. The atmosphere lets in the right amount of energy from the sun and provides the air we breathe. It also prevents extreme weather differences on the earth.

Contents of the Atmosphere

One part of the atmosphere is air. But what is air? **Air** is a mixture of nitrogen, oxygen, carbon dioxide, and other gases in the atmosphere. We cannot see or feel these gases, but they are very important to life on the earth. Plants need the nitrogen and carbon dioxide to produce food. People and animals need oxygen to survive. Providing an atmosphere with this blend of gases is one way God meets the needs of living things.

Another part of the atmosphere is dust particles. When you clean your bedroom, you probably stir up dust. Dust particles may seem annoying when you are cleaning. However, they are useful in the atmosphere. Dust helps water droplets and ice crystals in the clouds form rain, snow, and other types of precipitation.

Gases in the Atmosphere

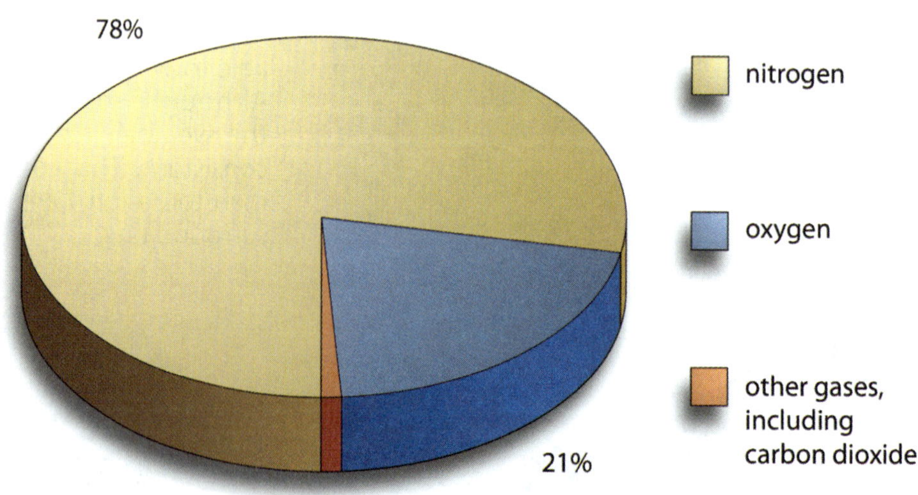

Air Pressure

Gravity pulls the atmosphere close to the surface of the earth. At any moment there are thousands of pounds of air pressing on you. The weight of the air is called **air pressure**. In fact each square inch of space has 14.7 lb of pressure. It does not seem that air would weigh very much, but there is a huge amount of air above the earth. As the air is pulled toward the earth by gravity, it causes great pressure.

Air pressure is greatest at the surface of the earth and decreases as you move away from the surface of the earth, or gain altitude. **Altitude** (OWL ti TOOD) is the measurement of the distance above sea level. The altitude affects air pressure. There is less air pressure on a high mountain than at the seashore. However, altitude is not the only factor that affects air pressure. Other factors, such as changes in temperature, also affect air pressure.

A *barometer* (buh ROM ih ter) is an instrument used to measure air pressure. Knowing the air pressure is important when forecasting the weather. Changes in air pressure may mean that a storm is coming. Pilots are also alert to changes in air pressure because the changes can affect flying conditions.

barometer

Creation CORNER

Some places in our bodies, such as our lungs and inner ears, are filled with air. When we breathe in and out, the air pressure in our lungs changes to equalize the outside air pressure. Our inner ears are often closed, however. This means the air pressure inside our ears may not be the same as the pressure outside. The inequality may cause our ears to hurt as we travel up and down mountains or fly in a plane. To help prevent this, God has designed our bodies with a tube that goes from our middle ears to our throat. When we swallow, we open the tube and allow the air pressure inside and outside our ears to equalize.

Layers of the Atmosphere

God designed the atmosphere to have several layers. Each layer is different. Together, though, these layers protect the earth and give it a controlled climate.

The **troposphere** (TRO puh SFEAR) is the layer of the atmosphere that is closest to the earth. But even the tallest mountain on earth, Mt. Everest, reaches only about halfway into the troposphere. About half of the air in the atmosphere is in the troposphere. The troposphere is also where weather occurs.

The air in the troposphere holds in the radiant heat from the sun. This helps keep the surface of the earth warm. At higher altitudes, the air in the troposphere gets thinner and cooler. Just as a thin sweater cannot keep you as warm as a thick coat can, the thinner air at higher altitudes cannot hold as much thermal energy as the denser air near the surface can.

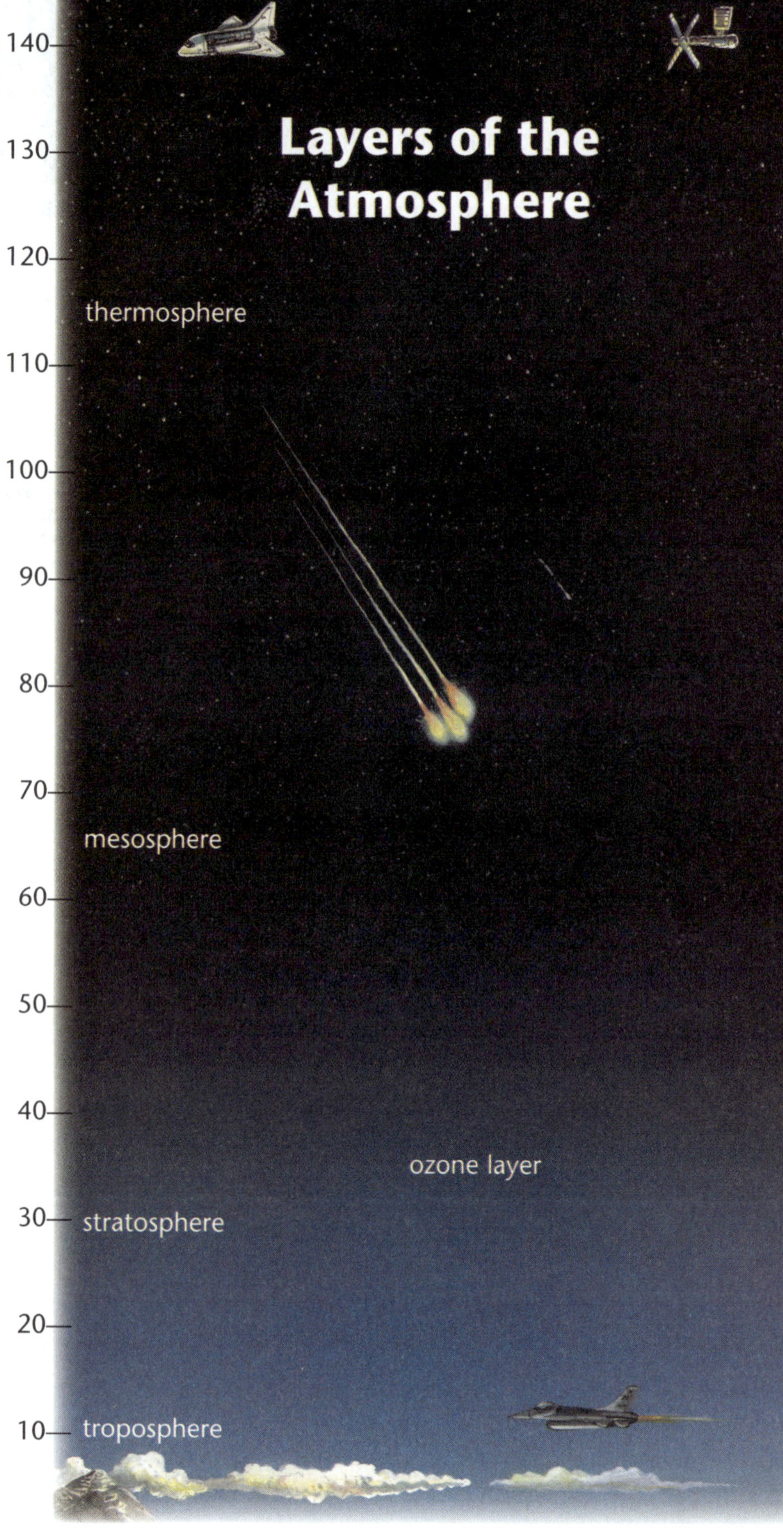

altitude in km

Weather is the condition of the atmosphere at any moment in time. The troposphere contains many particles and water droplets that affect the weather. These reflect light, allowing us to see colorful sunrises and sunsets.

The *stratosphere* (STRAT uh SFEAR) is the next layer above the troposphere. The air in the stratosphere continues to get thinner as you travel away from the surface of the earth. Unlike the troposphere, though, the stratosphere increases in temperature as the altitude increases.

God made the stratosphere to protect the earth. During the day, the stratosphere shields the earth from the harmful effects of the sun. At night, the stratosphere helps hold in some of the heat that the sun provided during the day.

The *ozone layer* is in the upper part of the stratosphere. Ozone is a form of oxygen. This layer of gas is one way the stratosphere protects the surface of the earth from the sun's harmful rays.

The higher layers of the atmosphere also help protect the earth. Meteors heading toward the earth burn up in the *mesosphere* (MEZ uh SFEAR). These burning meteors are the "shooting stars" we sometimes see. Many of our weather and communication satellites are in the *thermosphere* (THUR muh SFEAR). The *exosphere* (EK soh SFEAR) is the layer of the atmosphere farthest from the earth. This layer gradually fades into space.

Some people compare the atmosphere to a greenhouse. A greenhouse is a special building, often made of glass. It completely surrounds and protects the plants inside from extreme heat or cold. The sunlight, temperature, and moisture inside a greenhouse are carefully adjusted to provide the ideal environment for the plants. In a similar way, God designed the atmosphere to completely surround the earth. He planned for the atmosphere to protect the earth and provide the proper weather needed for each area of the earth.

QUICK CHECK

1. What is the atmosphere?
2. What is air pressure?
3. Which layer of the atmosphere is closest to the earth?
4. In which layer of the atmosphere is the ozone layer found?

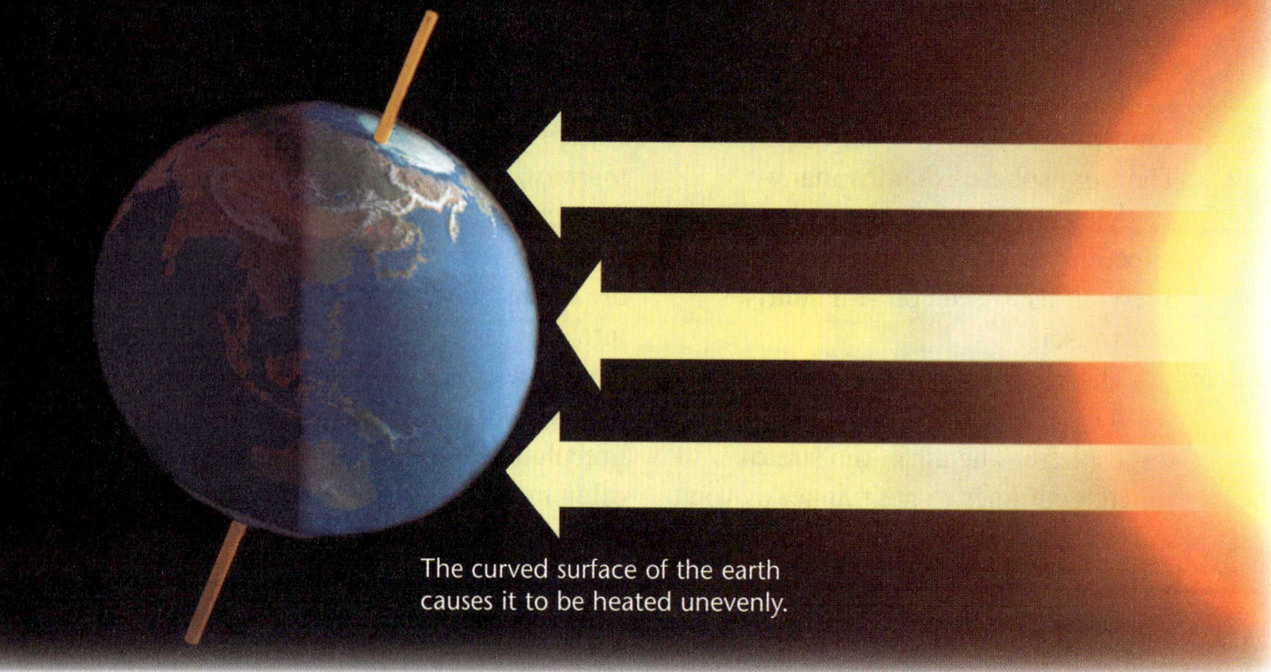
The curved surface of the earth causes it to be heated unevenly.

Moving Air

You are surrounded by air that is usually moving. Moving air is called **wind**. Sometimes wind moves so slowly that it seems to be perfectly still. Other times it blows violently and destroys everything in its path.

We can use and enjoy wind in many ways. A light breeze may cool us off after a ball game. A stronger wind may allow us to fly a kite high in the air. In times past, great winds pushed the ships of explorers across the oceans. Today we rely on wind to provide some of our electricity.

Air Temperature

Although the heat from the sun comes through the atmosphere, the sun does not warm the air much. Instead, the sun warms the earth's surface, which then warms the air above it. The air temperature is a result of the heating and cooling of the earth's surface.

However, the earth's surface does not heat evenly, so the air in the atmosphere does not heat evenly either. The part of the earth facing the sun receives heat and is warmer than the part facing away from the sun. This is why days are usually warmer than nights are.

The curved surface of the earth also affects temperatures. Sunlight hits some places directly and other places at a slant. The places that receive direct sunlight are warmer than those that receive sunlight at a slant.

Air Masses

A large body of air that has about the same temperature and moisture is called an **air mass**. An air mass often takes on different characteristics as it moves over the earth's surface. For example, an air mass over a cool area will become cooler. An air mass over an ocean will collect moisture. As a cool air mass moves over a hot desert, it will become warmer and drier.

Air masses also vary in density and air pressure. The gas particles in cool air are close together, causing cool air masses to be denser than warm ones are. Cool air also has greater pressure. The air pressure of a dense, cool air mass is called *high pressure*. Because of its greater density, a cool air mass cannot hold much moisture. For this reason, a high-pressure air mass usually has cool, dry air.

High-pressure air masses often move toward the surface of the earth. There, the warm surface of the earth heats the air, causing the gas particles to spread out. As the air becomes lighter and less dense, it rises in the atmosphere. This light, warm air can also hold more moisture. The air pressure of a light, warm air mass is called *low pressure*. Low-pressure air masses of warm, moist air generally move above cool air masses.

Science and HISTORY

Hot air balloons use changes in air density to move up and down. Heating the air in a balloon moves the air particles farther apart. As the air inside the balloon becomes less dense than the outside air, the balloon rises. As the air inside the balloon cools, the balloon drops.

Hot air balloons have been used by the military since the Civil War. The balloons were used to observe the location and size of enemy armies. Today some balloons are still used for surveillance along our country's borders.

Fronts

When two unlike air masses meet, the boundary between the masses is called a **front**. A cool air mass may push itself under a weaker warm air mass. This type of front is called a *cold front*. It often brings rainy weather that may include thunderstorms and hail. A cold front usually moves quickly through an area. After the cold front passes, the weather is usually cooler and drier than before.

A *warm front* occurs when a warm air mass moves over a slower cool air mass. A warm front moves slowly and may take several days to leave an area. As a result, a warm front often brings several days of light rain or foggy weather. When a warm front passes, the following days may have warm, moist weather.

Sometimes air masses push against each other but do not move. When this happens, the boundary is called a *stationary front*. A stationary front may stay in the same place for several days. It usually causes cloudy skies and rainy conditions.

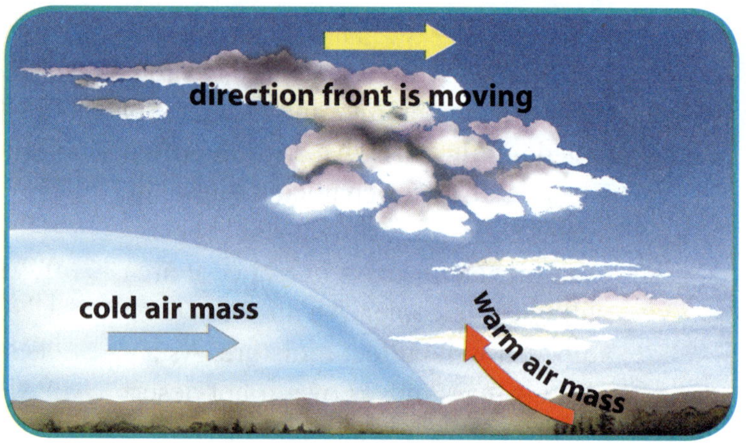

cold front

warm front

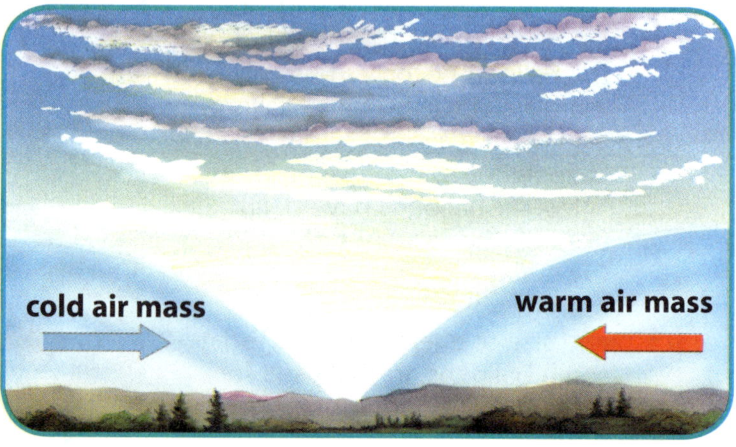

stationary front

Wind

Air varies in temperature. Many things, such as location, affect the air temperature and can make it warmer or cooler. For instance, air near the surface of the earth is warmer. But air at higher altitudes is cooler. Air is also warmer near the equator and cooler at the poles of the earth. Changes in temperature cause wind. Warmer air rises. Cooler air moves toward the earth to replace the warmer, rising air. These and other air patterns influence the movement of winds.

Global winds

The uneven heating of the earth causes global winds. **Global winds** move in large, circular belts around the earth. Global winds include trade winds, the prevailing westerlies, and the polar easterlies. Winds are identified by the direction from which they blow.

The prevailing easterlies, or *trade winds*, blow from the east toward the equator. Christopher Columbus used the prevailing easterlies when he sailed to the New World. These winds became known as the trade winds because trade ships relied on these strong winds to sail to the Americas. After trading their cargo, the ships would then return to Europe using the *prevailing westerlies*. In the Northern Hemisphere, these winds blow northward from the west. Near the North Pole and the South Pole, the *polar easterlies* blow from the east and move away from each pole.

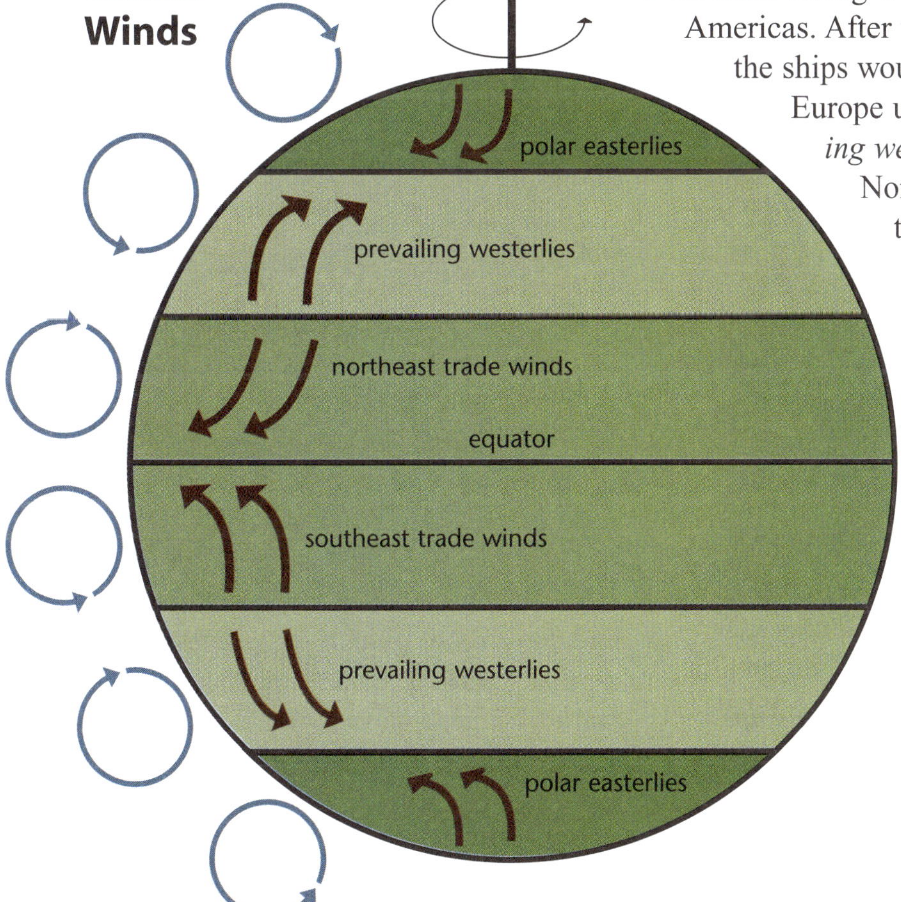

Local winds

Other winds, known as **local winds**, are influenced by temperature changes in a small area or place. During the day, both land and water absorb, or take in, heat from the sunlight. At night, the land and water cool as heat moves toward the atmosphere. God made land and water able to absorb heat and cool off at different rates, or speeds. Water warms and cools more slowly than soil and rocks do.

sea breeze

land breeze

Places where water and land meet often have local winds called *sea breezes* and *land breezes*. Winds form as cooler air moves to replace warmer, rising air. During the day, the air over land is warmer than the air over large bodies of water is. This causes sea breezes to blow inland from the cooler water. At night, the water and the air above it cool down slowly and stay warm longer than the land does. This causes land breezes to blow from the land toward the water.

Valley winds and *mountain winds* are other types of local winds and form in a similar way. Air is less dense at the higher altitudes of a mountain. Less dense air warms and cools more quickly than denser air does. During the day, the sun warms the side of a mountain and the air around it. As the air warms, it

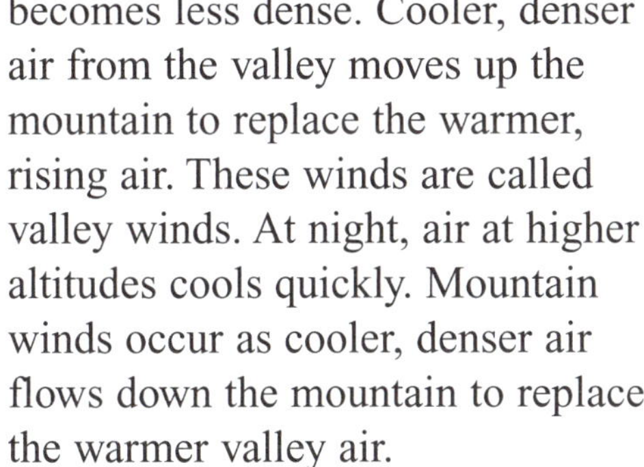
becomes less dense. Cooler, denser air from the valley moves up the mountain to replace the warmer, rising air. These winds are called valley winds. At night, air at higher altitudes cools quickly. Mountain winds occur as cooler, denser air flows down the mountain to replace the warmer valley air.

wind vane

A *wind vane* is an instrument that shows the direction wind is blowing from. The speed of wind is measured using an *anemometer* (AN uh MOM ih ter). An anemometer looks like several cups attached to a post. As the wind blows into the cups, they spin around the post. A dial that looks similar to the speedometer in a car shows how fast the wind is blowing. Usually, cooler winds blow more swiftly than warmer winds do.

anemometer

QUICK CHECK

1. What is wind?
2. Does a cool air mass have high pressure or low pressure?
3. How does a warm front form?
4. What are local winds?

Temperature Changes

Process skills
- Measuring
- Observing
- Inferring
- Recording data

When you swim, the water temperature does not always feel the same as the air temperature. On a hot day the water may seem cooler. On a summer night the water may feel warmer. Are there really differences in the temperatures, or are your senses fooling you?

As the "scientist" in this activity, you will compare the temperatures of soil and water.

Problem

Which substance warms and cools faster—water or soil?

Procedure

Materials:
- 2 containers
- potting soil
- centimeter ruler
- water
- 2 thermometers
- Activity Manual

1. Complete the hypothesis in your Activity Manual.
2. Put 4 cm of soil into one container. Fill the other container with 4 cm of water.
3. Place a thermometer into each container. Make sure that the bulbs of the thermometers are under the surface of the soil or water.

4. Check the temperature of each container and record the starting temperatures.
5. Place the containers outside in a sunny place. Check and record the temperature of each container after 30 minutes and then after 60 minutes.
6. Move the containers to a shady location. Check and record the temperature of each container after 30 minutes and then after 60 minutes.

Conclusions

- Which substance's temperature increased more in the sunny location?
- Which substance's temperature decreased more in the shady location?
- How do the results compare to what causes land breezes and sea breezes?

Follow-up

- Compare the temperatures after longer periods of time.
- Test pairs of containers in other temperature situations.
- Test the temperature changes of other materials such as sand or gravel.

Moisture in the Air

Isaiah 55:10–11 tells us that God planned for the living things on the earth to depend on the water that He provided. The Bible compares how water accomplishes its purposes to how the Word of God accomplishes the purposes of God.

All the water on the earth follows a cycle, or repeated path. Water falls to the earth as *precipitation* (prih SIP ih TAY shun). Plants, animals, and humans need this water to survive. Some water returns to the atmosphere through *evaporation*. Most of the water in the air is evaporated ocean water. When conditions are right, the water in the air changes to droplets and forms clouds through *condensation*. The clouds then produce more precipitation, continuing the cycle.

rain

Precipitation

Water vapor, or water in the air, cools at high altitudes. Water vapor cools around dust particles and forms water droplets or ice crystals. Gravity pulls the larger water drops and ice crystals toward the earth and causes precipitation. **Precipitation** is any type of moisture that falls from the atmosphere and reaches the ground. Rain, sleet, snow, and hail are all types of precipitation.

Rain forms when water droplets in the clouds join together to form larger drops. Raindrops can be big or small. Their sizes are determined by air temperatures, winds, the types of air fronts, and the types of clouds.

Sometimes, although the air is warm enough for the rain to fall as a liquid, the surface of the earth is below freezing. When this happens, the liquid raindrops freeze as they hit the earth. This *freezing rain* forms an icy glaze that coats objects on the ground, such as tree branches and fences.

Sleet occurs when liquid raindrops fall through air that is below freezing.

Get a spray bottle of water. Adjust the nozzle to spray a fine mist. Find a smooth outside wall or window. Aim the bottle at the wall or window and spray once or twice. Look at the tiny droplets. Spray more water. What happens to the size of the droplets? Compare the movement of your drops to that of falling rain.

Unlike freezing rain, the drops freeze on their way to the earth and land as tiny ice pellets. If the air temperature borders on freezing, a winter storm may have a mixture of freezing rain and sleet.

Snow forms when ice crystals in the clouds join together and fall to the earth. The air between the clouds and the earth must be at or below freezing for snow to fall. The size of snowflakes varies depending on the temperature and the amount of moisture in the air. Large, fluffy-looking snowflakes form at temperatures near 0°C (32°F). As temperatures drop, the flakes become smaller.

Because of the need for cold air temperatures, most frozen precipitation occurs during cold weather. But one type, *hail*, usually falls during warm weather. In some rain storms, the upward-moving warmer air pushes some raindrops higher into the tall clouds. There, the raindrops freeze into tiny pellets that fall back to the lower clouds. The upward-moving air pushes the pellets back up, starting the cycle again. Moisture in the clouds continues to add layers of ice to the pellets each time they are blown upward. Finally, the ice becomes too heavy and falls to the earth as hail. Hailstones vary in size from as small as a pea to even larger than a grapefruit.

freezing rain or sleet

Beth Hamil

snow

hail

Dew and Frost

Dew and frost are not types of precipitation. Precipitation falls from the sky, but the moisture that forms dew and frost does not. Instead, dew and frost are formed from water vapor in the air. Dew appears when water vapor condenses on the surface of objects. Early on a cool morning, you may see tiny dew drops on the blades of grass. During colder weather, the vapor quickly freezes into ice crystals and forms frost.

Humidity

As the sun warms the earth, some of the water evaporates into the atmosphere. Water vapor in the atmosphere is called **humidity** (hyoo MID ih tee). The temperature and air pressure influence the amount of humidity that the air can hold at a given time.

You may have heard a weather forecaster speak of relative humidity. *Relative humidity* is the amount of water vapor in the air compared with the amount that the air could hold at that temperature. Different temperatures can hold different amounts of water vapor. Relative humidity is identified as a percentage.

Science and the BIBLE

The Bible character Gideon sought God's will by observing dew. God told Gideon to conquer the Midianites. Gideon was uncertain, though, and wanted a sign from God. So Gideon laid a fleece, a sheep's woolly skin, on the ground. He asked God to make the fleece wet with dew but not the ground around it. God answered his request. The Bible says in Judges 6:38 that the fleece was so wet that when Gideon wrung it out the water filled a bowl. But Gideon was still afraid and asked God to send another sign. This time he asked that God make the ground wet with dew but not the fleece. God again answered Gideon's prayer. Finally Gideon was convinced of God's leading and obeyed His command.

Clouds

Clouds form from condensed water vapor or ice crystals. One way clouds are classified is by shape. The three basic shapes of clouds are stratus, cumulus, and cirrus. Clouds can be also classified according to altitude. The prefix *alto* is added to the names of some clouds. This prefix shows that the clouds are part of the middle altitude. They are neither very high nor very low clouds. A form of the word *nimbus* is added to the names of clouds that produce precipitation.

Stratus clouds look like flat blankets and are usually the lowest clouds in the sky. Sometimes they actually lie on the surface of the earth. In this case, the cloud is called fog. Nimbostratus clouds often produce light rain.

Probably the most familiar clouds are cumulus clouds. **Cumulus clouds** are large, fluffy-looking clouds with flat bottoms. These clouds mostly form in the middle of the troposphere. The tall, dark clouds that produce thunderstorms are called cumulonimbus (KYOOM yuh low NIM bus) clouds.

The thin, curly-looking clouds seen high in the sky are called **cirrus (SEAR us) clouds**. Because they are high in the troposphere, cirrus clouds are made of ice crystals rather than water droplets. Cirrus clouds often indicate that a warm front is moving into the area.

1. What is precipitation?
2. What is humidity?
3. Describe a cumulus cloud.

Meet the SCIENTIST LUKE HOWARD

A scientist does not have to work in a science profession. For example, Luke Howard was a British businessman. But he enjoyed studying nature, especially clouds. He kept accurate notes on weather observations for more than thirty years.

In the early 1800s, he wrote a paper based on his observations. He classified the clouds and gave them Latin names. The paper was published and used by other scientists. In fact, Mr. Howard's groups and names are the basis for the cloud classifications used today. He also wrote and gave lectures on many weather topics. His lectures were printed at one point and became the first textbook on meteorology.

Types of Clouds

cirrus—thin, wispy clouds sometimes called "mares' tails"

nimbostratus—thick mass of rain clouds that seems to cover the sky

stratus—wide, thin layer clouds that form at lower altitudes

cumulonimbus—rain clouds that produce heavy downpours of rain or hail

cumulus—fluffy, cottonlike clouds that indicate fair weather

Severe Weather

Weather includes temperature, winds, air pressure, and humidity. Severe weather conditions occur when various aspects of weather combine to form high winds, large amounts of precipitation, or extreme temperatures. Some types of severe weather can be very harmful. But knowing how and why this weather occurs can reduce the damage and loss of life.

Global winds influence the weather patterns around the world. For example, the prevailing westerlies cause most of the weather in the United States to move from west to east. Sometimes cold air masses move southward from Canada. Warm, wet air masses can blow toward the East Coast from the Gulf of Mexico. When large air masses like these meet, severe weather may result.

Thunderstorms

A **thunderstorm** occurs when a large, swift-moving warm air mass meets a cold air mass. All thunderstorms have lightning and thunder. Most also have strong winds, heavy rain, and sometimes hail. The tall, dark cumulonimbus clouds that produce thunderstorms are called thunderheads.

During a storm, air temperatures change rapidly. This causes strong air movements among the clouds. The resulting friction creates **lightning**, a type of static electricity. Lightning can move either between clouds or between the clouds and the earth. The temperature of lightning can reach up to 30,000°C (54,000°F). Imagine how quickly a lightning bolt heats the air around it! That rapid heat change produces vibrations in the air that we hear as **thunder**.

lightning

You can easily tell if a thunderstorm is moving toward you or away from you. Since light travels faster than sound does, you see lightning before you hear the thunder. Count the seconds between each flash of lightning and the sound of its thunder. As the thunderstorm gets closer, there are fewer seconds between the lightning and the thunder.

thunderstorm

Tornadoes and Hurricanes

Depending on the speed and strength with which the fronts hit, a thunderstorm may also produce tornadoes. A **tornado** (tor NAY doe) is a funnel-shaped cloud of swirling winds that reaches down to the ground. Tornado winds are powerful and can reach speeds of 400 km/h (250 mi/h). Their force may destroy anything in the tornado's path, including houses and trees. Most tornadoes, though, are small and last only a short time.

tornado

Another type of severe storm may form over a low-pressure area of an ocean. Winds gather warm, wet air from the ocean surface. As the warm air rises, towering cumulonimbus clouds form. Heavy rains pour from the clouds, and strong winds swirl around the low-pressure area. In the Atlantic Ocean or the eastern Pacific Ocean, a storm with spiraling winds that forms over the ocean is called a **hurricane** (HUR ih KAYN). A hurricane can cover hundreds of miles. In the western Pacific Ocean, these storms are called *typhoons* (tie FOONS).

In the Northern Hemisphere, hurricane winds spiral in a counter-clockwise direction. The *eye* of a hurricane is a calm, clear area in the center of the storm.

Other Severe Weather

Some areas of the earth may experience other types of severe weather. One type of severe weather is a blizzard. A *blizzard* is a snowstorm with strong, freezing winds and blowing snow. The blowing snow is dangerous because it reduces a person's ability to see very far. Another type of severe weather is a heat wave. A *heat wave* is a period of time with higher-than-average temperatures. The humidity is usually also higher than normal. During a heat wave, people should avoid being outdoors for long periods of time.

Storm Safety

Severe weather can be very dangerous. An organization that tracks the weather in the United States is the National Weather Service. Sometimes the National Weather Service issues a *weather watch*. This means that the conditions are right for a type of severe weather but that the weather is not currently happening. A watch alerts people to get ready for the possibility of a storm. Once the storm begins and people report having seen it, a *weather warning* is announced. You should always look for safe shelter if you hear a weather warning.

Listen to the radio for watches and warnings if you think a severe storm is on its way. Always try to stay inside a building during a storm. If the storm has very strong winds, go to a basement or another sturdy place inside the building. Plan ahead. Find out about what to do and where to go if severe weather comes.

Throughout the Bible, God uses storms to show His power. God has given man dominion over the earth to use and care for it. But man has very little influence on the weather. Only God can control it. In Nahum 1:3, the Bible says that "the Lord hath his way in the whirlwind and in the storm, and the clouds are the dust of his feet."

1. What are some characteristics of a thunderstorm?
2. What is a tornado?
3. What is a weather watch?

Explorations Dangerous Extremes

Extreme weather often brings hazards and dangers. Severe weather conditions such as tornadoes and hurricanes bring strong winds and heavy rains. Strong winds may destroy buildings. Heavy rains may result in flooding or mudslides. Extreme conditions such as blizzards and heat waves can be dangerous to humans, livestock, and plants.

In this exploration, you will make and present an awareness poster or pamphlet for a specific type of severe, or extreme, weather.

What to do

1. Choose a type of severe weather.
2. Make an awareness poster or pamphlet about your chosen type of weather. Provide a description of the weather conditions that people should watch for. Include the dangers caused by that type of weather. List actions people should take to avoid these dangers. Include telephone numbers or other information that people living in your area would need in case of this type of emergency.
3. Present your poster or pamphlet. Emphasize the weather conditions to watch for and the precautions that should be taken to avoid injury.

Forecasting the Weather

God designed and maintains the weather patterns. Air moving over water collects moisture. Cooler air moves to replace warmer, rising air. Global winds blow in set paths around the earth. These, and other predictable conditions, provide some of the information needed to forecast the weather. A **weather forecast** is a prediction of future weather conditions.

Making Predictions

The scientists who study the atmosphere and weather are called **meteorologists** (MEE tee uh ROL uh jists). Much of their work involves gathering data, or information, about the atmosphere and environment. They use thermometers, barometers, anemometers, and other basic equipment to provide some of this data. More advanced equipment such as radar and satellites can also provide useful data.

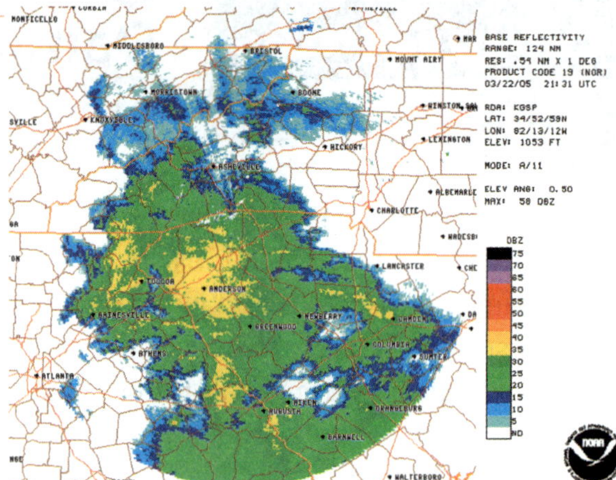

radar image of northwest South Carolina

Throughout history people have watched the skies for weather patterns. By studying these patterns, people hoped to predict the coming weather. Farmers and sailors, who depended on the weather, found many predictable patterns. One of these patterns is even mentioned in the Bible. Matthew 16:2–3 tells us that the people of Christ's day had observed that the weather would be fair if the evening sky was red but would be stormy if the morning sky was red.

Modern meteorologists work in a similar way. They daily gather weather data to find and study weather patterns. In this way meteorologists can use present conditions to make fairly accurate predictions about future weather.

satellite map of North America

Reading Weather Maps

Meteorologists put some of their data onto weather maps. These maps allow us to understand the data more easily. Some weather maps are colored to show differences in temperature. Other maps have circular lines that show differences in air pressure. Lines with shape symbols are used to show fronts. Many weather maps also have symbols to indicate different types of precipitation.

1. What is a weather forecast?
2. What is a meteorologist?

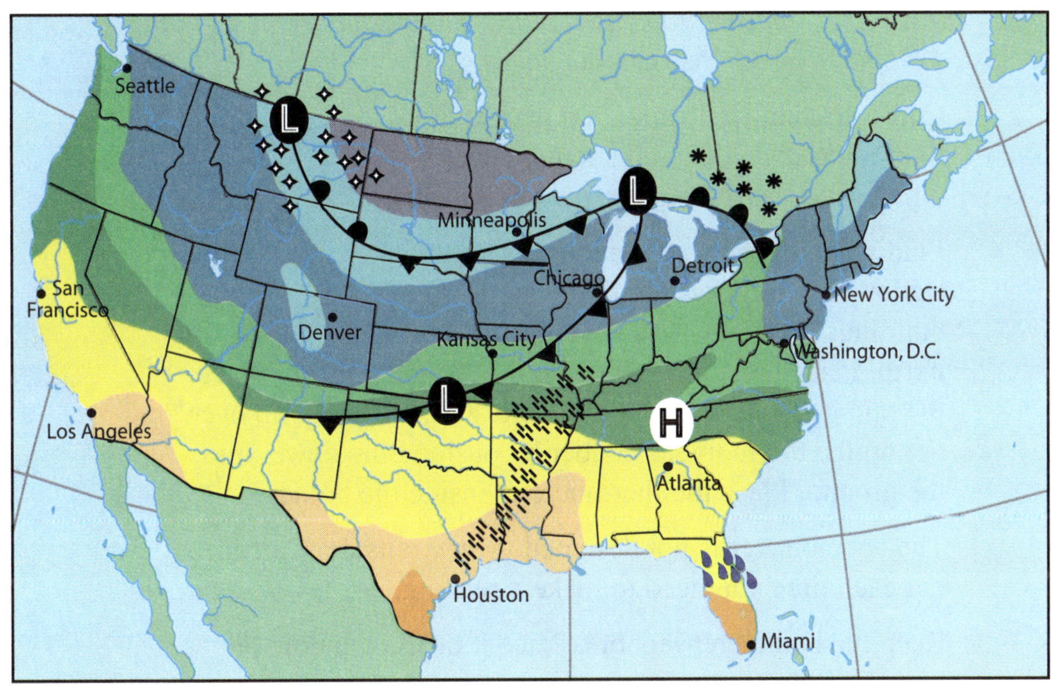

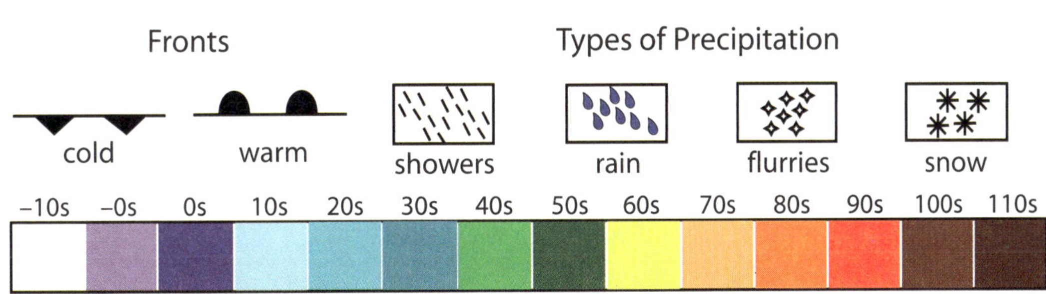

ACTIVITY

Weather Observatory

Meteorologists use a variety of instruments to collect data related to weather conditions. In this activity, you are the meteorologist. You even make some of the equipment!

Process skills
- Measuring and using numbers
- Making and using models
- Observing
- Collecting, recording, and interpreting data

Purpose

Make and use weather instruments.

Procedure

Note: The materials needed to construct the weather instruments are listed on the Weather Instruments *pages.*

Materials:
- barometer
- *Weather Instruments* pages
- Activity Manual

1. Construct the wind vane, rain gauge, thermometer holder, and anemometer as directed on the *Weather Instruments* pages.
2. Find an outdoor location to use as a weather station. The location should be away from buildings and trees. Use the compass to find north. Place the wind vane with the *N* facing north. Place the rain gauge in a level place so it will not easily tip over. Set up the thermometer holder by pushing the dowel into the ground. Place the thermometer inside the holder.
3. The anemometer is not designed to stay outside. Carry it out each time you need to make a reading.
4. Keep the barometer indoors. Place it near a window or outside wall.
5. Use the Cloud Chart in your Activity Manual to determine what types of clouds are present. Record your observations on the Weather Log in your Activity Manual.
6. Check the wind direction, amount of precipitation, temperature, wind speed, and air pressure. Record your observations on the Weather Log.
7. Continue to record your weather observations for 10 days.

Conclusions

- Were there any patterns or relationships between your observations and the types of weather that occurred each day?
- Can you predict the weather for tomorrow based on your observations from today?

Follow-up

- Compare your observations each day with the daily weather maps and reports from newspapers, the Internet, or other sources.
- Make your own weather maps based on your observations.

Answer the Questions

1. How is the atmosphere like a ball that falls toward the earth?

2. Why do air masses containing warm, moist air usually move above air masses of cool, dry air?

3. Why is there usually a breeze at the beach?

Solve the Problem

For a special occasion, you are invited to spend the night with your friend. While playing games in the room over the garage, you hear on the radio that the National Weather Service has issued a tornado warning for your area. What does a tornado warning mean? What should you do?

Biomes

6

REMEMBER now thy CREATOR

Imagine you are shivering in cold, windy weather. You step through a door. Suddenly you feel as if you were in a tropical rainforest. The temperature is hot and humid. Tropical birds freely fly and nest among large tropical plants. This aviary, or bird house, is a common part of many modern zoos. Here, the zoos try to provide a natural setting for the birds. And visitors can enjoy seeing the birds in a setting that is similar to the birds' natural environment. The building is made of glass, and artificial heat keeps it very warm. Systems in the building control the moisture in the air. The heat and humidity make it feel like a tropical rainforest. By using technology man is able in a small way to copy part of God's wonderful creation.

When God created the earth, He made many kinds of animals and plants. He knew exactly what each living thing needed and prepared the right living conditions for it. So, just as there are many plants and animals, there are many places where they live. Scientists refer to all of the areas where life can exist and the living organisms that live there as the **biosphere** (BYE uh SFEAR).

The biosphere is very large, though. A person could not study all of it. So scientists divide it into sections called biomes (BYE OHMS). A **biome** is a large area of the earth in which plants and animals share a similar environment. A biome might be a desert, a forest, a prairie, or even an ocean. These smaller sections are easier to study.

Land Biomes

Land biomes are influenced by their climate. The **climate** is the usual weather of a region over a long period of time. Climate includes

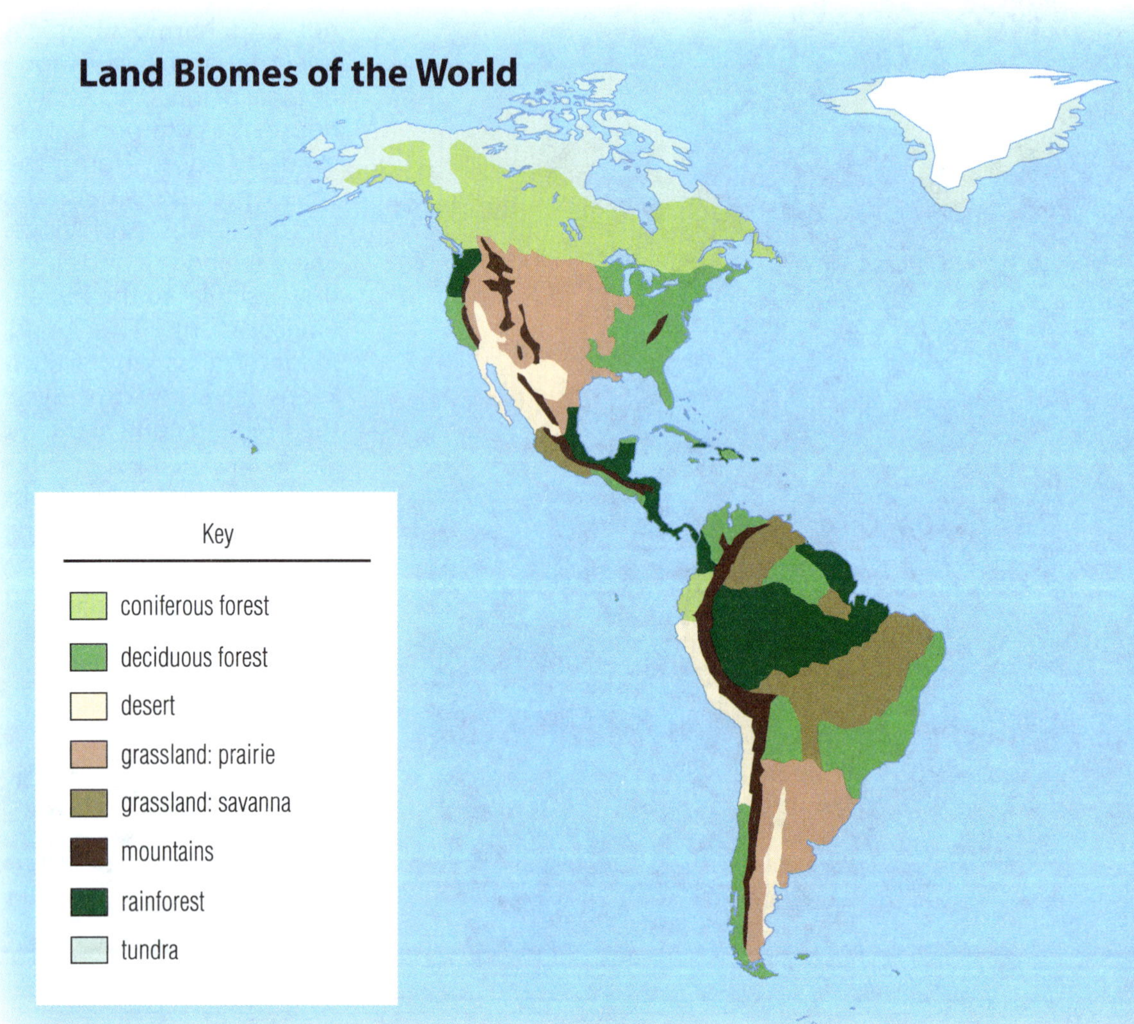

the temperature and the amount of precipitation in an area. The climate of a biome determines what types of plants and animals can live there.

Scientists have divided the earth's land into several major biomes. These land biomes can be very different. The tundra around the Arctic Circle is cold and frozen. But the tropical rainforests near the equator are very hot and humid.

The Northern Hemisphere has more biomes than the Southern Hemisphere does. The main reason for this is that there is more land in the Northern Hemisphere. Also, most of the land in the Southern Hemisphere is in or near the tropics. Because the conditions do not vary much, there are only a few types of biomes. The Northern Hemisphere, however, has land stretching from the equator all the way to the Arctic Circle. This allows the Northern Hemisphere to have many biomes.

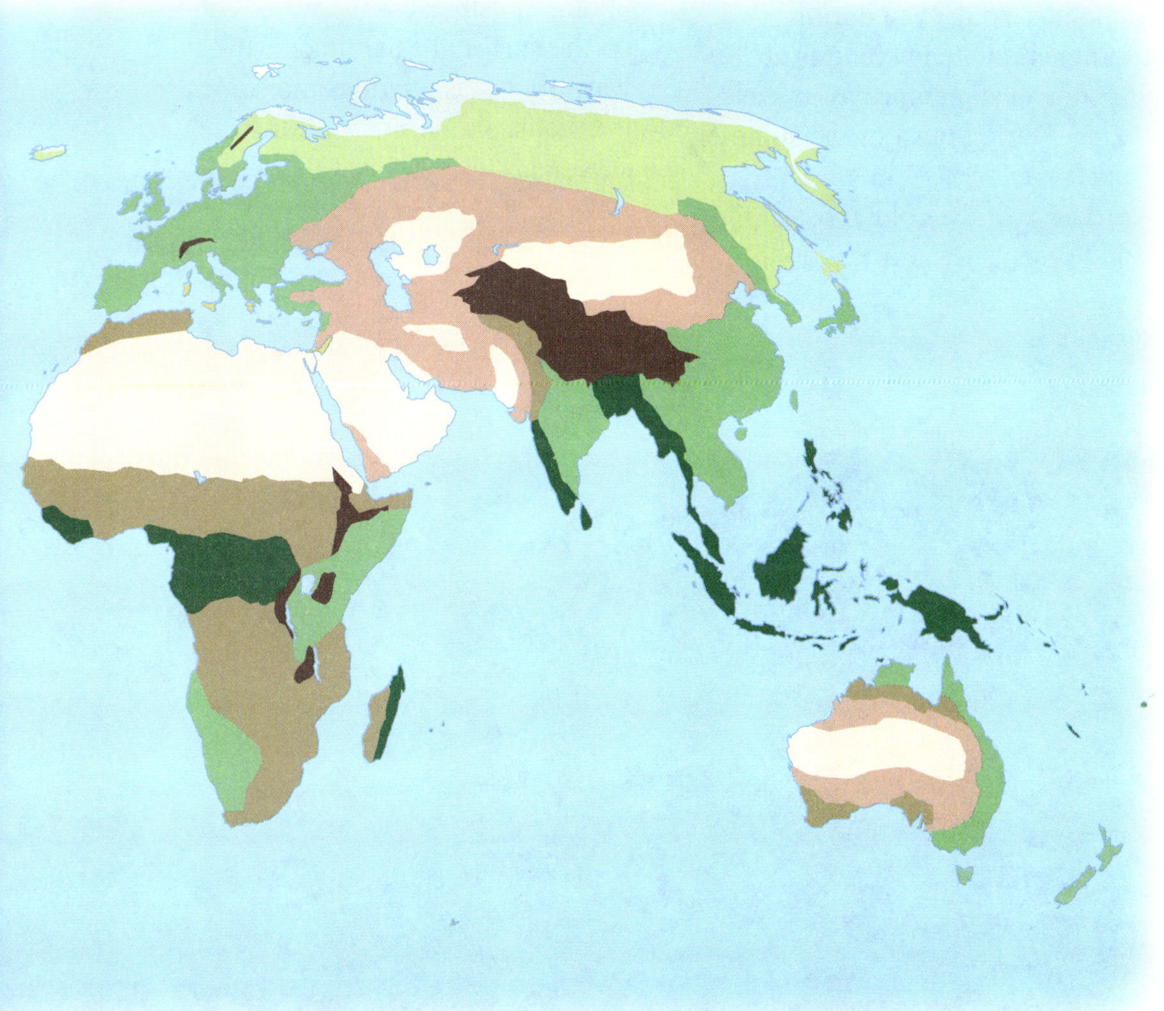

Tundra

The coldest biome is the tundra. This biome is found in the northern latitudes around the Arctic Circle. Winter and summer are the two main seasons in this biome.

The tundra has long, cold winters, with temperatures that are far below freezing. In fact, the tundra stays below freezing for at least nine months of the year. For part of the winter, the sun never rises.

The summer is the growing season. But in the tundra it is very short—sometimes less than two months. And, even during the summer, the temperatures are still cool and sometimes as low as freezing. During most of the summer, the sun never sets.

Because of the cold, most of the ground stays frozen all year long. This permanently frozen soil is called **permafrost** (PUR muh FROST). A thin layer of soil on the surface thaws a little during the summer. However, the permafrost below is still frozen. Trees cannot grow on the tundra because their roots cannot get through the frozen soil.

The tundra is not just cold, though. It is also very dry. Only a small amount of precipitation falls during the year. Most of this precipitation is in the form of snow. When the snow melts in the summer, the permafrost is too frozen to soak up the moisture. So the water collects on the surface of the tundra. In this way, the water provides moisture for the plants and animals during the summer.

tundra in the summer in Denali National Park, Alaska

musk ox

God designed animals and plants on the tundra to be able to keep warm in cold weather. One tundra animal, the musk ox, has a double coat of hair. The animal has a thick undercoat of soft fur and a thick overcoat of coarse, straight hair. The undercoat provides warm insulation during the winter months. During the warm months, the musk ox sheds its undercoat, but it grows back again in time for winter. The outer hair is so long that it reaches almost to the ground. The hair resists water and keeps the musk ox from getting wet and cold.

The woolly lousewort has "hair" that helps trap heat in the cold tundra.

Plants also need to keep warm in order to grow. Some tundra plants are "hairy." The woolly lousewort, for instance, has fuzzy coverings on its buds and stems. This "hair" traps heat and keeps the surface of the plant warmer. Other plants have dark red leaves instead of green leaves. The red color helps the plants absorb more sunlight and keeps the plant warmer. Most plants on the tundra are also small and grow in groups. Being close to the ground protects them from the wind and allows the plants to absorb heat from the ground.

tundra in the winter in Alberta, Canada

1. How is a biome related to a biosphere?
2. How does the climate affect a biome?
3. What is permafrost?

Coniferous Forest

The coniferous (koe NIF ur us) forest is the largest land biome. This biome, also called the *taiga* (TIE guh), is located just south of the tundra. The biome is so large that it stretches across most of Canada and into some of the northern United States. It also covers large parts of Europe and Asia.

The coniferous forest has two main seasons: summer and winter. Spring and autumn do occur. They are so short, however, that they are barely noticed.

The winters are long and cold. The temperatures usually stay below freezing for at least six months of the year. Winter days are also short. During part of the winter the sun is up for only 4–6 hours!

In contrast, the sun may shine for 20 hours a day during the summer. The growing season lasts longer in the coniferous forest than in the tundra. The summer is still short and cool, however. Most of the year's precipitation occurs during the summer.

circumpolar map of the tundra and the taiga

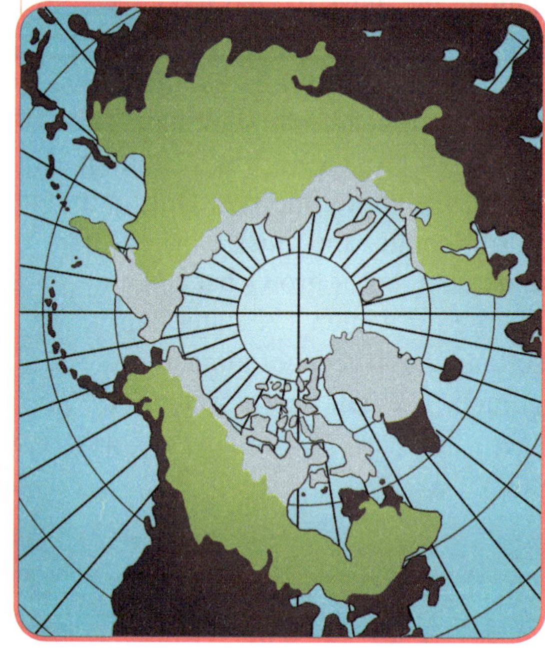

coniferous forest in Manitoba, Canada

Fantastic FACTS

The taiga has many ponds, bogs, and lakes. One type of bog, a *muskeg*, can be found in some areas of the taiga where water does not drain through the soil. This swamplike ground may appear firm because of the moss, grass, or trees growing on it. But, underneath, the land is soggy and wet. In some areas in Manitoba, Canada, stepping on certain parts of the ground causes the trees to move.

snowshoe hare

Most of the trees in the coniferous forest are **conifers**, or cone-bearing trees. Some of the most common conifers are spruce, fir, and pine trees. Many conifers are evergreens. These trees do not lose their leaves during the winter. This enables evergreens to make food even during the long winter season.

Winter temperatures in the coniferous forest are usually so cold that the snow does not melt between storms. So the trees must be able to support a lot of heavy snow. Otherwise, the weight of the snow would break the tree branches.

So God designed many conifers to be shaped like cones. This shape helps some of the snow to slide off the tree without causing damage. He made other trees able to bend with the weight of the snow. Some trees can bend so much that they become almost flat to the ground. But when the snow melts, the tree stands straight again.

God also gave the animals in the coniferous forest special characteristics that help them survive. For example, the snowshoe hare's fur changes to brown in the summer and then to white in the winter. This color change helps camouflage the hare. The white fur is not only for camouflage, however. Inside the white hairs are air-filled spaces. These spaces help insulate the hare and keep it warmer during the winter. The hare also has large back feet that act like snowshoes, helping it stay on top of the snow. Stiff hairs on the bottom of these feet form fur pads that keep the hare's feet warm and insulated.

Deciduous Forest

Deciduous (dih SIJ yoo us) forests line the eastern coast of North America. They are also found in other parts of the earth, such as in Europe and in Asia. This biome gets its name from the trees that make up the forest. Most of these trees are **deciduous**, meaning that they lose their leaves in the winter. Deciduous trees usually have large, wide leaves.

The weather in the deciduous forest is not constant but changes with the seasons. The spring is usually warm and rainy. Summer is hot and humid. Autumn is cool and crisp. Winters are often cold and snowy.

The deciduous forest is a wet biome. It receives precipitation throughout the whole year. In fact, a deciduous forest gets more rain than any other type of biome except a rainforest.

The warm growing season lasts about half of the year. This longer time allows the biome to get warmer than those biomes with shorter summers do. This longer growing season provides time for plants and trees to grow. Many shrubs, berry bushes, flowers, and other plants cannot survive in colder biomes. But these plants flourish in the warmer climate of the deciduous forest.

deciduous forest in Quebec, Canada

A cardinal is a common bird in the deciduous forest.

The plants and trees in a deciduous forest must change with the seasons. If deciduous trees kept their broad leaves throughout the winter, the water in the leaves would freeze. This could damage the tree. So God designed deciduous trees to lose their leaves.

During the summer, deciduous tree leaves use sunlight to make food. Some of this food is used for growing. But some is stored in the trees' roots. In autumn, the days get shorter, and the temperatures become cooler. These changes cause deciduous trees to block nutrients and water from the leaves. The leaves can no longer make chlorophyll, so their green color begins to fade. The other colors that had been hidden by the green begin to show. Leaves fall to the ground, decay, and add nutrients back to the soil. In the spring the trees use their stored food energy to form new leaves.

God, the Creator, also provides for animals to survive the changing seasons. Some birds, butterflies, and large mammals move to warmer areas for the winter. The animals then return to the forest in the spring when it is warm again.

Other animals remain in the forest year-round. Some, like the deer, grow thick winter coats of fur. They shed these winter coats when the temperature gets warmer. Other animals, such as the woodchuck, hibernate.

A deer grows a thick winter coat to stay warm in the deciduous forest during cold weather.

1. What is the largest land biome?
2. How are the trees in deciduous forests different from the trees in coniferous forests?

Grasslands

Grasslands are usually found between deserts and forests. Some grasslands are flat. Others have gently rolling hills. The main *vegetation* (VEJ ih TAY shun), or plant life, is grass. Grasslands also have wildflowers and small bushes but very few trees.

Prairies

The prairie is one kind of temperate grassland. Temperate areas are located between the polar and tropical regions. Much of the central area of North America is covered by wide, grassy prairies. Prairies have four regular seasons. The winters are usually cold, and the summers are warm.

Most precipitation on the prairie falls in late spring and early summer. The amount of rainfall is usually low to moderate. A prairie receives about the same amount of precipitation as a coniferous forest does. However, water evaporates faster on the prairie than in the forest. This means that prairie plants do not have as much water available as the trees in the coniferous forest do.

Prairies have a wide variety of grasses. Most prairie grasses, though, do not look like the grass growing on people's lawns. Instead, prairie grasses vary in height. Some, such as buffalo grass, are short. Others, such as prairie cordgrass, can grow over 3 m (10 ft) tall. The wheat, corn, rice, and rye that we use as food are also types of grasses.

The roots of prairie grasses usually are matted together and spread deep underground. This prevents seeds from trees and other plants from taking root. It also enables the grasses to grow again even after a fire or after grazing animals have eaten them.

Many kinds of animals live on the prairies. However, prairies are very open spaces, so animals can easily be seen by other animals that could eat them. To protect themselves, some animals, such as prairie dogs, hide in their underground holes. Snakes and birds often hide in the grass. Other animals simply run fast to escape. The pronghorn antelope, for instance, can run as fast as 96 km/h (60 mi/h).

prairie in Manitoba, Canada

Science and the BIBLE

In Psalm 103:15–16, the Bible compares man's life to the grass. Both grow quickly and then are gone. But God's mercy lasts forever. The next verse says, "But the mercy of the Lord is from everlasting to everlasting upon them that fear him."

The baobab tree loses its leaves during the dry season. Some people think that it looks like it has been planted upside down.

Savannas

Tropical grasslands are called savannas. They are located in tropical areas of Africa, Australia, South America, and India. The vegetation is similar to that of a prairie. Savannas have a much warmer climate, though. Because savannas are close to the equator, they are hot all year.

Savannas have only two main seasons—dry and wet. Savannas receive anywhere from 64 to 152 cm (25 to 60 in.) of rain. Most of that rain falls during the wet season. During the dry season, these tropical grasslands usually receive less than 10 cm (4 in.) of rain.

This long dry season makes it hard for plants. The grasses and trees that grow on a savanna have to be able to survive through the long dry season. So God designed the grasses to grow quickly during the wet season. During this time, they store food and water in their roots. Later, during the dry season, the grasses turn brown and appear to die. But the roots are still alive. When the wet season returns, the grasses will grow again.

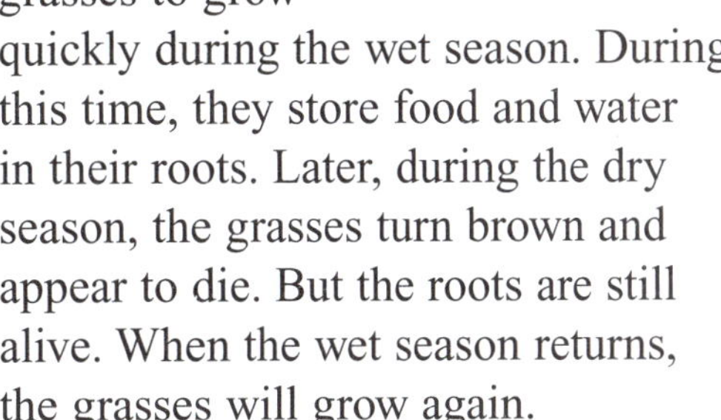

One of the biggest differences between savannas and prairies is the number of trees each can support. Savannas have more trees than prairies do. These trees have special features that allow them to survive the dry season. For instance, the baobab (BAY oh BAB) tree, found on the African savanna, stores water in its trunk during the wet season. During the dry season, the tree depends on the stored water.

Serengeti Plains, Tanzania, Africa

Deserts

What are deserts like? Do you think of hot, dry places when you think of deserts? Although some deserts are hot and dry, others are very different. Some are cold and covered with snow! Others have rocks and gravel instead of sand.

All deserts, though, have one thing in common. They receive very little precipitation. Most get less than 25 cm (10 in.) of rain each year. Because deserts are so dry, the temperatures are usually extreme. During the day the temperature might reach 38°C (100°F) or higher. But at night the temperature drops quickly. Sometimes it can even get below freezing.

Deserts can be found all over the world. Many deserts are located in tropical areas on either side of the equator. These hot deserts are warm year-round but get even hotter in the summer. The Sahara Desert, the largest desert in Africa, is an example of a hot desert.

Cold deserts have cool winters and warm summers. These deserts are usually located between the tropics and the polar region. One cold, dry desert is the Atacama Desert in Chile. The Gobi Desert, another cold desert, is located in China and Mongolia. Deserts can at times be found in very cold places, though. For example, some parts of Antarctica are considered desert.

Great Basin Desert, Nevada

God created desert animals with the ability to live in dry places with extreme temperatures. For example, the jackrabbit has large ears that help its body get rid of excess heat. Many desert animals are **nocturnal** (nok TUR nul), or active at night. During the day, they sleep. Some desert animals, such as kangaroo rats, burrow under the ground to stay cool. At night, they come out to hunt and eat. Other animals, such as rattlesnakes, are most active at dusk and at dawn. Resting during the hot part of the day helps them conserve energy and water.

God also provided for desert plants. Some have the ability to store water. The saguaro cactus is able to store as much as 757 L (200 gal) of water in its stem. This water can provide enough moisture for the cactus for an entire year! A plant that can store water in its stem or leaves is said to be **succulent** (SUK yuh lunt).

Desert plants usually have either long, deep roots or a system of wide, shallow roots. Some plants have both. Long, deep roots allow plants to reach water located deep under the ground. Shallow roots spread out in many directions and can get water from a larger area of soil.

Plants lose water through the small pores on their leaves and stems. Because of this, many desert plants, such as cactus and aloe, have waxy surfaces that help keep water inside the plant. Some plants have small leaves or only a few leaves. Other plants remain as seeds until the rain comes. Then the plants quickly grow, flower, and produce new seeds while water is available.

1. How are savannas different from prairies?
2. What is true about all deserts?

Death Valley National Park, California

ACTIVITY Help Prevent Water Loss!

Process skills
- Predicting
- Measuring
- Making and using models
- Inferring
- Recording data

All plants lose water through tiny pores in their leaves called *stomata* (STOH muh tuh). But if a particular biome does not receive much precipitation, the plants in that biome could lose more water than they receive. So God made some plants to be very water efficient. These plants have characteristics that help them lose very little water.

Some plants, such as cacti, have fewer stomata than other plants do. Other plants open their stomata only at night when temperatures are cooler. A waxy surface also helps some desert plants keep water inside.

In this activity, you will use a model to discover how much an outer coating affects the amount of water that evaporates.

Problem

How will coating the surface of a sponge affect the amount of water that evaporates from the sponge?

Materials:
- 2 flexible, thin sponges
- rubber bands
- petroleum jelly
- 100 mL water
- metric measuring cups
- container
- waxed paper
- balance (mass scale)
- pie plate
- Activity Manual

Procedure—Part 1

1. Complete the hypothesis in your Activity Manual.
2. Roll each sponge into a tube shape and fasten it with a rubber band. Arrange the rubber bands so that the two sponges look the same.
3. Coat the sides and top of one sponge with petroleum jelly. Make sure the bottom is not coated. Do not coat the second sponge.
4. Pour 100 mL of water into the container.

5. Stand the sponges in the water. Be sure that the coated sponge is standing on its uncoated end. Do not allow the sponges to touch each other. Allow the sponges to absorb water for three minutes.
6. Remove the sponges from the water. Place waxed paper on the balance. Measure and record the mass of each sponge.
7. Stand each sponge on its end in the pie plate. Place the plate in a sunny or well-lighted area.

Procedure—Part 2

8. Let the water evaporate from the sponges for one hour.
9. Measure and record the mass of each sponge.
10. Continue to measure and record the mass of each sponge at the times given by your teacher.
11. Graph the mass of each sponge for each given time.

Conclusions

- Was your hypothesis correct?
- How did this activity model the way some plants survive?

Follow-up

- Place the wet sponges in a windy area.
- Use flat sponges instead of rolled sponges.

Tropical Rainforests

Rainforests receive abundant rainfall throughout the year. More rain falls in this biome than in any other type. A few rainforests are located in temperate areas. But most are located near the equator and are very humid and rainy. They are known as tropical rainforests.

Rainforests are known for their great biodiversity. **Biodiversity** (BYE oh dih VUR sih tee) refers to how many species of plants and animals are found in a specific area. Scientists think that about half of all the plant and animal species on the earth live in the rainforest.

Scientists have divided the rainforest into four main layers. The crowns, or tops, of tall trees form a green canopy for the rainforest. A few taller trees stick out above this canopy. These trees form the *emergent layer*. They receive the most sunlight, but they also must face the strongest winds and the hottest temperatures.

In the *canopy layer*, the trees grow closely together. The upper branches of these trees are often covered with vines. Plants such as ferns, orchids, and mosses often grow on the branches in the trees of the canopy. Very little sunlight gets through the canopy to the plants below. The canopy also keeps moisture from evaporating. The little sunlight and the extra moisture make the areas under the canopy very warm, dark, and damp.

Underneath the canopy is a third layer made up of younger trees and leafy plants. The plants in this *understory layer* do not need much sunlight. Most have large leaves to help gather sunlight. Many leaf-eating animals live in this section of the rainforest and eat these large leaves.

Even less sunlight reaches the fourth layer, the *forest floor*. A few plants grow there, but most cannot. The forest floor is home to organisms such as termites, fungi, and bacteria.

Some trees in the rainforest have stilt roots to help support them and to help them gather nutrients from the shallow soil.

The trees in a rainforest need sunlight, but they also need nutrients to grow and stay healthy. Only the top layer of the rainforest soil has the nutrients that the trees need. So the roots spread out horizontally under the ground and intertwine with other roots. Because the roots are so near the surface of the soil, the trees need extra support to keep from falling over. Some tall trees have roots that grow out of the sides of their trunks. These above-ground roots give the trees extra support.

Many rainforest animals live in the treetops and rarely touch the ground. Some of these animals use their tails to swing through the trees. Other animals glide or jump from branch to branch. Some tree frogs have large, webbed feet that they use like parachutes as they glide. Their feet also have soft, flat toes that act like suction cups to help the frogs stick to the branches.

One kind of tree frog, Wallace's flying frog, has flaps of skin along the sides of its body. These flaps of skin and the frog's webbed feet enable this flying frog to glide for distances of up to 15 m (50 ft).

Wallace's flying frog

Fantastic FACTS

Have you ever heard of a pond on top of a tree? Bromeliads (bro MEE lee ADS), plants similar to pineapples, often grow on the branches of trees in rainforests. Their long, stiff leaves collect water. Some bromeliads can hold as much as 7 L (2 gal) of water! The small ponds that form in the leaves are homes to many kinds of insects and amphibians.

Mountains

Biomes are a general way to classify sections of the biosphere based on climate. But sometimes a large area such as a mountain may have more than one biome in it. As you travel up a mountain, the air becomes thinner and colder. These changes create different climates. The climates, in turn, affect what types of plants and animals can survive.

In dry regions, desert or grassland biomes are usually at the base of a mountain. As you go up the mountain, less desert or grassland vegetation grows, and more trees do. These mountain forests are usually deciduous forests.

Farther up the mountain side, the climate may change again. The deciduous forest now changes to a coniferous forest. Mountain forests are often called *montane (mon TAYN) forests*.

Above the coniferous forest is a biome that is similar to the tundra. This cold biome is called the alpine tundra. Above the alpine tundra is the snowy top of the mountain. The mountain biomes are similar, but not identical, to the major land biomes.

Mountain Biomes

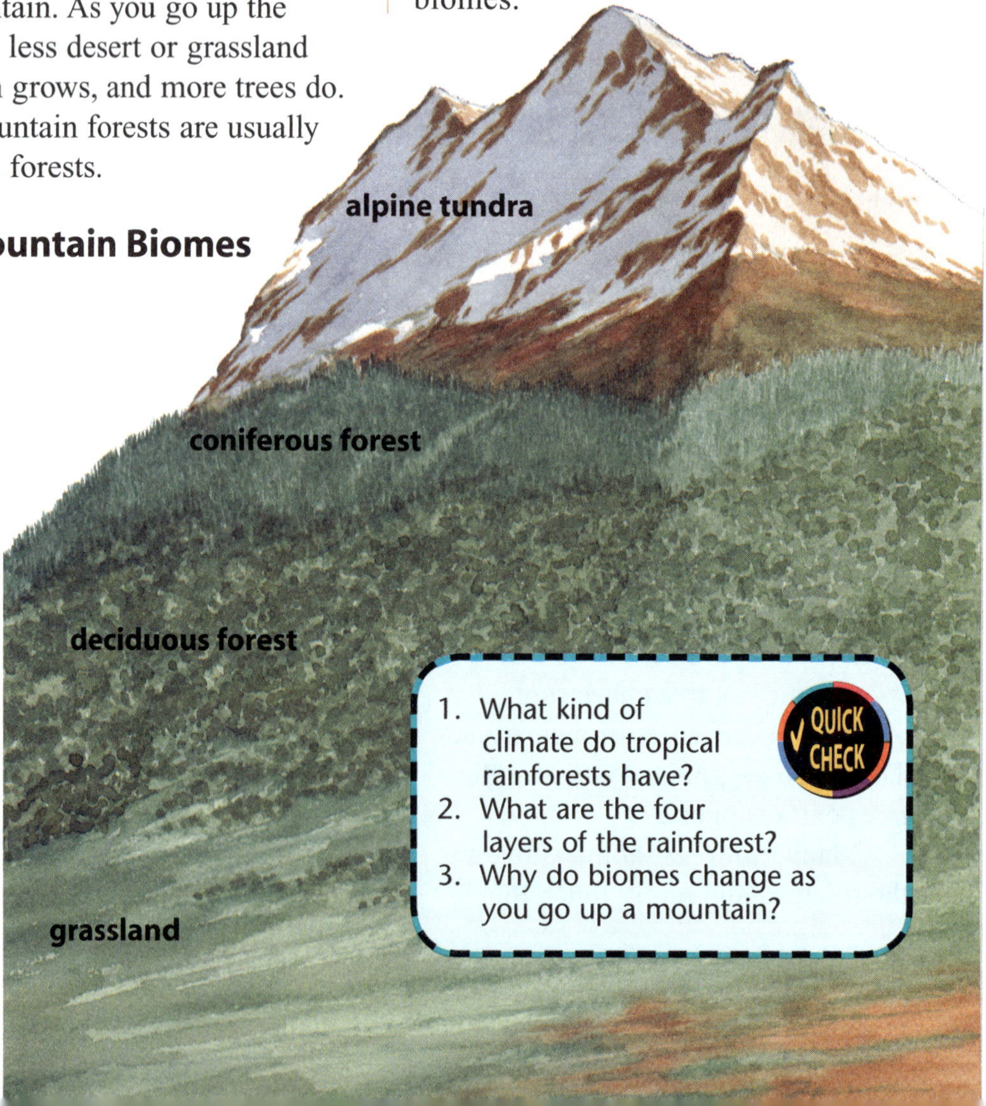

alpine tundra

coniferous forest

deciduous forest

grassland

QUICK CHECK

1. What kind of climate do tropical rainforests have?
2. What are the four layers of the rainforest?
3. Why do biomes change as you go up a mountain?

Explorations Build a Biome

What do you think of when someone mentions a tropical rainforest? Maybe you think of parrots, monkeys, and thick vines. In contrast, you probably think of cacti and sand as belonging in a desert. Each biome has characteristics that make it unique and different.

For this exploration, you will build a model of one of the biomes.

What to do

1. Choose one of the biomes mentioned in this chapter.
2. Decide on the location and characteristics of the biome that you chose. For example, if the chosen biome is a deciduous forest, will your model represent the forests of North America or those of Europe? Which species of broad-leaved trees will you include?
3. Display the dominant vegetation, or most common plants, for that biome. Include a variety of plants and animals in the model.
4. Research and find some interesting facts about at least two of the plants and two of the animals included in your model. Record those facts on note cards. Include this information in your model.
5. On your model, identify the type of biome and its location. Include information about the climate and other characteristics of the biome. Present your model.

Aquatic Biomes

Land biomes are influenced directly by the climate. However, aquatic (uh KWAHT ik), or water, biomes do not have one specific climate. One example is the Pacific Ocean. It stretches from cold Alaska to the warm tropics and then to the cold shores of Antarctica.

Aquatic biomes are classified as either saltwater or freshwater. The **salinity** (suh LIN ih tee), or amount of dissolved salt in the water, varies with each biome. Salt water has a higher concentration of salt than fresh water does. But even fresh water contains a little salt.

Most fish can live in only one type of water. However, God created some aquatic animals and plants with special characteristics. These animals and plants can adjust to the salinity, temperature, and speed of the water more easily than others can. Salmon and eels, for example, are able to live in both kinds of water.

Saltwater Biomes

Saltwater biomes are also called **marine biomes**. The largest one is the ocean. Because it is so large, scientists divide it into different zones, or sections. One of these zones is the place where the ocean and shoreline meet.

As the ocean tide comes in and out, it sometimes forms tide pools. Tide pools are low places along the shore that are exposed by low tides. The conditions in the tide pool change as the water goes in and out. When the water is low, clams snap their shells shut to keep water inside. Sea anemones pull in their tentacles and keep moist by covering themselves with slimy mucus. As the waves rush back into the tide pool, sea urchins wedge into rocks and sand dollars burrow into the sand to keep from being pulled back into the ocean.

tide pool

coral reef

Another part of the ocean, coral reefs, is found in or near the tropics. These reefs are formed by living animals called coral. Corals prefer the clear, warm, shallow salt water of the tropics. Certain types of coral take salt from the sea and use it to build limestone skeletons on underwater objects. The skeletons of these stony corals form the coral reefs.

Many plants and animals live in the coral reefs. In fact, coral reefs have such great biodiversity that they are sometimes called "the rainforests of the sea." Many brightly colored fish, such as angelfish and parrotfish, live in the coral reef.

Another zone is the open ocean. It is often divided into layers based on the amount of sunlight each layer receives. The top layer receives the most sunlight. Some tiny plants and organisms can live in only the top layer of the ocean. They need sunlight to grow. Many fish and sea mammals also live in this layer because they depend on the plants and organisms for food.

The deeper layers of the ocean are dark and cold. They also have a lot of water pressure. So God designed some animals that can thrive in these conditions. Some fish that live deep in the ocean have large eyes to help them see in the dark waters. Other fish, such as lantern sharks, have light-producing organs. These lights help them attract their prey.

Viper fish live deep in the ocean.

Fantastic FACTS

Have you ever seen a fish fly? Some surface fish, such as the California flying fish, can "fly" to escape being a larger fish's meal. These fish have tails that allow them to swim very rapidly in the water. When in danger they can gather speed, head to the surface, and launch themselves out of the water. Their large side fins act like wings and allow the fish to soar above the water. The fish do not actually fly but glide. Some can stay aloft for distances of several hundred meters. That is longer than two football fields! Sometimes the fish unexpectedly land on the decks of small boats.

Great Lakes, United States

Freshwater Biomes

About three-fourths of the earth's surface is covered by water. But only a little bit of that water is fresh water. Freshwater biomes include ponds, lakes, streams, and rivers. God designed these biomes for the many animals and plants that could not survive in the marine biomes.

Freshwater biomes are classified as either standing water or moving water. The term *standing water* is used for any water that is not constantly moving. Ponds and lakes have standing water. This water comes from rivers, springs, rain, and melting snow. These bodies of water can be found in both cold and hot climates.

Ponds and lakes are similar, but ponds are not as deep. This allows plants such as cattails and reeds to grow in the pond as well as at its edge. Because lakes are deeper, many lake plants grow only at the edge of the lake. Some plants, such as the water lily, live on top of ponds and lakes. The rounded leaves of these plants help protect them from the wind.

Many animals also live in ponds and lakes. Dragonflies dart among the plants. Bullfrogs and snapping turtles live along the water's edge. Freshwater fish, such as perch and large-mouthed bass, swim in the water. Beavers may use nearby trees to build their dams in the water.

Creation CORNER

If you put a leaf on the surface of a pond or stream, the leaf will eventually sink. But God planned for water lilies to stay afloat. Water-lily leaves have air pockets that help them float. The leaves are also covered with a waxy surface that helps water slide off the leaf. The lily's flowers also help it stay on top of the water. On rainy days the lily does not open its flower. If it did, water would collect on top of the plant and cause it to sink.

Underneath the water, the water lily's stem is anchored in the mud. This stem is very strong but is also flexible. The flexibility helps the plant adjust to the height and movement of the water.

The water in other freshwater biomes, such as rivers, is constantly moving. River water comes from snow, rain, glaciers, and ground water. Gravity keeps this water flowing downhill to the ocean.

headwater

The beginning of a river, or the *headwater*, is usually a little stream. This water is usually clear and moves quickly. As the river winds along, other smaller rivers, called tributaries (TRIB yuh ter ees), join it. The river gets wider, slower, and warmer as it flows toward the ocean. The river may also get muddy as dirt and debris get mixed in. The *mouth*, or end, of the river empties into the ocean.

The temperature and speed of the water affect what kinds of plants and animals can live in freshwater biomes. Plants and animals that live in fast-flowing water must be able to either move with the water or anchor themselves against the current. Plants such as moss attach themselves to rocks in a stream. Many fish, including some kinds of trout, prefer the cool, fast-moving water.

The plants and animals that live in the slower water can be very different from those in the fast-flowing water. Plants along the edges of slower water may be similar to those around ponds and lakes. Some fish, such as certain kinds of catfish, feed on the bottom of rivers. They prefer the slow-moving water. Some large river mammals, such as the manatee, also live in slow-moving rivers. They eat the water plants that can grow in slower water.

river mouth

Florida Everglades

Wetlands

Scientists often disagree about how many land and water biomes exist. This is because biomes do not have set boundaries. They often merge into each other. One biome gradually turns into a different one. This transition zone can happen in places such as where grasslands meet a forest or where water meets the land. It can even happen where a river meets the ocean.

Wetlands are land that is almost always wet. Some wetlands are covered in water all year round. Other wetlands do not have water part of the year. The water in some wetlands comes and goes with the ocean tides. Wetlands are usually classified as marshes, swamps, or bogs.

Marshes and Swamps

The most common wetlands are marshes. They are found in many places and can have either fresh water or salt water. Most marsh plants are grasses such as reeds and cattails. Trees usually do not grow in marshes. Animals such as muskrats and alligators sometimes live in freshwater marshes. Saltwater marshes are home to oysters, crabs, and water birds such as pelicans and cranes.

Swamps, on the other hand, have many trees. The types of trees vary depending on where the swamp is located. The type of water also determines what kinds of trees can grow there. Saltwater swamps usually have mangrove trees. Freshwater swamps may have maple, willow, or bald cypress trees. Wading birds and snakes are common in swamps. Some also have alligators.

Bond Swamp National Wildlife Refuge, Georgia

Bogs

Swamps and marshes can have fresh water or salt water, but bogs can have only fresh water. The water is usually cold as well. This is mainly because bogs are often found in cooler northern climates. Bogs sometimes form near lakes, ponds, or other places where water cannot drain easily through the soil. Most of the water in bogs comes from precipitation.

When leaves fall or plants die, the dead plant material usually decays, or rots. Sometimes, though, it does not completely decay. When this happens, the partially decayed plant material called **peat** piles up into dense layers. The swampy soil in bogs forms from this peat. Moss, grass, and even some trees can grow in it. The surface of the bog may look firm and solid, but it is not. It is really mostly water.

Man's Stewardship

People often disagree about how to use wetlands and biomes. Sometimes people want to change the land to make way for more buildings and roads. At other times, people want to cut trees down to make more farmland. People usually have strong opinions about these changes.

God has given man dominion over the earth. But He has also given man the responsibility to be a good steward of the earth. To be a good steward, man must use his resources wisely and not waste them.

QUICK CHECK

1. What are the two ways water biomes are classified?
2. What keeps river water flowing towards the ocean?
3. What are the three main types of wetlands?

From Dirty to Clean

Process skills
- Making and using models
- Observing
- Inferring

Marshes, bogs, and swamps are important to both man and animals. Many animals lay their eggs or raise their young in wetlands. Some animals, such as migrating birds, use the wetlands as a "rest stop." After a little while, the animals continue on their journey.

Wetlands can also help control flooding. They act like sponges by absorbing some of the water from the tides or an overflowing river. Wetlands often clean the water as well by filtering out dirt and pollutants. As water flows into a wetland, some of the sediment carried by the water sinks. Plants trap sediments and pollutants from the water as well. When the water flows back out of the wetland, the dirt and pollutants stay behind.

In this activity, you will demonstrate how wetlands filter water.

Purpose

Demonstrate how wetlands filter water.

Procedure

Materials:
- foam cup, 16 oz
- scissors
- cheesecloth
- dried moss
- 4 jars with lids
- 500 mL water
- metric measuring cups
- potting soil
- spoon
- Activity Manual

1. Cut a hole in the bottom of the foam cup. Line the cup with cheesecloth. Some of the cheesecloth should hang over the sides of the cup.
2. Pack moss into the bottom one-third of the cup. This is your "wetland." Balance the cup over one of the empty jars.
3. Select two other jars and pour 250 mL of water into each. Add a spoonful of soil to each jar of water. Close the jars and shake well.
4. Set one jar of dirty water aside. You will be comparing this jar of water to the water that you filter through your wetland.

5. Shake the other jar of dirty water again. Pour the water from that jar into the cup so that the water will drip down through the moss and into the empty jar.
6. Compare this filtered water with the jar of dirty water. Record your observations in your Activity Manual.
7. Once all the water has dripped through, move the cup to the clean jar that has not been used yet. Put the lid on the jar of water that has been filtered. Shake the jar and pour the water through the wetland again.
8. Compare the jars of water and record your observations.
9. Carefully remove the moss and cheesecloth from the cup. Examine the moss and cheesecloth and record your observations.

Conclusions

- How does the activity model the way wetlands filter water?

Follow-up

- Use a different amount of dirt in the water.
- Add a few drops of food coloring to the water to represent pollutants.

Answer the Questions

1. How does the climate of a biome determine which organisms can live there?

____

____

____

2. Why are coral reefs sometimes called the "rainforests of the sea"?

____

____

____

3. Why might a mountain have several different kinds of biomes?

____

____

____

Solve the Problem

In November you are planning to visit a friend who lives in the Great Basin Desert in the western United States. You are looking forward to the hot, sunny weather in the desert. When you talk to her next, though, she tells you to bring a heavy coat, gloves, and a hat. Why would you need such heavy clothes in a desert?

____

____

____

____

____

In Perfect Balance

It is said that a metal chain is only as strong as its weakest link. Chapter 7 describes a chain that depends on the strength of each of its living parts.

A thunderstorm often provides rain for plants. In Chapter 8 find out how a storm's lightning also helps plants.

In Chapter 7 learn how God designed a type of shrimp that operates a cleaning service.

Interactions in an Ecosystem

REMEMBER now thy CREATOR

God gave many animals the ability to blend into their surroundings when they are not moving. This camouflage helps the animals survive. But God designed some animals with a disguise that works even when the animal is moving.

In 2005 the United States Army changed their combat uniforms, or fatigues. The new fatigues hide the soldiers better than the old ones did. The faded grays and tans on the new fatigues help disguise the soldiers in both wooded and desert areas. The army also changed the pattern of the material to camouflage soldiers as they move. Human eyes tend to focus on sharp changes of shape or color. So the new pattern has fuzzy edges that make it harder to see a moving soldier. Advanced computer graphics made this camouflage pattern possible. But the pattern is simply copying God's design.

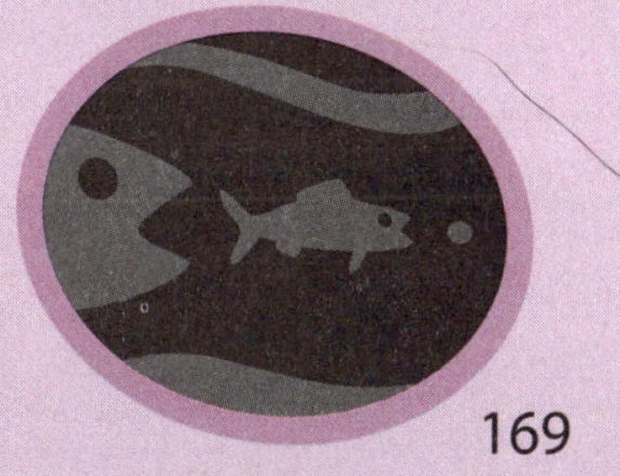

At first, the forest seems to be quiet. The leaves of tall trees rustle softly in the evening breeze. Then the silence is broken by the soft hoot of an owl. As you look for the owl, you become aware of other animals. A small mouse scurries across the forest floor. A red fox watches the mouse. These are just some of the living organisms in the forest. Many organisms are so small that you cannot see them.

Each organism, whether big or small, is part of an ecosystem. An **ecosystem** (EE ko SIS tum) consists of all the living organisms and their environment in a certain section of the earth. Ecosystems vary in size. Some, such as a tropical rainforest, are as large as a biome. Others, such as a rotting tree stump on the forest floor, are small. Even your skin is an ecosystem for many tiny organisms.

Parts of an Ecosystem

One part of an ecosystem is its environment. The **environment** (en VIE run ment) is the nonliving part of an ecosystem. This part includes the soil, water, sunlight, temperature, and air. The environment determines the kinds of organisms that can live in that ecosystem. For example, plants that need a large amount of water could not live in a desert. An animal with thick, long fur would not survive in the hot, humid climate of a tropical rainforest. Nor could a reptile that depends on warmth from the sun for its body heat live in the cold arctic tundra.

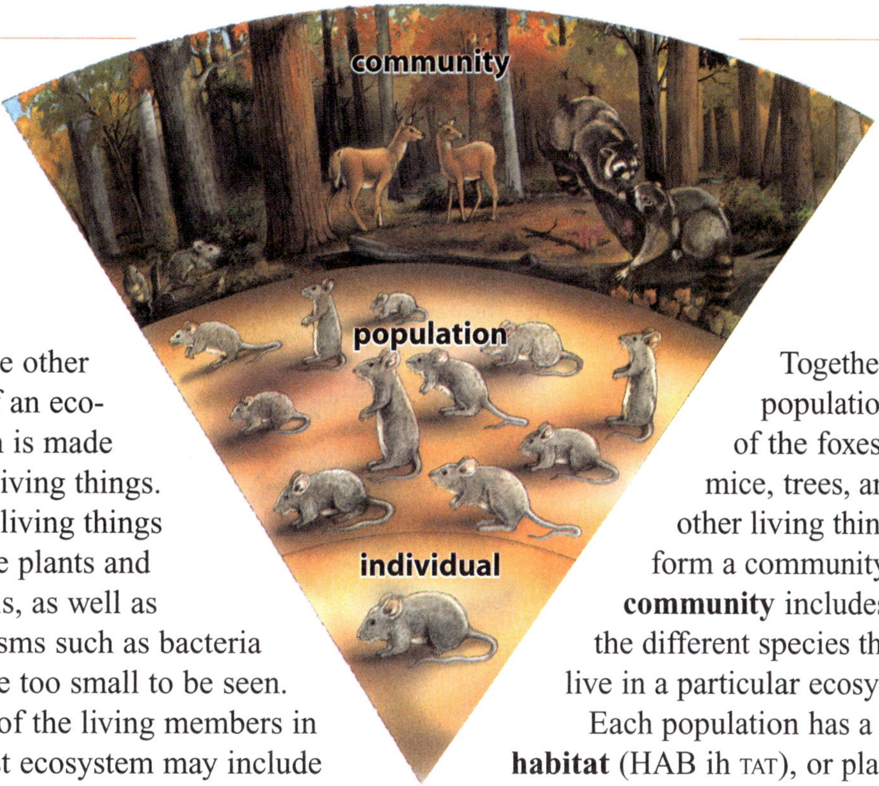

The other part of an ecosystem is made up of living things. These living things include plants and animals, as well as organisms such as bacteria that are too small to be seen. Some of the living members in a forest ecosystem may include trees, bushes, foxes, and birds. A desert ecosystem, on the other hand, may include cacti, scorpions, and lizards. Some ecosystems have many living things. Other ecosystems have only a few.

Each living member of an ecosystem is an **individual**. One red fox is an individual. All the red foxes in the forest, though, make up the forest's red fox population. A **population** consists of all the organisms of the same species that live in an ecosystem.

Populations can be different sizes. One forest might have a population of only a few foxes. That same forest could also have a red oak tree population of hundreds and a white-footed mouse population of thousands.

Together, the populations of the foxes, mice, trees, and other living things form a community. A **community** includes all the different species that live in a particular ecosystem.

Each population has a **habitat** (HAB ih TAT), or place to live. Several populations can share one habitat. One area of the forest may be a habitat for trees, mice, owls, and foxes. Each population also has its own niche. A **niche** (NICH) is an organism's specific function, or job, in the ecosystem. A niche includes all the different ways that an organism uses its *resources*, or available supplies. An animal's niche includes what the animal eats, when it eats, how it protects itself, and how it raises its young.

Populations can share a habitat and may even eat similar foods. But two populations cannot share exactly the same niche. For example, both hawks and owls eat mice. However, hawks hunt by day and owls hunt at night.

Roles in an Ecosystem

Animals eat food to get energy. But where does this energy come from? The source of this energy is the sun. God designed the sun to provide energy for all living things. Plants use energy from sunlight to make food from carbon dioxide and water. This process of making food is called *photosynthesis* (FOE toe SIN the sis). Plants use most of this food energy to grow and reproduce. The rest of the energy is stored in the roots, stems, or leaves of the plant.

Because plants make their own food, they are called **producers**. All life depends on producers. They change the energy from the sun into a form that other organisms can use.

Many living things cannot get their energy directly from the sun. These living things that depend on producers for food are called **consumers**. Consumers, such as animals and humans, must eat food in order to get energy. In an ecosystem there are usually more producers than consumers.

consumer

producer

herbivore

Some consumers, such as rabbits and grasshoppers, eat only plants. These animals are called *herbivores* (HUR buh VORS). They get their energy from the plants. However, not all herbivores eat the same part of the plant. Some herbivores eat only the leaves. Others eat the seeds or roots.

Some consumers eat both plants and other animals. These consumers are called *omnivores* (AWM nih VORS). For example, the red fox usually eats mice, but it also eats berries and grass. Many omnivores change their eating habits when the seasons change.

omnivore

carnivore

Consumers that eat other consumers are called *carnivores* (KAR nih VORS), or meat eaters. These animals usually do not eat plants. Instead these animals get their energy by eating other consumers. Many carnivores, such as cougars and weasels, eat several different species of animals.

Some consumers help keep the ecosystem clean. These animals, called *scavengers* (SKAV in jers), eat things that have already died. Cockroaches and vultures are two common kinds of scavengers. Most scavengers are carnivores.

Another group of organisms are called decomposers. **Decomposers** (DEE kum POE zers) help break down dead things and wastes. Decomposing adds minerals and nutrients back into the environment. Plants then use the nutrients to grow and produce more food. There are many kinds of decomposers. Most, like bacteria, cannot be seen without a microscope. Other decomposers include molds, mushrooms, and earthworms.

Scavengers and decomposers are an important part of the ecosystem. Without them, the ecosystem would be full of wastes and dead things.

decomposer

1. What are the two parts of an ecosystem?
2. Which is larger—a population or a community?
3. What is different about the way producers and consumers get energy?

Habitat Investigation

Process skills
- Observing
- Classifying
- Collecting and recording data
- Defining operationally

What do you think of when someone mentions habitats? Perhaps you think about large animals and their homes. Or you might think of a plant that is unique to a certain environment.

Both plants and animals have habitats. Some are big. For example, a pond, forest, or savanna can be a habitat for many different populations. But some habitats are so small that you might not even notice them at first.

In this activity, you will be investigating a very small habitat.

Purpose

Investigate a habitat.

Materials:
- meter stick
- small sticks or stakes
- string
- scissors
- magnifying glass
- toothpicks
- garden trowel
- Activity Manual

Procedure

1. Go outside to an area that your teacher has selected. Choose a spot of ground to mark as your habitat.
2. Measure a square that is 1 m on each side. Push a stake or stick into the ground to mark each corner of the square. Outline your habitat by connecting the stakes with string.

3. Carefully observe your habitat without disturbing it. In your Activity Manual use terms such as *grassy*, *wooded*, or *sandy* to describe the area around your habitat.
4. Notice whether any living things are interacting. Record your observations.
5. List the nonliving things that are part of the habitat.
6. Use toothpicks to carefully move pieces of plant matter. Look for any living things that might be hiding under the plant matter. Use toothpicks or the trowel to gently move

some of the soil. Look for living things that might be in the soil. Use the magnifying glass as needed.

7. List all the living things that you observe in your habitat. Remember to include plants as well as animals. If you cannot identify a plant or animal by name, describe it as well as possible. Draw a small picture of it if necessary.

8. Identify the living things as either producers or consumers. Try also to identify the consumers as herbivores, omnivores, or carnivores.

Conclusions

- How many different populations did you observe in your habitat?
- How does the environment affect the organisms that make up your habitat?

Follow-up

- Enlarge your square habitat to 2 m on each side. Notice any differences in populations.
- Observe a different habitat. Compare this habitat to your earlier one.

Energy in an Ecosystem

Chains and Webs

A grasshopper nibbling on a leaf might become dinner for a mouse. Later, a fox might catch and eat the mouse. The energy that the leaf got from the sun has been passed from one organism to another. This transfer of energy and nutrients through a community is called a **food chain**.

Food Chain

A food chain always begins with a producer. The second link of a food chain is usually a herbivore. The animals that make up any additional links are predators. A **predator** (PRED eh ter) is any animal that hunts and eats other animals. Predators are either carnivores or omnivores. The animals that a predator hunts are called its **prey**.

A food chain shows only one source of food for each animal. However, most animals are part of more than one food chain. This is because animals usually eat more than one kind of food. And most animals are eaten by more than one kind of predator. A **food web** con sists of several food chains linked together. For example, a grasshopper may be eaten by a mouse, but a grasshopper can also be food for a spider, bird, or salamander.

Changing one part of a food web affects all the other organisms in that web. For example, weasels are often eaten by hawks. If you removed all the hawks, the weasel population would probably increase. But then the ecosystem might not have enough resources for all the weasels. Weasels eat mice and small birds. If there were more weasels, there would be fewer mice and small birds. And other animals that eat mice and birds would have less food. Food webs show how organisms depend on each other.

Forest Food Web

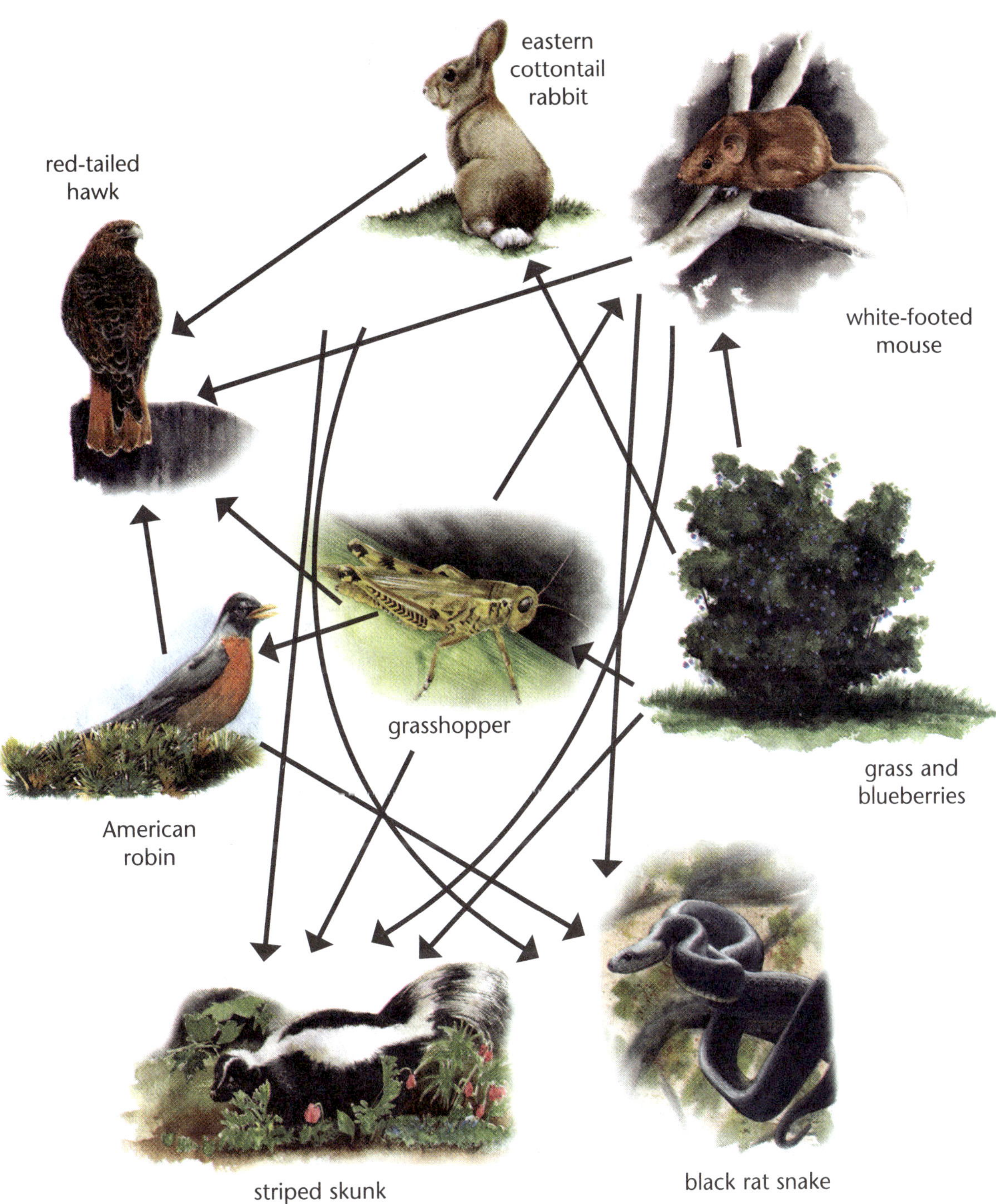

Energy Pyramid

Energy is transferred at each link of a food chain. However, the amount of energy transferred becomes smaller each time. A grasshopper gets energy from eating grass. It uses most of that energy for its own needs. Some of the energy, though, is stored in the grasshopper's body. That stored energy later transfers to the mouse that eats the grasshopper.

Scientists use an energy pyramid to show how energy moves through an ecosystem. An energy pyramid shows only one food chain. Producers, such as plants, form the base of the pyramid. The producers receive the most energy because they get it directly from the sun.

The other levels represent the different links of a food chain. The pyramid shows how the amount of energy changes at each level. There are fewer animals at the top of the pyramid because less energy is available. Each organism uses about 90% of its energy to live and grow. That means only about 10% of its energy is passed on to the next organism.

Energy Pyramid

On a prairie, grasses and wildflowers may have to compete for space and sunlight.

Competition occurs when two or more organisms are trying to use the same resources. This happens when wildflowers compete with grasses for space and sunlight. Competition also happens when two animals need to eat the same kind of food. Competition can occur between members of the same species or between members of different species.

Competition helps keep the ecosystem balanced. For example, owls eat white-footed mice. If there are not enough mice, the owls will have to compete for the same limited prey. Some of them may not be able to find food in that ecosystem. They may move to another area, and some of them may die. The population of owls will adjust based on the populations of their food. If the population of mice increases, the population of owls may also increase again. Or other animals such as foxes might move into the area and help keep the mice population balanced.

owl hunting a mouse

1. How are food chains different from food webs?
2. Why are there fewer animals at the top of an energy pyramid?
3. When does competition occur?

Food-Web Connections

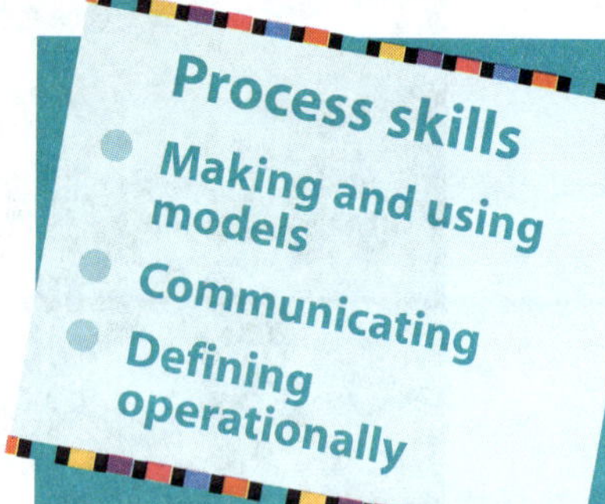

A food web consists of many food chains mixed together. Because animals eat more than one type of food, a food web can have many different connections.

In this activity, you and your partners will make a model of a food web.

Purpose

Model a food web.

Materials:
- food-web cards
- pieces of string, each 2 m long

Procedure

1. Get a food-web card and some pieces of string from your teacher. Look at your card and determine whether you represent a producer, a herbivore, an omnivore, or a carnivore.
2. Check the identities of the other members in your group. Decide which people represent your food sources. Use string to connect yourself to your "food sources." See how many different connections your group can make.

Conclusions

- How does your food web compare to an actual food web for an ecosystem?
- If something happened to one organism in your food web, how would that affect the other organisms?

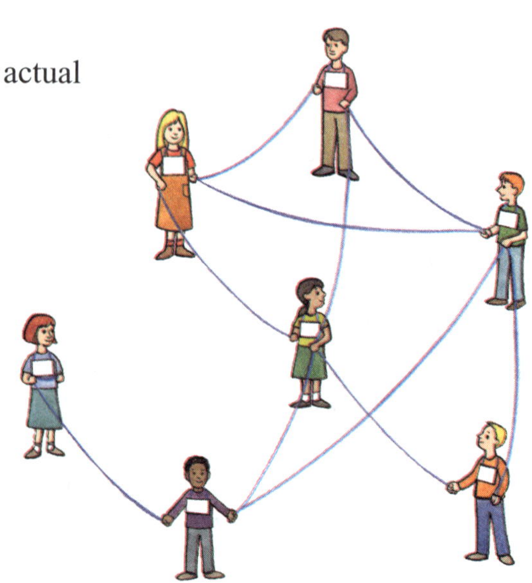

Follow-up

- Research the consumers in your food web to find out which foods they prefer to eat.
- Add more consumers to your food web.

Explorations A Tangled Web

Ecologists (ee KOL oh jists) are scientists who study how living things interact. This interaction may be between living things or between living things and their environment. Ecologists often use a food web to study predator and prey relationships.

In this exploration, you are an ecologist. You will make a visual to represent one of the food webs in an ecosystem.

What to do

1. Choose an ecosystem that you would like to study. Make a list of several plants and animals that are common to that ecosystem. Be sure to include smaller living things as well as bigger living things. Separate your list into producers and consumers. Try to include at least eight different living things.
2. Research to find out which animals are herbivores. Identify the plants that each of those animals eats. Which animals on your list are omnivores? Identify the plants and animals that each of those animals eats. Next, look at the carnivores. Which consumers does each of them eat?
3. Using the information you gathered about the living things in your ecosystem, make a visual that shows a food web for your ecosystem.

Meeting Needs

All living things have the same basic needs: food, water, protection from consumers, and shelter. To meet these needs, God designed living things with a variety of adaptations. **Adaptations** (AD ap TAY shuns) can include any special characteristics or skills that help a living thing survive in its environment.

Plant Adaptations

Most plants make food through photosynthesis. This process is not possible, though, without sunlight. Some plants need a lot of sunlight. Others need only a little. God gave each plant exactly what it needs to survive in its environment.

Plants that grow in shady places sometimes have large leaves. These leaves have a large surface area for collecting sunlight. Vines often climb on objects or other plants. Climbing helps the vine get up higher so that it can get more sunlight.

However, plants need more than just sunlight for photosynthesis. They also need carbon dioxide and water. So plants have tiny pores in their leaves. These holes are called stomata. Stomata allow air and water to move in and out of the plant.

Venus flytrap

A few unusual plants, such as sundews and Venus flytraps, catch their food as well as make it. These carnivorous plants are able to make food through photosynthesis. However, the soil in their swampy habitats often lacks some of the nutrients these plants need. So God provided these plants with a unique adaptation. These plants attract insects and other small animals. When an insect or animal gets close enough, the plant traps and eats it. The trapped insect or animal provides extra nutrients for the plant.

Plants also need protection from predators. Some plants are protected by thorns, spines, or stinging hairs. Acacia (ah KAY shah) trees have long thorns. These thorns protect the trees from many animals that would eat the leaves. Other plants, such as stinging nettles, are covered with tiny hairs. When touched, the tiny hairs "sting" the predator.

Sometimes plants use poisons to protect themselves. The poisonous plants often taste bad. For example, acacia trees are often eaten by giraffes. These trees release a chemical that makes the leaves taste bitter after a few mouthfuls. The giraffe soon moves to a different tree. A plant's poison can sometimes cause sickness or death. But poisons that harm one animal might not hurt another species. God carefully designed adaptations so that animals and plants can meet their basic needs.

giraffe and acacia tree

Animal Adaptations

Animals use a variety of ways to find food or protect themselves from predators. Some animals, such as the opossum, lie still when threatened and pretend to be dead. Both predators and prey use camouflage to blend in with their environment. Predators use camouflage to sneak up on their prey. Prey use it to avoid being seen.

Other animals use mimicry (MIM ih kree) and disguises. The scarlet king snake has colors and markings similar to those of the poisonous coral snake. This mimicry helps the scarlet king snake avoid hungry predators.

The tawny frogmouth uses a disguise to hide from predators. The nocturnal bird's feathers are silver, gray, black, and white. During the day, the sleeping bird looks like a dead tree branch.

school of fish

Living in groups is another way that animals meet their needs. Many species of animals live in groups. These groups have different names. Lions live in *prides*. Groups of fish stay together in *schools*. Termites live in *colonies*. Elephants travel in *herds*. No matter how a group is named, though, its advantages are the same. Living in a group makes it easier for the animals to find food. Being in a group also helps the animals protect and care for their young.

Sometimes a whole group of animals leaves one ecosystem and moves to another ecosystem. This adaptation is called **migration** (my GRAY shun). Animals migrate for different reasons. Some animals, such as salmon and sea turtles, move to a new place in order to reproduce

migrating birds

or to raise their young. Other animals migrate when their food supply is low. Animals on the African savanna often migrate in search of food and water. Some animals, such as birds and monarch butterflies, migrate when the seasons change. This migration helps them avoid weather that is too hot or too cold. Even huge gray whales move to warmer waters during the winter.

Some animals do not need to eat food during winter. They sleep through the winter and wake up in the spring. This deep sleep, called **hibernation** (HI bur NAY shun), is one way that animals adapt to their climate. Animals that hibernate eat large amounts of food during the summer and autumn. This food is stored as body fat and provides energy for the animal while it sleeps.

When an animal hibernates, its body temperature drops. In fact, its body temperature might be almost as cold as the weather outside its den. The animal's breathing rate and heart rate also drop. These lowered rates allow the animal to use very little energy during the winter.

Most ground squirrels hibernate during winter.

Fantastic FACTS

One hibernating animal has its own holiday! Americans celebrate Groundhog Day on February 2. Folklore and tradition state that a groundhog will come out of its hole on the second of February. If the groundhog sees its shadow, it will return to its hole. That supposedly means that there will be six more weeks of winter. If it does not see its shadow, then spring is coming and the worst of winter is over. Actually, groundhogs usually begin their hibernation in September or October and end in March.

1. What are some of the basic needs of living things?
2. How are Venus flytraps adapted to their swampy habitats?
3. What are three reasons that animals migrate?

Relationships

Plants and animals sometimes compete to meet their needs. But at other times, they share their resources. Several different forest animals might live in the same tree. Many different populations of herbivores live together on a savanna. Some of them prefer different plants. Others eat different parts of the same plant or eat at different times of the day. Zebras prefer to eat the top part of the grass. Wildebeests eat the middle stems and leaves, and gazelles prefer the part of the grass that is closest to the ground.

Some organisms share their resources by forming special partnerships. Scientists use the term *symbiosis* (SIM bee OH sis) to describe this kind of relationship. **Symbiosis** occurs whenever two species interact with each other over a long period of time. There are several types of symbiosis.

One type of symbiosis is parasitism. *Parasitism* (PAIR ah sih TIZ um) is an interaction that helps one partner and harms the other. A **parasite** (PAIR ah SITE) is any organism that lives on or inside another organism and takes food from that organism. The plant or animal that a parasite lives on or in is called its **host**. The parasite usually does not kill its host, but it does cause harm to the other organism. In another type of symbiosis, the

Parasitism

Fleas can really cause a lamb to itch! Fleas and lambs have a parasite/host relationship.

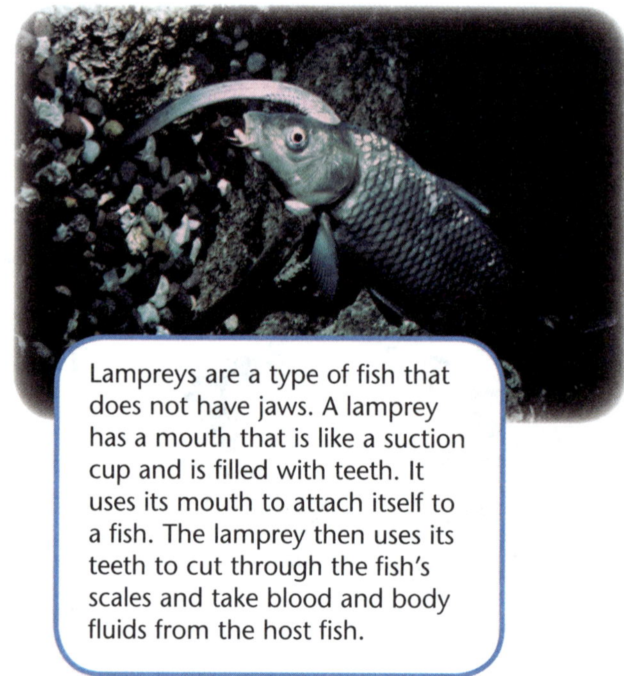

Lampreys are a type of fish that does not have jaws. A lamprey has a mouth that is like a suction cup and is filled with teeth. It uses its mouth to attach itself to a fish. The lamprey then uses its teeth to cut through the fish's scales and take blood and body fluids from the host fish.

interactions benefit both partners. This type of symbiosis is called *mutualism* (MYOO choo ah LIZ um). A relationship that benefits one partner but does not help or harm the other partner is called *commensalism* (ka MEN sah LIZ um).

Mutualism

Oxpeckers, a type of bird, have a special relationship with gazelles. The bird rides on a gazelle and eats ticks and other harmful insects. The bird gets food and protection from predators, and the gazelle gets rid of its insect pests.

Bees visit flowers to collect pollen and nectar. When a honeybee visits a flower, some of the pollen sticks to the fuzzy hairs on the bee. This pollen usually falls off when the bee visits another flower. The flower gets pollinated and the honeybee gets its food.

The scarlet cleaner shrimp runs an underwater cleaning service! It picks off parasites, bacteria, and dead skin from coral reef fish. Even fierce predator fish wait in line for cleaning. The fish get rid of parasites, and the scarlet cleaner shrimp gets a meal.

Commensalism

Very little sunlight comes through the canopy of a rainforest. Some plants, such as tropical orchids, get a boost from the tall trees. The flower is not rooted in the soil. Instead, it attaches itself to the tree's broad branches and grows high on the tree. The tree supports the orchid, and the orchid is able to get sunlight without harming the tree.

Behaviors

How do animals know how to form partnerships? How are birds able to migrate thousands of miles without getting lost? What tells the squirrels and groundhogs when to hibernate? God designed His creatures with **instincts** (IN STINGKTS), the basic knowledge and skills that are needed for survival.

Instincts are behaviors that are inherited. They are automatically passed down from generation to generation. Migration and hibernation are instincts. No one has to give hummingbirds travel directions from North America to Central America. No one has to teach a groundhog how to hibernate. Instincts are not unique to one individual. Every member of a species is born with the instincts it needs to survive.

Some behaviors, though, are learned. A **learned behavior** is a behavior that cannot be inherited. For example, a chimpanzee might learn how to use rocks to crack open nuts. This chimpanzee can teach its offspring how to crack nuts, but the baby chimpanzees are not born with the knowledge of how to crack nuts.

Sometimes it can be hard to decide whether a behavior is an instinct or is learned. For example, lions are born with the instinct to kill and eat meat for food. But to be good hunters, they need to learn from other lions. So lionesses teach their cubs how to hunt. The instinct to hunt and the learned ability to hunt well work together. But they are not the same.

God planned for all of His living things to interact with each other. Every plant and animal in an ecosystem has its specific niche. This does not mean that ecosystems never change. Ecosystems are constantly changing! Changing one part of an ecosystem affects all the other parts. But change is part of God's plan and purpose for the earth.

Science and the BIBLE

Before man's sin, animals did not hunt and kill each other for food. However, when man sinned, death became part of the natural order of the food chain. God provided animals with the necessary instincts to survive in a sin-cursed world. But one day God will change these instincts. Isaiah 11:6–9 tells us that predators and prey will live together peacefully on God's new earth. God tells us that this will be possible because in that day all "the earth shall be full of the knowledge of the Lord."

QUICK CHECK

1. What name is given to special partnerships in which two different species interact with each other over a long period of time?
2. What are instincts?
3. How are instincts and learned behaviors different?

Answer the Questions

1. What is the difference between a food chain and a food web?

____

____

____

2. Why are decomposers so important to an ecosystem?

____

____

____

3. Why are there fewer living things at the top of an energy pyramid than at the bottom?

____

____

____

Solve the Problem

For several weeks you have observed migrating flocks of geese flying overhead. You know that there is a lake north of you where the geese stay during the spring and summer. You tell your friend that, when the geese migrate the direction that you observed, it is a sign that spring is coming soon. In what direction are the geese flying, and why does that mean spring is coming soon?

____

____

____

____

____

Changes in an Ecosystem

REMEMBER now thy CREATOR

Man's technology allows him to live for a little while in space. But he must transport supplies from the earth to help meet his basic needs. Most scientists believe that for long stays in space man must reproduce the cycles of nature that exist on the earth.

God's patterns of nature efficiently provide for the needs of living things. For example, plants are an important part of many cycles. Plants provide food, but they also help clean the air. The carbon dioxide that people exhale is part of what plants need to produce food. The oxygen that plants release is needed by people to breathe. Waste materials produced by living things can fertilize plants. By using plants in his space environment, man could reduce some of his costly supplies. God's plan works better than even man's best technology does.

spring in Washington, D.C.

summer in Seattle, Washington

Cycles of Change

Change is always happening in our world. Some changes occur quickly. In just a few short hours, heavy rains can flood roads and houses. Fires can quickly destroy whole forests. Other changes, such as the growth of a plant, take place slowly. Sometimes changes happen so slowly that they are not even noticed for a long while. The weathering of rock is an example of this.

However, changes do not happen by chance. Each change, big or small, is planned and controlled by God. Some changes are part of a **cycle**, or regular pattern of change. God uses these cycles to maintain His earth. He promises that they will continue. In Genesis 8:22, God says, "While the earth remaineth, seedtime and harvest, and cold and heat, and summer and winter, and day and night shall not cease."

Seasonal Changes

One of the earth's cycles is the **seasons**, or the regular divisions of the year. Many parts of the earth change temperature as the seasons change. These areas usually have four different seasons: spring, summer, autumn, and winter.

The season of spring is a time of new growth for living things. Fresh grass and new flowers appear. Trees put out new leaves. Migrating animals return in search of food. Other animals come out of hibernation. Many animals give birth to their young in the spring.

During the summer, the baby animals grow and learn. Plants grow and produce food both for themselves and for animals. Some animals begin to gather food and store it for the coming winter.

In autumn, the temperatures get cooler. The leaves on many trees

autumn in West Virginia

winter in Clinton, New Jersey

change color. Animals continue preparing for the winter. Some animals migrate to warmer places. Other animals grow thick coats of fur.

Winter has the coldest temperatures of the year. Many tree branches are bare of leaves. Some animals stay in their holes or burrows and are inactive. Others hibernate in dens until the warm spring comes again.

In some areas of the earth, however, the temperature does not change very much, but the amount of rain changes a lot. The seasons in these areas are based mostly on rainfall. They usually have two seasons: the wet season and the dry season. During the wet season, most of the rain for the entire year falls. In the dry season, very little rain falls.

Monsoons (mon SOONS) are winds that change direction with the seasons. These winds control the wet and dry seasons in some areas. For example, the winds blow across the Indian Ocean for several months and bring heavy rains to India and Southeast Asia. Then the winds reverse their direction and blow across the land for the rest of the year. India and Southeast Asia have a very dry climate for these remaining months of the year.

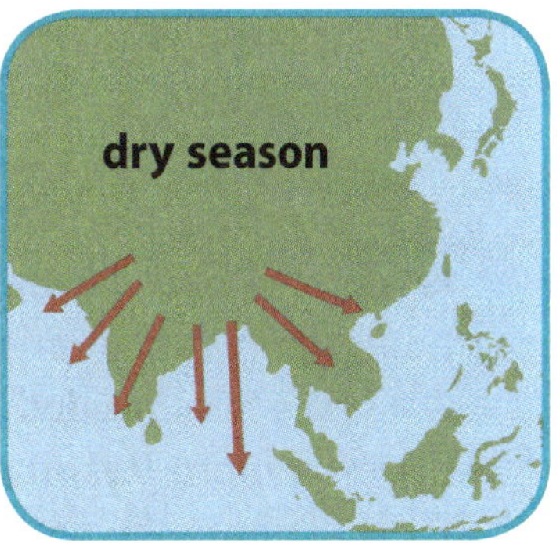

Monsoons control the seasons in India and Southeast Asia.

Carbon Cycle

Another cycle is the carbon cycle. Every living thing needs carbon. Carbon combines with other elements to form the compounds that make up living things.

When carbon combines with oxygen, it forms a gas called carbon dioxide. Plants take in and use this gas. During **photosynthesis** plants use water, carbon dioxide from the air, and energy from the sun to form sugar molecules and oxygen. The sugar molecules contain carbon. The plants use some of the sugar molecules to provide for their own needs. The rest of the sugar molecules are stored in the plant. The stored sugar will provide food for other organisms. The oxygen that was formed during photosynthesis is released into the air. Animals and humans breathe in this oxygen.

Oxygen is needed for the process of respiration. **Respiration** (RES puh RAY shun) is the process in which organisms use sugar molecules and oxygen to produce energy. This process also produces carbon dioxide and water. Respiration takes place in almost all living things, including plants. In plants, respiration is the opposite of photosynthesis.

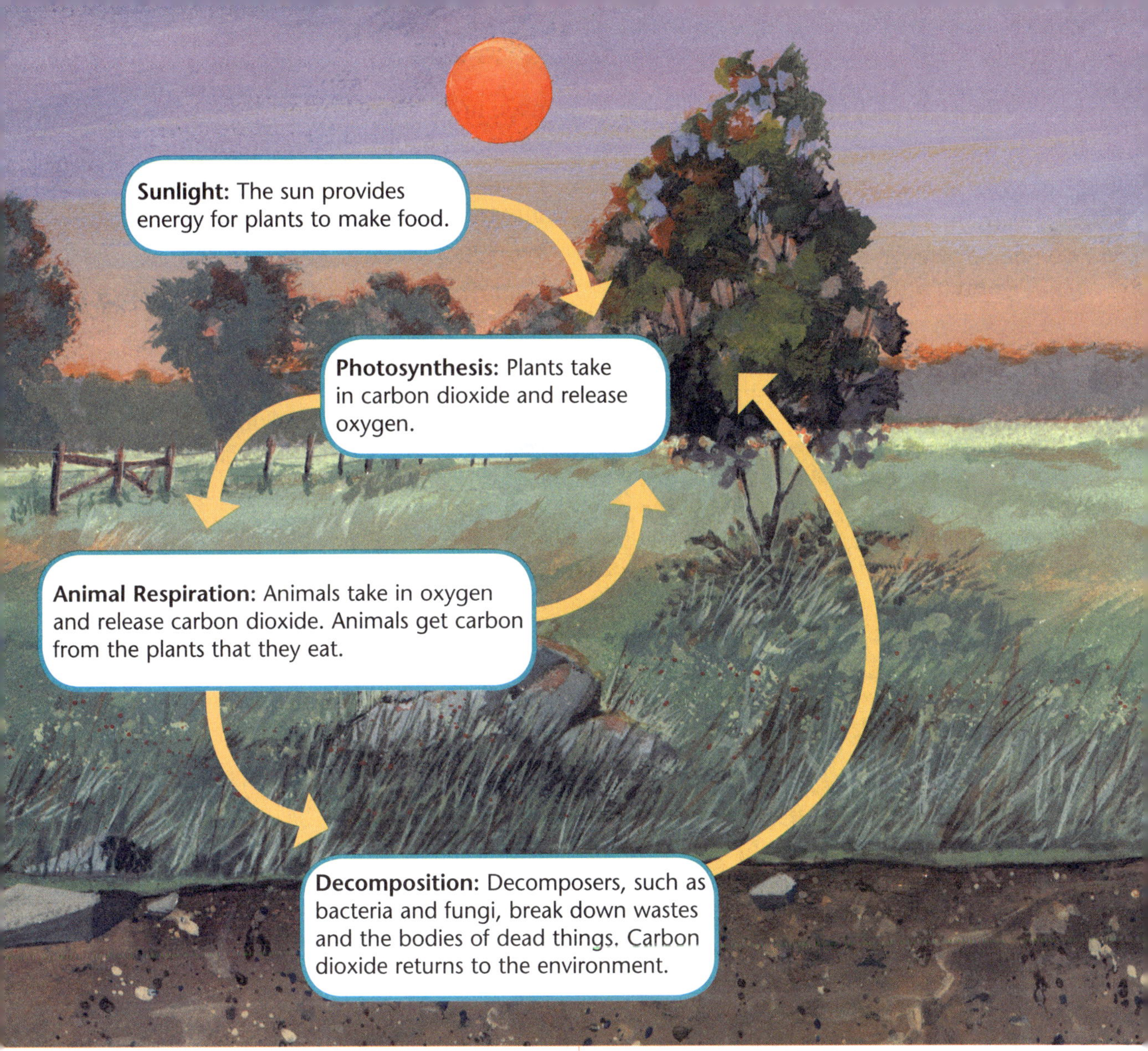

Sunlight: The sun provides energy for plants to make food.

Photosynthesis: Plants take in carbon dioxide and release oxygen.

Animal Respiration: Animals take in oxygen and release carbon dioxide. Animals get carbon from the plants that they eat.

Decomposition: Decomposers, such as bacteria and fungi, break down wastes and the bodies of dead things. Carbon dioxide returns to the environment.

When living things die, carbon remains stored in their bodies for a while. Gradually, bacteria, fungi, and other decomposers break down the bodies of dead things. The carbon is then released into the air as carbon dioxide.

1. What is a cycle?
2. What is the name of the winds that change directions with the seasons?
3. What process in the carbon cycle uses sugar molecules and oxygen to produce carbon dioxide and water?

Nitrogen Cycle

The nitrogen (NYE truh jun) cycle is also important to life. Like carbon, nitrogen is essential to life. Living things depend on this element. Without it, they could not grow and function normally.

Nitrogen gas is part of the air that we breathe. In fact, the air is mostly made up of nitrogen gas. However, plants, animals, and people cannot use nitrogen in this form. To be usable, nitrogen gas must combine with other elements.

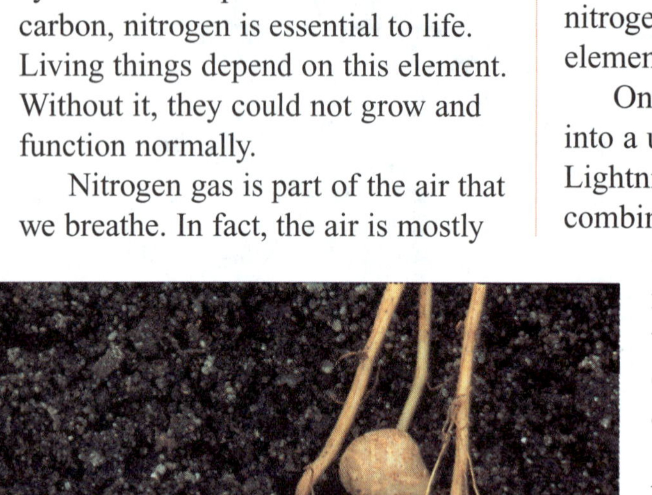

One way nitrogen can change into a usable form is by lightning. Lightning causes nitrogen gas to combine with oxygen. Rain then carries these compounds of nitrogen and oxygen down to the earth. Lightning can change only a small amount of nitrogen at a time.

Most nitrogen is changed by bacteria. There are many kinds of nitrogen-changing bacteria. These bacteria are found in the soil. They live in little bumps, or nodules (NOJ ools), on the roots of plants such as peanuts, peas, and beans. The tiny bacteria absorb nitrogen gas from the soil and combine it with other gases to form nitrogen compounds. These compounds help plants to grow. The plants, in turn, provide a habitat for these helpful bacteria.

The nodules on the soybean plant contain the bacteria that change nitrogen into useful compounds.

Plants use the nitrogen compounds both to grow and to make proteins. Animals get the proteins and nitrogen by eating the plants or other animals. In this way, animals get a form of nitrogen that they can use.

When plants and animals die, other kinds of bacteria act as decomposers. These bacteria form compounds from nitrogen and other gases. These compounds are used by some plants. Some of the compounds are broken down completely to form nitrogen gas. This returns nitrogen gas to the air so that the cycle can begin again.

Water Cycle

Water is always moving between the atmosphere and the earth. The sun warms bodies of water, such as oceans, lakes, and rivers. This heats the water and causes some of it to evaporate. **Evaporation** is the process of liquid water changing into a vapor, or gas.

Plants, animals, and humans also release water vapor into the air. Plant roots absorb water from the soil. The water is then carried to the stems and leaves. Tiny openings, called stomata, allow water vapor to move out of the plant. This is called **transpiration** (TRAN spuh RAY shun). Animals and humans also breathe out water vapor when they exhale.

As the water vapor rises high above the earth, it cools. The cooling causes it to change back to a liquid. The process of water vapor changing to a liquid is called **condensation**. Rain droplets form from condensation. The droplets collect in the clouds and then fall to the earth as **precipitation**.

Some precipitation soaks into the ground and is stored there. This

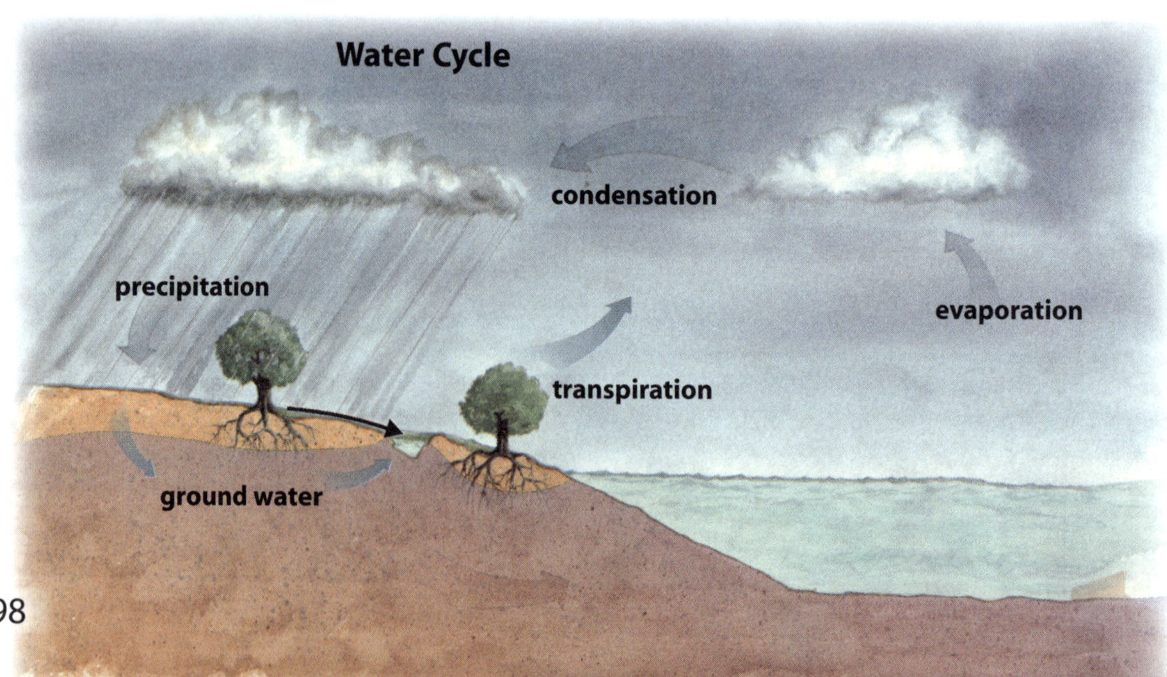

water is known as **ground water**. It provides water for plants, streams, rivers, and oceans. Water that does not soak into the ground collects on the earth's surface. The collected water may be as small as a puddle or as large as an ocean. Evaporation of some of this water begins the cycle again.

Creation CORNER

You may be surprised to see all the benefits that God has provided for us in a single tree. A tree absorbs and uses carbon dioxide and then releases oxygen. However, through its leaves and trunk, the tree also absorbs some of the excess carbon dioxide and other gases that are harmful to life. Even a tree's roots are useful. They help filter and clean ground water.

A tree may also change the temperature around it. For example, a single average-sized oak tree not only provides shade from the sun to lower the temperature, it also transpires a lot of water. In fact, it can transpire as much as 375 L (99 gal) of water each day! Just like evaporation, transpiration helps cool the tree and the air around it. And, of course, the tree provides beauty for us and a habitat for animals. A tree shows how God's creation can be both beautiful and useful.

God's Perfect Plan

Our world did not begin by chance. Our great Creator planned and created every detail. He planned for each cycle to depend on the other cycles. Water is needed for the water cycle. Water is also used in the carbon cycle during photosynthesis. Nitrogen compounds are made available to plants through precipitation and by being dissolved in ground water.

Seasonal changes also affect other cycles. Autumn leaves fall to the ground. Bacteria break down the leaves to form nitrogen compounds. This adds many nutrients to the soil. Plants need these nutrients so that they can grow. During the spring, plants grow and produce new leaves. The leaves are needed for photosynthesis to occur. Through these cycles, God is continually providing for what He has created.

QUICK CHECK

1. How is most nitrogen changed into usable compounds?
2. What is the process through which plants release water vapor into the air?

ACTIVITY

Decomposers at Work

Process skills
- Hypothesizing
- Experimenting
- Observing
- Identifying and controlling variables
- Recording data

Decomposers are an important part of many cycles. Without decomposers, living things would not be able to get the nutrients that they need. Some decomposers, such as worms and mold, are large enough to be seen. But others are too small to be seen without a microscope.

In this activity, you may not be able to see the decomposers, but you will be able to observe their work.

Problem

How does water affect how quickly carrots and lettuce decompose?

Materials:
- 3 containers
- potting soil
- centimeter ruler
- 9 carrot pieces
- 60 mL shredded lettuce
- 60 mL water
- metric measuring cups
- spoon
- plastic wrap
- 3 rubber bands
- Activity Manual

Procedure

1. Label one container *wet*, another one *moist*, and the last one *dry*.
2. Predict which condition will allow the carrots and lettuce to decompose the fastest. Complete the hypothesis in your Activity Manual.
3. Put 3 cm of soil in each container.
4. Add three carrot pieces and 20 mL of shredded lettuce to each container.
5. Pour 40 mL of water into the container labeled *wet*. Add 20 mL of water to the container labeled *moist*.
6. Stir the mixture in each container.
7. Cover each container with plastic wrap, and secure it with a rubber band. With a pencil, poke an equal number of small holes through the plastic wrap on each container. Set the three containers in the same location.

 8. Observe the containers every two or three days for two weeks. Record your observations. Stir the mixtures each time you check them. Be sure to cover each container again after observing it.

Conclusions

- In which container did the mixture decompose the fastest? Was your hypothesis correct?
- What are some other things that could have influenced how quickly the mixture decomposed?

Follow-up

- Test the mixtures in a cooler or warmer area.
- Add fertilizer and observe whether it affects how quickly the mixtures decompose.
- Use the same amount of water in each container, but use a different kind of soil in each.

Stresses on an Ecosystem

An unexpected change in the environment can cause an ecosystem to not be able to function normally. A river might overflow its banks and flood nearby fields and towns. Fires might burn forests and force animals and people to flee to safety. Droughts can dry up the water supply, causing crops to fail and soil to erode.

A **stress** is any physical hazard to life caused by having too much or too little of things needed for life. These stresses change the environment. Sometimes they seem like tragic disasters. Animals may die or be forced to move. Plants may be uprooted or burned. However, these stresses are all part of how God maintains the earth.

Fire

Many forest fires are started through man's carelessness. Other forest fires are caused by lightning. Either way, a fire can cause ecosystems to undergo quick and sudden changes. Fires are often thought of as destructive and harmful. Sometimes, though, a fire can be beneficial to an ecosystem. Forest fires get rid of dead trees, branches, pine needles, and other things that could cause larger fires. For this reason, some fires are allowed to burn themselves out. People carefully watch these fires, though, so that they do not get out of control. Any fire that threatens the safety of people is put out as soon as possible.

lodgepole pine

New trees grow in the burned area of Yosemite National Park in California.

Fires cause nutrients from dead trees and plants to be recycled into the soil. These nutrients make the forest soil rich and fertile. Some plants have seeds that will sprout only after a fire. For instance, the lodgepole pine's cone needs heat in order to open and release its seeds.

Over time, new forests grow to replace those that were burned. This may take many years. The new forest, though, is not exactly like the one that it replaces. It often has a greater variety of plants and animals than the old one did.

Flood

A **flood** occurs when an ecosystem receives more water than it can use or store. A flood can move large amounts of earth and rock. The force of water can uproot trees and move houses. Sometimes a flood can carry away rich topsoil. Without topsoil, crops may not be able to grow. The floodwaters may also destroy crops and growing plants by covering them with water.

Sometimes flooding occurs when a river overflows its banks into surrounding land. It may take a while for floodwaters to recede back into the river. When they finally do, the river may have a new water level or even a new route.

Like fires, floods are often seen as harmful and disastrous. However, floods too can be beneficial. Floods can distribute fertile soil and seeds. Plants may grow in areas where they would not have grown before. Some trees depend on annual floods. Without them, the trees' seeds could not sprout.

Mississippi flood in 1993

Drought

A **drought** occurs when an ecosystem receives less rainfall than it needs. Sometimes a drought is so severe that there is not enough water to meet the needs of the plants and animals. Lower water levels in rivers and streams cause many problems for the fish and wildlife that depend on the water.

The lack of rain causes topsoil to be dry and dusty. It can be easily eroded by the wind. Some plants die without a good water supply. These things all cause food for animals and humans to become scarce. In poorer countries, drought often leads to famine.

Droughts also make an area more susceptible to fires. Dry vegetation burns easily. So, once a fire starts, it can spread rapidly. In extreme heat, some fires can even start all by themselves.

A drought does not have a definite beginning or ending. In this way, a drought is different from other natural disasters. The beginning of a drought may not be noticed for weeks or even months. The end of a drought also occurs gradually. Some droughts last only a few months. Others can last for years and completely change an ecosystem.

dried-up river bed in San Luis Obispo, California

Succession

Ecosystems are changing all the time. Many of these changes are due to stresses such as fires, floods, and droughts. After a stress occurs, the size of the populations and the types of organisms are often different. For

Science and the BIBLE

Sometimes God uses natural disasters as a judgment for sin. During the reign of King Ahab of Israel, the king and the people of Israel had been involved in idol worship and great wickedness. In 1 Kings 17–18, the Bible tells us that God sent Elijah to King Ahab to announce a drought. Elijah said God would punish Israel for its rebellion against God. So for three years God did not send dew or rain. A disaster is not always a judgment of God. But it can be the tool that God uses to bring His people back to Himself.

example, new trees and plants grow to replace a destroyed forest. However, the species of trees and plants may be different from those in the original forest. Animal populations also change according to what foods are available. These gradual changes in the populations of organisms in an ecosystem are called **succession** (suk SESH un).

Succession happens when part of the environment changes. The environment determines what kinds of living things can exist in an ecosystem. A change in the climate, amount of sunlight, or available nutrients causes the living things in an ecosystem to change.

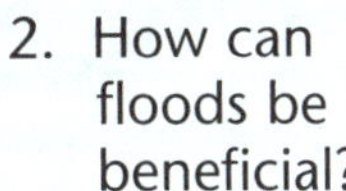

1. What is a stress?
2. How can floods be beneficial?
3. What is succession?

Beavers cut down trees and dam a forest stream. The stream floods and makes a pond.

Trees in the flooded area die. Pond plants, such as reeds and cattails, grow at the edges of the pond.

Over the years, sediment builds up in the pond, and the pond becomes shallower. The dam eventually breaks, and most of the pond water drains away.

As the pond dries out, plants at the edges of the pond gradually take over the center of the pond. The pond has become a meadow.

Shrubs replace the meadow grasses. Fast-growing trees, such as pines and poplars, replace the shrubs.

Explorations Stress Alert

Have you ever heard a news report about an emergency situation? News reporters cover these events so that the public can be informed. Often a reporter is sent "on location" to be near where the storm or disaster is taking place. The reporter can then give an eyewitness report about what is going on. He might also warn people to evacuate the area or tell them where to go for help.

In this exploration, you are the news reporter. You will cover a flood, a fire, a drought, or another kind of stress just as if you were on location at the scene.

Materials:
- *Stressful Events* page
- resource books about stresses
- Activity Manual

What to do

1. Choose one event from the *Stressful Events* page.

2. Research to find out facts about your chosen event. Remember that a reporter always looks for information to answer the questions *who*, *what*, *when*, *where*, and *why*. Record your facts in your Activity Manual.
3. Organize your information into a news report. Pretend that you are presenting your news report for the evening news on the day that the event occurred. Include pictures or drawings of the event. You may include other materials as well to make your news report seem more realistic.
4. Present your report.

Current Events

Process skills
- Classifying
- Communicating
- Defining operationally

Ecosystems never stay the same. Sometimes they change in small ways that are barely noticed. At other times, they change in big ways because of events such as floods and fires. Sometimes the changes are mentioned in the news.

In this activity, you will collect current news articles and information about ecosystem changes that are happening right now.

Purpose

Identify current events that involve changes in ecosystems.

Materials:
- current magazines and newspapers
- notebook
- scissors

Procedure

1. Look through newspapers and news magazines, and cut out any articles that are about an ecosystem. Listen to news reports. If you hear one about an ecosystem, record the date and time of the report and write a brief description about what was said.
2. Organize your articles and information into a notebook. Arrange the notebook in a logical way. You might group your news reports by topic, by type of event, by date, or by geographical location. Include a table of contents in your notebook.
3. Share your information with your classmates.

Ecosystems and Man

Man's Responsibility

When God created the world, He placed Adam and Eve in the Garden of Eden. God gave man dominion over His creation. But God also gave man responsibility. Adam's job was to be a steward, or keeper, of God's creation. Like Adam, we also must be good stewards of what God has given us.

However, people have very different views about how to use our resources. Some people believe that man should use and benefit freely from all of the earth's resources. This attitude can lead to a waste of natural resources. Other people believe that preserving an ecosystem is more important than any benefit man might receive from it. They do not believe that God gave man the earth to use. Still other people think that there should be a balance. They feel that resources should be used but not wasted. These people believe that man honors God most by using His resources wisely.

Man's Interactions

Ecosystems often undergo many kinds of stress. Some are natural stresses, such as droughts, floods, and fires. Many, though, are man-made stresses.

Probably the largest man-made stress is *habitat destruction*. Man often destroys plant and animal habitats when expanding his own. Forests are cut down to provide lumber or farmland. Wetlands are drained to make room for shopping centers. Dams are built across some rivers to provide electricity.

fish ladder at the Bonneville Dam in Washington

wildlife refuge in Crystal River, Florida

Construction and development are often good. However, they can be harmful if not done with care. There are many ways that man can lessen the harm done to an ecosystem during development. New trees can be planted to replace ones that are cut down. Areas of land can be set aside as wildlife refuges or national parks. Artificial wetlands can be built to replace wetlands that have been drained. Dams can have fish ladders added. These step-like waterways help fish travel safely around the dam.

Pollution (puh LOO shun) is another major man-made stress. Living things need clean water, air, and land. *Pollution* is anything that makes the water, air, or land dirty. Most people think of oil spills and factory chemicals as pollution. But littering and car exhaust also pollute the environment. Other trash and chemicals can cause pollution as well. If not disposed of properly, they can harm plants, animals, and humans.

Excessive hunting and fishing can also be a problem. Laws today control, or regulate, fishing and hunting. These laws try to help keep the animal populations in an ecosystem balanced. For example, hundreds of years ago many Atlantic puffins lived in North America. By the early 1900s, though, the number of puffins had decreased greatly. Many puffins had died because of excessive hunting and habitat loss. Today, because of laws that protect them, the number of puffins in North America is increasing again.

puffin

Unexpected Dangers

nene

mongoose

Plant and animal species that originally live in an ecosystem are called **native species**. Species that are not native to the area and can cause harm are called **invasive species**.

Introducing new species into an ecosystem often brings problems. For example, years ago ships accidentally brought rats to Hawaii. The rats were an invasive species. They preyed on the eggs of the nene (NAY nay), the Hawaiian goose. To control the rat population, the mongoose, a member of the weasel family, was brought to Hawaii. But the mongooses did not eat the rats. Instead, they preferred nene eggs. This introduction of a non-native species only made the problem worse.

Besides preying on native species, invasive species can also bring other problems. Sometimes native species die from diseases brought in by the new species. Many times the invasive species also has no natural predator in the new habitat. This allows the population of the invasive species to grow rapidly. With more species, there is more competition for the same resources, such as water or food. Native populations may then decline.

Science and HISTORY

The water hyacinth (HIE uh sinth) is a plant native to South America. In 1930, the plant was taken to China to provide food for cattle. The plant is beautiful, and many people admired it. They used it to decorate ponds and other water ecosystems.

However, the water hyacinths quickly became a nuisance and danger to China's aquatic ecosystems. The plants grow very quickly. Sometimes the number of plants can double in just 12 days. The plants also block waterways and crowd out native plants. The plants can even kill fish by preventing sunlight and oxygen from reaching the water. Many methods are currently used to control the spread of the plants.

passenger pigeon

Extinction

At one time huge flocks of passenger pigeons used to fill the North American skies. But the last known passenger pigeon died in captivity in 1914. Most of the birds died from hunting or loss of habitat. The species is now considered extinct. Scientists consider a species to be **extinct** (ik STINGKT) when its last known member dies.

A species becomes **endangered** (en DAYN jerd) when its population is so small that the species may become extinct. Many animal and plant species are considered to be endangered. Hunting, loss of habitat, and man's carelessness are most often the reasons a species becomes endangered.

A species is **threatened** if its population could become endangered in the near future. A species that can live in only one habitat is in more danger of becoming threatened, endangered, and eventually extinct than a species that can live in several different areas is.

Thinking It Through

Ecosystems are always changing in one way or another. Some changes are part of a natural cycle. Other changes are sudden and unexpected. But God controls each change. He uses them to maintain the earth He created.

Many people refuse to admit that God is the Creator and Sustainer of the universe. They worry that man will use up all the earth's resources or that the land and atmosphere will become too polluted.

We have a duty to be wise stewards of the earth. We must take care of what God has given us and should avoid adding unnecessary stresses. However, we must keep in mind that God is in control. Man can cause great damage. But man cannot destroy what God has created and is maintaining.

✓ QUICK CHECK

1. What are some ways that man can lessen the harm done to an ecosystem during development?
2. What makes a species invasive?
3. How is an extinct species different from an endangered species?

Answer the Questions

1. How is a drought different from other stresses on an ecosystem?

___

___

___

2. Clover is a plant that has roots with nodules containing nitrogen-changing bacteria. Why might a farmer plant clover in a field that is not producing well?

___

___

___

3. What usually causes succession?

___

___

___

Solve the Problem

While coming back from a trip overseas, you notice that there are people who are checking objects coming in from other countries. These people will not let a lady bring a foreign bird into the country. The lady says that it is a pet that she bought. Why is she not allowed to bring the bird into the country?

___

___

___

___

___

UNIT
5
By Waves of Energy

Musicians tune their instruments to a standard pitch. In the past, though, many great composers used a different standard pitch. Chapter 9 tells us how the pitch has changed.

Have you ever mixed red and green to get yellow? In Chapter 10 you will learn how this is possible.

The Israelites willingly gave their possessions to build the tabernacle. In Chapter 10 find out what item that reflects light was given by the women.

Sound

9

Microphones often make sounds louder. But some microphones help produce silence. In an airplane cockpit there are many low, unwanted sounds. Some pilot headsets only muffle this noise. However, headsets with active noise reduction (ANR) technology use sound wave properties to actually get rid of the noise. A microphone in the headset picks up a low, unwanted sound in the cockpit. The headset then produces an opposite sound wave. The two sound waves cancel each other out. The result is no sound at all!

The ANR headset removes unwanted sounds but does not affect the pilot's ability to hear voices or a sudden change in engine sounds. But the headsets work only because sound travels in predictable ways. As always, man's technology relies on God's design.

Properties of Sound Waves

Sit quietly for a moment and listen. You may hear the hum of air moving through a vent or the ticking of a clock. Perhaps a noisy truck or train is passing nearby. A chair may squeak or shoes may rustle on the floor. Although each sound is different, all sounds are made in a similar way. Each sound started because an object moved.

Vibrations and Waves

The movement of an object causes vibrations. A **vibration** (vie BRAY shun) is a rapid, back-and-forth movement. **Sound** is a vibration that can be heard. The ticking that comes from a clock is caused by the movement of the parts inside the clock. The parts vibrate as they touch each other. They cause the air around them to vibrate too. These vibrations blend together to make the ticking sound that you hear.

Sound moves through matter in waves. A **wave** is a disturbance that moves energy from place to place. The matter through which a wave travels may be a solid, liquid, or gas. Most of the sounds that we hear travel through the air.

Sound energy moves from the vibrating object to the ear. You hear

Imagine if you had to put your head against your friend's head in order for him to hear your voice! Having a conversation would certainly be more difficult. This is one way that astronauts talk to each other while in space, though. Outside a spacecraft, there is no air. This means there is no matter for the sound to travel through. By touching their helmets, the sound vibrations of their voices have matter to move through. This allows them to hear one another. However, the best way for them to communicate is by using two-way radios.

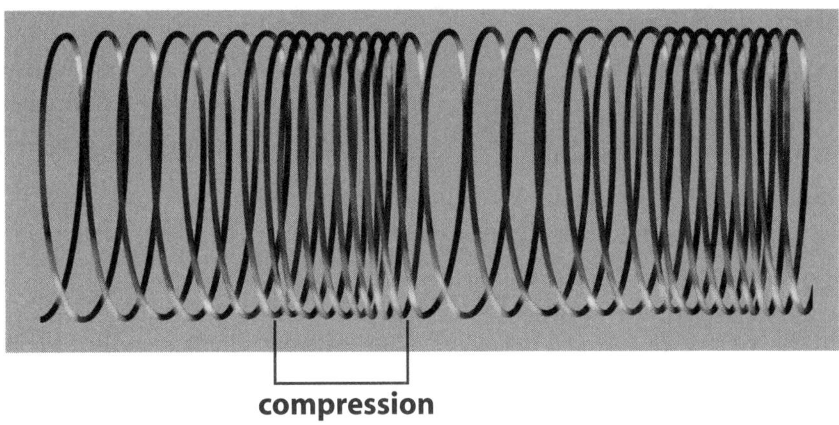

sounds because the vibrations of sound energy cause your eardrum to vibrate. As the vibrations are carried through the bones of your middle ear, the vibrations are changed into nerve messages. Your brain then interprets these messages and tells you what you hear.

Sound waves can be described as mechanical (mih KAN ih kul) waves. Mechanical waves must have matter to travel through. Energy causes particles in the matter to move and vibrate. Sometimes you can feel sound waves. When you hum, you can feel the vibrations that your throat makes. Those vibrations cause the sound that you hear. Other sounds that you might feel are loud thunder or the beats of a bass drum.

In a sound wave the particles of matter vibrate back and forth in the same direction that the sound energy is moving. The motion of each vibration pushes together some of the particles of the matter. This part of the wave is called a *compression* (kum PRESH un). As the motion of the vibration moves away from the compression, the particles spread apart again. Compressions continue to form as long as the object vibrates.

The way sound waves move is similar to the way a spring toy moves. If you stretch out a spring toy and push one end, the coils of the spring move back and forth as the wave passes to the end of the spring. The particles of matter are not carried along with the sound wave. Each particle vibrates but remains in its place. Imagine what would happen if air particles were carried with the sound waves. Sound waves from a choir's singing would cause a wind to blow!

Frequency and Speed

Even though sound waves cannot be seen, they can be measured. The distance from one compression to the next is called a **wavelength**. Different sound waves have different wavelengths. These lengths are determined by how quickly the source of the sound vibrates. Sounds that vibrate quickly have short wavelengths.

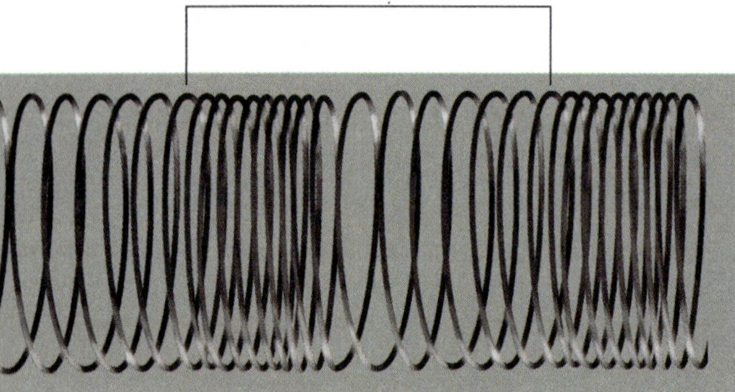

To help study sound waves, scientists have designed machines called oscilloscopes. An *oscilloscope* (uh SIL uh SKOPE) changes the sound waves into electrical pictures that are seen on a graph. Stereos and computers often have oscilloscopes on them. Types of oscilloscopes are also found on heart monitors and other medical equipment.

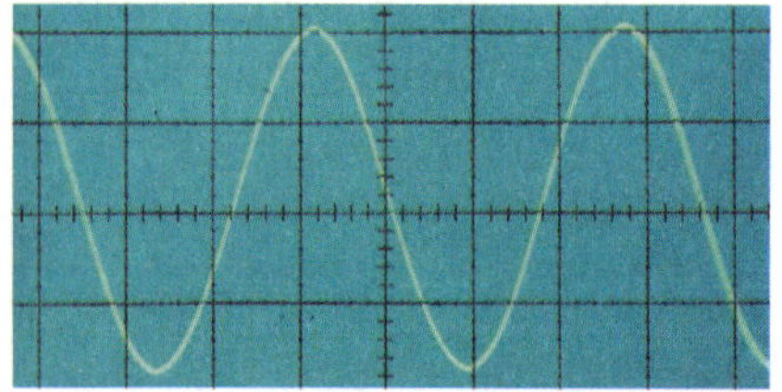

oscilloscope screen

The number of sound waves per second produced by a vibration can vary. As the number of waves changes, so does the frequency of the sound. **Frequency** (FREE kwun see) is the number of waves that pass a point in one second. Frequency is measured in a unit called hertz (HURTS).

Sound waves travel in all directions away from the source of the sound. A sound wave can also travel through different types of matter. The siren of an ambulance can be heard whether you are in a house, in a tree, or underwater in a pool.

Sound waves move at different speeds in different types of matter, though. The density, or how close the matter molecules are, affects how quickly the vibrations move from one particle to the next. The density of the matter also affects how far the sound waves can travel.

Sound needs particles in order to move. Of the three states of matter, gas is the least dense, so sound moves the slowest through gases. The sound cannot easily move from particle to particle. Also, some of the energy gets used up as it travels through the spaces between the particles. This slows the movement of the waves.

Air is the most common type of matter through which we hear sounds. The **speed of sound** in air is about 335 m (1,100 ft) per second. This is how fast sound travels through

Speed of Sound Through Matter

(Distance traveled in one second)

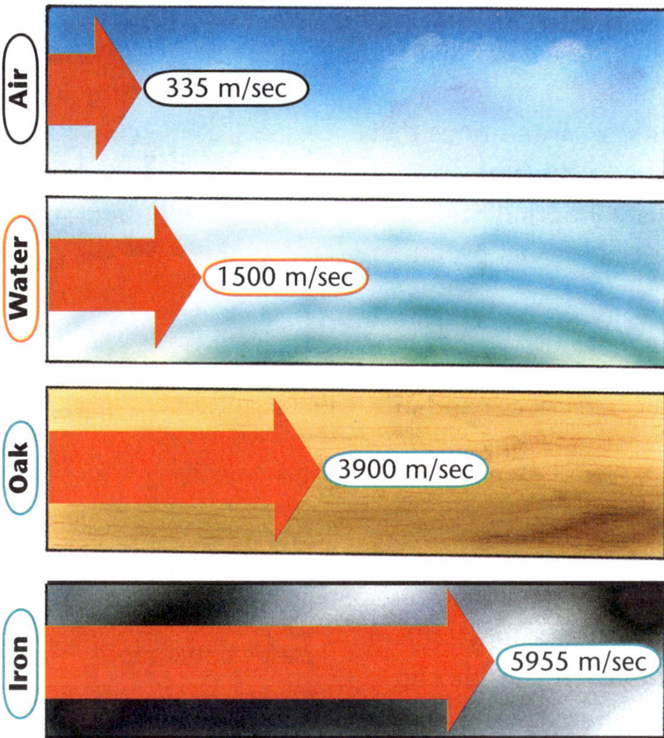

the air under specific atmospheric conditions. In different conditions, such as a hotter day, the speed of sound will be different.

The particles in liquids are denser than the particles in gases are. So sound moves more quickly through liquids than it can through gases. The waves can also travel farther than they can in a gas.

Solids are the densest state of matter. Their particles are very close together. The sound waves easily move from one particle to the next. So sound waves can also travel faster and farther in a solid than in a liquid or a gas.

The speed of sound is not the same as the frequency of sound vibrations. Think of watching cars traveling on a straight highway. Suppose all the cars on this highway are traveling at 50 km per hour (km/h). That is the speed of the cars. However, the frequency of the cars is the number of cars that pass you in a set period of time. In the first minute, perhaps only one car passes. In the next minute, five cars may pass. The speed of the cars stayed the same, but the frequency changed. The speed and frequency of sound waves are related in much the same way as the speed and frequency of the cars on a highway are related.

QUICK CHECK

1. What is sound?
2. What is a wavelength?
3. Through which type of matter can sound travel faster—a gas or a solid?

Sound Slide

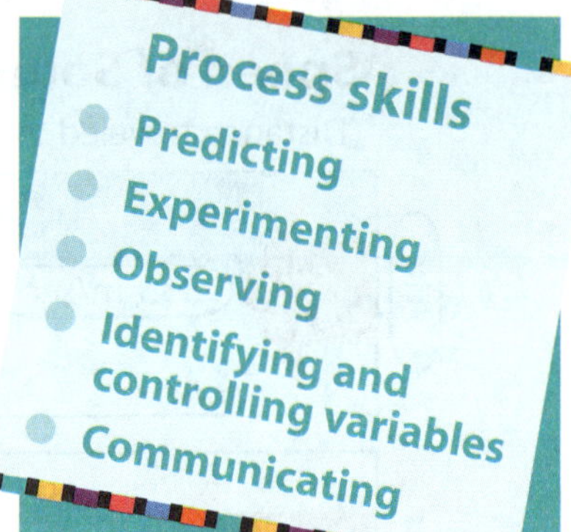

Anything that moves makes sound. Sometimes one item can make a variety of sounds depending on different conditions. Conditions that can change are called *variables*.

In this activity, you will make a Sound Slide and use it to identify and control variables that produce changes in the sound.

Problem

How does changing the length of a rubber band affect the sound it makes when plucked?

Procedure

Materials:
- centimeter ruler
- assorted rubber bands
- plastic bottle cap
- marker
- Activity Manual

1. Prepare your Sound Slide by stretching a rubber band lengthwise over the ruler. Use the marker to make a mark down the side of the bottle cap. Place the bottle cap between the rubber band and the side of the ruler that shows the measurements. Adjust the bottle cap so that the mark faces toward the lower numbers of the ruler. The bottle cap is called a slide.
2. Move the slide so that the mark is at 15 cm. Press the rubber band against the slide. Pluck the part of the rubber band that is over the lower numbers and listen to the sound. Observe the vibrations. This is the setting that you will be comparing the other sounds to. You may return the slide to 15 cm at any time to compare the sounds better.
3. Move the slide to 10 cm. Predict whether the sound will be higher or lower. Pluck the part of the rubber band that is over the lower numbers. Notice any changes in the sound and vibrations from when the slide was set at 15 cm. Record your observations.

4. Move the slide to 20 cm. Predict whether the sound will be higher or lower than the sound when the slide is at 15 cm. Pluck the part of the rubber band that is over the lower numbers. Observe the changes in sound and vibrations. Record your observations.

5. Choose three additional markings at which to set the slide. Predict the changes in sound and vibrations. Test your predictions and record your observations.

Conclusions

- Were your predictions correct?
- How did the length of the rubber band affect the sound?

Follow-up

- Use other rulers, slides, or rubber bands. Test how changing a different variable affects the sound and vibrations.
- Try playing a simple song on your Sound Slide. Record the numbers that you use.

Characteristics of Sound

The characteristics of sound help us compare and describe individual sounds. You experience many different sounds each day. A songbird trills a high, happy song. The horn of a tugboat makes long, low blasts. The siren of a police car may change between loud and soft sounds.

Pitch

Pitch is how high or low a sound is. The pitch of a sound is related to its frequency. Remember that the frequency is the number of waves in one second. These waves result from vibrations. A slowly vibrating object has a low frequency. This produces a low pitch. As an object vibrates faster, its pitch gets higher. Your ear can hear differences in pitch.

You can hear changes in pitch by listening to the different sounds made by an electric mixer that has several settings. When the mixer is at the lowest setting, the motor vibrates slowly and you hear a low pitch. As the motor is turned to a higher setting, the motor vibrates faster. The pitch of the motor sounds higher.

God gave the human ear the ability to hear certain frequencies. Most people can hear sounds with frequencies between 20 and 20,000 hertz (Hz). The lowest note, or pitch, on a piano has a frequency of about 26 Hz. The frequency of the highest note on a piano is a little over 4,000 Hz. The pitch of most sounds, however, is a blend of frequencies.

Some creatures, such as bats, dogs, and insects, can hear higher frequencies than humans can. If you blow a dog whistle, you cannot hear the sound, but a dog nearby can.

The ticking of a grandfather clock has a low pitch.

The beating of a hummingbird's wings has a high pitch.

When musical instruments play together, they must be tuned to the same pitch. If they are not, they will produce sounds that clash rather than blend. The standard pitch used today is not the same as the one musicians used in the past. The tuning fork of the eighteenth-century composer George Frideric Handel tuned the A above middle C to the frequency of 422.5 Hz. Today the same note is usually tuned to 440 Hz.

Hearing Ranges

(Frequencies given in Hz.)

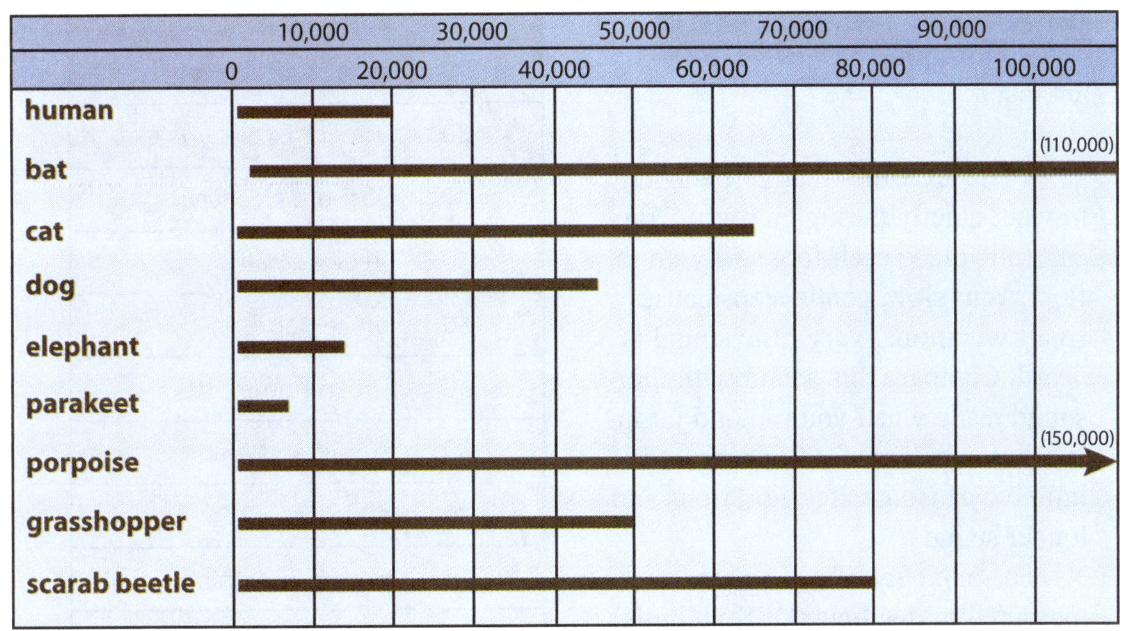

Volume

Volume is how loud or soft a sound is. The volume of a sound changes as the amount of force used to make the sound waves changes. A greater force, or *intensity*, will produce larger vibrations. Large vibrations make louder sounds than smaller vibrations do.

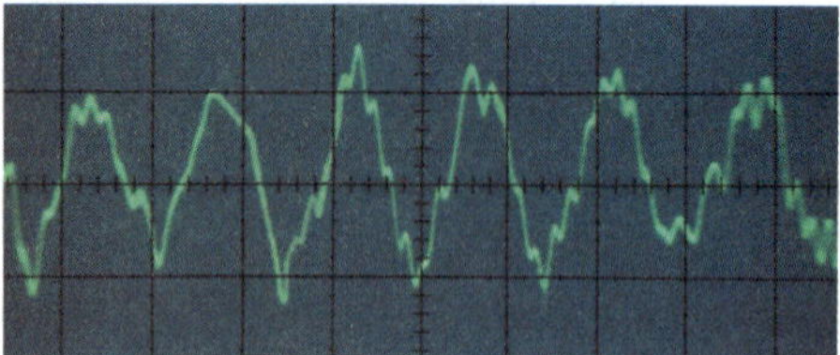

loud sound

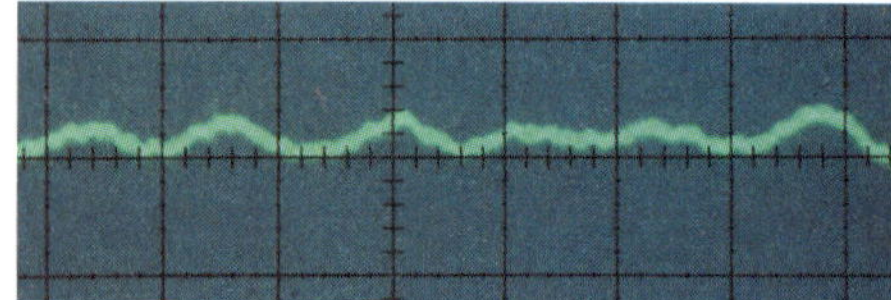

soft sound

There are times that you may try to walk quietly through a room. You carefully place each foot softly on the floor. Your slow, gentle steps cause small vibrations. Very little sound is heard. Compare this sound with the sound made when you run and jump in a basketball game. Running and jumping cause greater vibrations and louder sounds.

The intensity of a sound is measured in **decibels** (DES uh bulls). The sound of your breathing is about 10 decibels. Talking in a normal voice to your friend is about 60 decibels. The sound of a jet taking off is about 160 decibels.

Decibel Levels

180	rocket engine
170	
160	jet plane taking off
150	
140	warning siren
130	rock music concert
120	(threshold of pain)
110	riveting machine
100	large circular saw
90	jet aircraft flyover
80	interior of a sports car
70	vacuum cleaner
60	freeway traffic
50	office noise
40	urban home
30	suburban home
20	whisper
10	normal breathing
0	(threshold of hearing)

The human ear can be damaged by too many large, loud vibrations. Because sounds cause the parts of your ear to vibrate, the force of strong vibrations can cause pain. Exposing your ears to loud sounds for a long period of time may permanently damage your eardrums' ability to vibrate correctly. This may cause hearing loss. A sudden sound, such as a firecracker going off, can cause temporary hearing loss. You should wear hearing protection any time your ears are exposed to very loud sounds.

Quality

Timbre (TAM bur) is the quality of a sound that distinguishes it from other sounds of the same pitch and volume. Before a band concert, the instruments tune to the same pitch. However, the trumpets sound different from the clarinets, and the clarinets sound different from the flutes. They all play the same pitch, but the timbre of each instrument is unique.

Most of the sounds that we hear are a blend of several waves. Each of these waves has different characteristics. As these waves blend, the sound has a certain timbre. If one sound wave is added or removed, the timbre will change.

A clarinet has a wooden reed that vibrates. The reed is not the only part of the instrument that vibrates, though. When a musician blows into the clarinet, the long tube that forms the instrument vibrates as well. The air inside the clarinet also vibrates. A skilled musician must control all these vibrations so that they blend to produce a pleasant sound.

clarinet

An oscilloscope image of a single, pure sound, such as that made by a tuning fork, looks smooth. Many musical instruments, however, do not have a pure sound. Instead, musical instruments produce sounds that are a blend of different vibrations, or sounds. On an oscilloscope, these blended sound waves look rough or wiggly.

You recognize many sounds without thinking about it. You may be playing with a group of friends when someone's mother calls. You know immediately whether it is your mother or not. The timbre of her voice helps you know.

QUICK CHECK

1. What is another name for how high or low a sound is?
2. What causes the volume of sound to change?
3. What is timbre?

Uses of Sound

Some sounds are annoying and distracting. We often describe these sounds as noise. We usually think of a noise as a type of sound that is harsh, unwanted, or surprising. A jackhammer, children yelling, or the pop of a balloon are usually considered noises.

However, many of the sounds that you hear are pleasant. People usually enjoy talking with friends or listening to music. Voices and music are useful sounds. These sounds can communicate information or give us pleasure.

Seeing with Sound

The meanings of sounds are useful. The sound of a dog's barking lets you know that a dog is nearby. But sound waves themselves can also be useful. A sound wave uses up its energy as it moves away from its source. As the energy is used up, the sound gradually fades. You can try to estimate how close the barking dog is by how strong the sound waves are.

Sometimes an object interferes with the movement of a wave. A sound wave may bounce, or reflect, when it hits an object or a surface. A sound wave that bounces back toward its source and is heard is called an **echo**. Distance and the type of surface affect the clarity of an echo. To hear a clear repetition of the original sound, the distance between the source and

Science and HISTORY

A variety of devices have been developed to help visually-impaired people move around more easily. Some use sonar technology. One device has a small instrument attached to the grip of a cane. The user wears small earphones. He learns to listen to and interpret the beeps and other sounds he hears. The sounds help the user identify the closeness and size of the objects around him.

Oilbirds use echolocation to help them "see" in caves.

the place of reflection must be at least 9 m (30 ft). A smooth surface produces a clearer echo than a rough surface does.

God designed several animals to use echoes. For example, a tropical bird called the oilbird lives in caves. It uses echoes to "see" inside its dark home. An oilbird makes clicking sounds at a frequency of about 7,000 Hz. These sounds hit surrounding objects and bounce back to the bird. The time it takes the echoes to return depends on how far the sound waves traveled before hitting an object. The oilbird hears and senses these echoes. In this way, the echoes tell the bird how far it is from objects.

Scientists call this ability to see with sound *echolocation*. Sonar is a type of echolocation developed by man. Sonar was first used to help locate items underwater. A ship or submarine sends beeping sounds through the water. The length of time the wave takes to travel back as an echo helps the listener tell how far away an object is. The echoes can also give other clues about the object such as its size, the type of material it is made of, and how fast it is moving.

Ultrasound technology also uses echoes from high-frequency sound waves. Special instruments change the waves of the echoes to electrical images or pictures. Ultrasounds are often used by doctors to "see" inside a person's body without using surgery. For example, doctors can use ultrasounds to observe the growth of unborn babies. Many organs and even some large blood vessels inside the body can also be seen in this way.

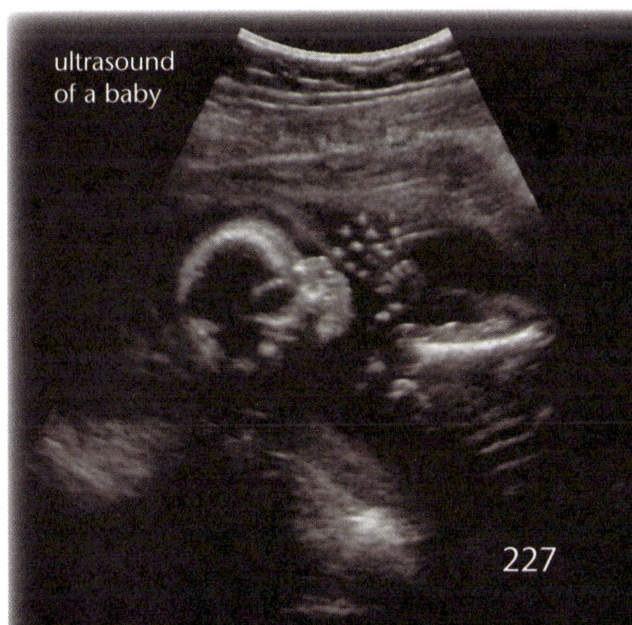

ultrasound of a baby

Communicating with Sound

God gave man the need to fellowship and communicate both with Him and with other people. One of the most common forms of communication is through sound. Man can praise and glorify God through speech and singing. Through his voice, man can also tell others about God's love and salvation.

Singing and speaking are much alike. Both are a result of vibrations of the vocal cords inside the larynx (LAR ingks), or voice box. The muscles of the larynx lengthen and shorten the vocal cords to produce different pitches. The force of the air moving through the larynx controls the volume.

Music

Music can communicate ideas and feelings. Psalm 150 says that music can be used to praise God. In 1 Samuel 16:14–23, the Bible tells us that David played music to calm the troubled spirit of King Saul. Today, music is still used for these purposes. Hymns express our praise to God. A mother may sing a soft lullaby to help her baby calm down and go to sleep.

God created man with the desire to express his thoughts and feelings in song. People sang long before they understood pitch and frequency. They built instruments long before they knew how sound waves travel. In fact, many of the early ideas and theories about sound developed through the study of music, not the other way around.

Composers use the characteristics of sound as they write music. They choose specific notes as well as the voices or instruments to play those notes. The results of their choices combine to communicate ideas and feelings. The combinations of sound waves can blend, or they might clash. These effects can be heard as pleasing or upsetting. On an oscilloscope, the waves of calm sounds are usually seen as smooth curves. The waves of harsh sounds look rough and jagged.

Creation CORNER

You know that you and your friend cannot both be in exactly the same place at the same time. However, God designed sound waves so that they can do just that. If you stand on a busy street corner, you might hear the sounds of traffic moving, people talking, and pigeons cooing. The sounds do not have to take turns entering your ear. They do it all at once. This is because many sound waves can occupy the same space and not disturb one another. Without this amazing design by God, we would not be able to enjoy combined sounds such as choirs, bands, or orchestras.

Composers use many characteristics of sound to produce pleasing music.

Musical instruments and voices can imitate other sounds in nature and our surroundings. To do this, the instruments or voices must copy the pitch, volume, and timbre of the original sound. Some musical compositions can cause you to imagine specific scenes or events.

Electronic sounds

God's design of the ear is remarkable. The ear receives sound vibrations. It then changes them into electrical messages that are interpreted by the brain. Microphones, recording equipment, and speakers are types of technology that use this same basic design.

A microphone receives the sound vibrations. The vibrations are then changed into electrical messages. The messages can be copied by a recorder or sent out through speakers. Speakers produce new sounds that can travel to your ears.

A sound recording studio uses many types of sound technology.

Building design and sound

Acoustics (uh KOO stiks) is the science of sound. The term comes from a Greek word that means "hearing." An acoustical engineer is a person who studies sound.

Most sounds are intended to be heard only once. You would not want to hear a person's words repeated every few seconds. You would find it difficult to understand what he was saying.

The design of buildings affects how sound is heard. Sounds reflect more clearly from smooth, hard surfaces than from rough or soft surfaces. This is why echoes are often heard in rooms with smooth walls, such as gymnasiums. For most buildings, acoustical engineers use materials that absorb sound, or stop it from continuing, instead of reflecting it. Materials that absorb sound may be rough, soft, or fuzzy. The energy of the sound waves is absorbed into the material.

Acoustical engineers also try to control the direction and strength of sound waves within a room. They may design the walls, ceilings, and even the floors with a slant or curve. These slants and curves reflect sound waves to certain areas of the room and away from others.

God created sound and the ability for us to hear it. Without it, we would not be able to enjoy music or hear friendly voices. But God did not create sound just for our enjoyment. He also intended for us to use sound. Through it, we can help others and spread God's Word.

1. What is an echo?
2. How are singing and speaking alike?
3. What is the name for the science of sound?

Science and HISTORY

People traveling to Greece and Rome are often amazed at the acoustics of the ancient outdoor theaters there. These amphitheaters use clever building designs that allow a large audience to clearly hear the performers. The seats are sloped, and the stage is placed in a precise location.

The theater at Epidaurus, Greece, was built in the fourth century BC. Its remarkable acoustic design can still be experienced today. Even visitors in the highest seating areas can hear sounds from the stage. Sounds as quiet as someone snapping his fingers can clearly be heard.

Explorations A "Medium" Exploration

The matter through which a wave travels is called a *medium*. Sounds travel more quickly through solids than through liquids and gases. Does the type of matter also make a difference in how you hear the sounds?

To test this, try listening to the same sound through a variety of mediums. You may not be able to tell how quickly the sounds travel. However, try to hear other differences between the sounds.

What to do

1. Get a stethoscope and two metal spoons.
2. Have a partner tap the two spoons together. Use the stethoscope to listen to the sound of the tapping as it travels through the air, through water, and through a table or other solid. For each test, make sure that your stethoscope is about the same distance from the tapping spoons.

3. Notice similarities and differences of the tapping sounds in the different mediums. Write a paragraph comparing and contrasting the characteristics of the sounds.
4. Present your findings and challenge your audience to conduct their own "medium" tests.

Shhh, Quiet Please

Process skills
- Hypothesizing
- Predicting
- Observing
- Communicating

Acoustical engineers identify and control how sound waves move. The engineers know that some materials are able to reflect, slow, or stop the movement of sound. Some rooms would be very noisy if certain materials were not used to block or absorb sounds.

In this activity, you are the acoustical engineer. Your task is to find which material absorbs the most sound. You will send sound waves through different materials that could be used in a room. Then you will determine which material absorbs sound the best.

Problem

Which building material absorbs sound the best?

Materials:
- metal fork
- ceiling tile scrap
- carpet scrap
- metal, such as a baking pan
- wood, such as a piece of board
- Activity Manual

Procedure

1. Predict which material will most effectively absorb sound. Complete the hypothesis in your Activity Manual.
2. Test the sound of your fork. Place your ear against your desk. Have a partner hit the tines of the fork quickly on the edge of the desk and immediately place the tip of the handle of the fork on the desk. You should hear a high, vibrating sound. This is the sound that you will listen for as you do the activity.
3. Choose the first material to test. Hold the material against your ear. Have a partner hit the tines of the fork against the desk and place the tip of the handle on the material. Listen for the sound.
4. Rate the loudness of the sound that you hear on the chart in your Activity Manual. Use the numbers 0–4 to rate the sounds. A score of 0 means you heard no sound. A score of 4 means the sound was loud.

5. Repeat steps 3–4 for each material.
6. If needed, you may repeat the test of any of the materials to determine their ratings.
7. As time permits, switch places with your partner.

Conclusions

- Which material absorbed sound the best?
- What characteristic of that material made it most effective?
- Why might different people get different results?

Follow-up

- Use other materials or other sources of sound.
- Test the effect of layers of different materials between the sound and your ear.

Answer the Questions

1. Why do sound waves travel more quickly in a solid than in a gas?

2. How can you tell that different musical instruments are playing even when you cannot see the instruments?

3. Why is it often difficult to understand a speaker in a room such as a gymnasium?

Solve the Problem

The dogs in the yard next to your house always bark when they hear a siren. You notice, though, that they do not react the same to all sirens. Unlike for other sirens, they often start barking at a fire engine siren even before you can hear it. Why would the dogs bark at the fire engine siren before you can hear it but not at the other types of sirens?

Light

REMEMBER *now* thy CREATOR

Sunlight is necessary for the growth and health of plants. However, sunlight also directly affects our health. Sunlight helps our bodies make Vitamin D that is necessary for strong bones. Scientists now know that the part of sunlight that helps produce Vitamin D is an invisible part. They call this part ultraviolet (UV) light.

Although we cannot see UV light, we can see its effects whenever we get tanned or sunburned. UV light can also affect our bodies on the inside. It can help prevent some bone diseases and can treat some other diseases. Doctors use equipment that produces UV light to treat some skin diseases. Research is also being done to see if UV light may help prevent some kinds of cancer. UV light is just one way light helps man. In His wisdom God has provided different parts of light to benefit man in many ways.

Light Energy

When God created the world, light was the very first thing He made. Genesis 1:3 says that God spoke, and light came into being. This light that God made is a form of energy. So, from that first day, energy has existed.

Characteristics of Light

Light is a form of wave energy. It is constantly moving throughout the universe. A light wave moves up and down as waves on an ocean do, but the light wave is much faster. If you could travel at the speed of light, you would be able to go around the world about seven and a half times in just one second!

Though light waves carry energy just as other waves do, light waves are different from many other kinds of waves. The energy of water waves and sound waves must move through matter. Light waves, though, can move through both matter and empty space. Because light waves can travel through space, light from the sun and other stars can reach the earth.

Light waves also move faster than other types of waves, such as sound, do. Light can travel through space at about 300,000 km/sec (186,000 mi/sec). The sun is about 150 million km (93 million mi) away from the earth. Yet light from the sun reaches the earth in about eight minutes. Scientists do not know of anything that can travel faster than light does.

Comparing Waves

Sometimes scientists classify waves by whether or not they can move through empty space. Waves that can move through space are called *electromagnetic (ih LEK troh mag NET ik) waves*. Light is an

Science and HISTORY

One of the first scientists who tried to measure the speed of light was Galileo. In the 1600s, Galileo and his assistant stood on top of two hills that were about a mile apart. Each of them had a shuttered lantern. Galileo flashed his lantern. As soon as the assistant saw Galileo's light, he flashed his own lantern. Galileo tried to time how long it took before he saw the answering flash of light. Since light travels so fast, Galileo was not able to measure the speed.

More than 200 years later, another scientist, Albert Michelson, was able to make an accurate measurement of the speed of light. He used a special eight-sided revolving mirror on top of a mountain in California.

electromagnetic wave. Waves that can move only through matter, such as sound waves, are called *mechanical waves*.

Scientists also classify waves by the direction in which they move. Sound waves move in the same direction as the matter is vibrating. Waves that travel this way are called *longitudinal (LON jih TOOD in ul) waves*.

Light waves move differently. They move in a manner similar to the way a wave moves along a rope. If you make a wave with a rope, you can see the wave traveling from one end of the rope to the other. As the wave travels forward, the rope moves up and down. The direction that the wave travels is perpendicular to the up-and-down movement of the rope. This is an example of a transverse (trans VURS) wave. Waves that move perpendicular to the way that the matter is moving are called **transverse waves**. Light waves are an example of transverse waves.

direction matter is moving

direction of wave

longitudinal wave

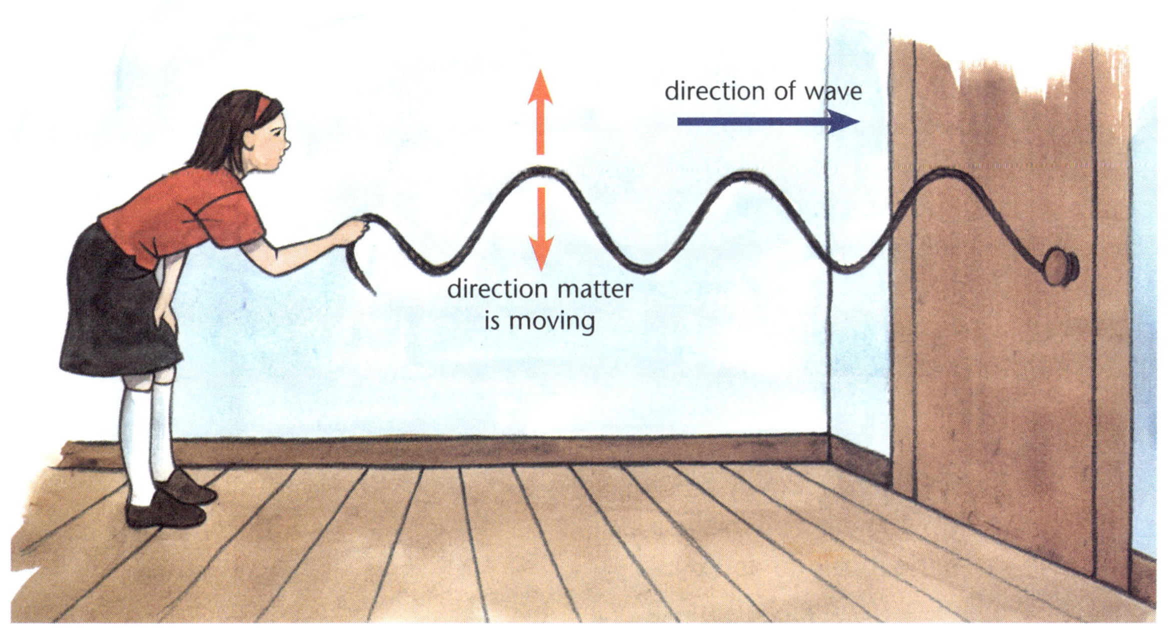

transverse wave

Properties of Waves

There are many different kinds of waves. Some are tall. Others are short. Some move quickly, but others move slowly. All waves, though, have the same basic properties, or characteristics. These properties include wavelength, amplitude, frequency, and speed.

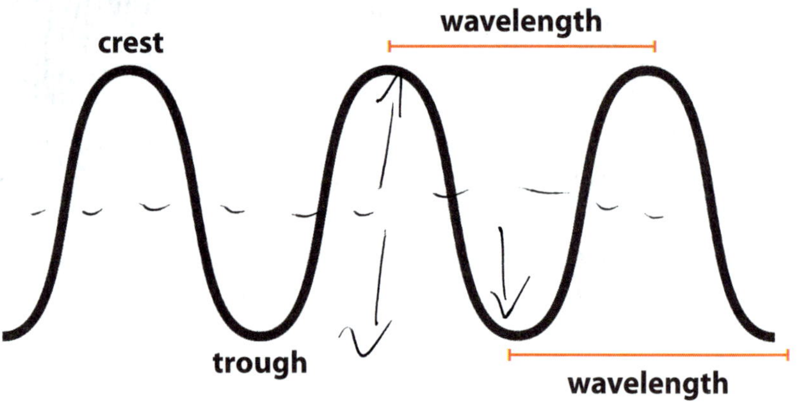

Transverse waves look like a series of hills and valleys. The top part of a "hill" is called the *crest*. This is the highest point of a wave. The *trough* is the lowest point, or "valley," of a wave. Scientists use the crests and troughs of a transverse wave to measure the length of that wave. Its **wavelength** is the distance between two crests or between two troughs. Waves with short wavelengths have more energy than waves with long wavelengths do.

Another property of a wave is its amplitude. **Amplitude** (AM plih TOOD) is the height of a wave. If you stretch a rope tightly, it will be in a straight line. Think of this straight line as the *rest position* of a wave. Moving one end of the rope will make the rope vibrate up and down. Part of the rope will move above the rest position and make the crests of the waves. The rope will also move below the rest position, forming the troughs of the waves. The distance that the rope moves above or below the rest position is the amplitude, or height, of the wave.

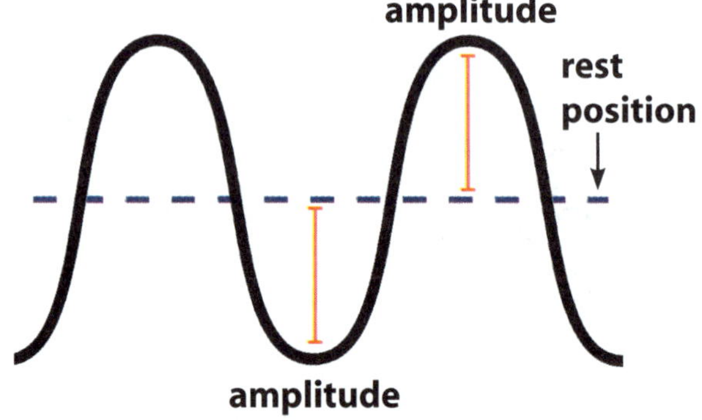

The frequency of a wave is the number of waves that pass a point in one second.

Frequency = 7

one second

As the rope moves up and down, many waves move through it. You can count the waves by counting each crest or each trough. The number of waves that pass a certain point in one second is the **frequency**. Waves with longer wavelengths have lower frequencies. Waves with shorter wavelengths have higher frequencies.

A wave's frequency is not the same as its speed. Frequency refers to how many waves pass by a point in a second. **Speed** refers to the distance that one wave travels in one second. All waves have specific speeds, frequencies, amplitudes, and wavelengths.

Science and MATH

The speed, wavelength, and frequency of a wave are related mathematically. If you know the wavelength and frequency of a wave, you can calculate its speed. Suppose a wave had a wavelength of 6 cm and a frequency of 5 waves per second. The speed of the wave would be 30 cm/sec.

Wavelength × Frequency = Speed

1. What are two ways that light waves are different from other waves?
2. What are transverse waves?
3. What is the distance between two crests of a wave called?

Visible Spectrum

If you try to walk through a dark room, you may stumble or bump into things. Without light, there is no vision. You see the objects around you because light bounces off them. Light makes things visible, or able to be seen. Light also gives objects color.

In 1672, Sir Isaac Newton proved that light is made up of many different colors. Newton used a prism to separate white sunlight into a band of many colors. The different colors of light are called the **visible spectrum** (SPEK trum).

Refraction and Reflection

Light always travels in a straight line. The direction and speed may change, but its path will always be straight. The matter through which a wave travels is called a *medium*. The speed of light changes as light enters different mediums. Light travels the fastest in empty space. It slows down a little when it enters air. Things such as a glass or water make the light slow down even more. When it enters a new medium, the light slows, bends, and changes direction. **Refraction** (rih FRAK shun) is the bending of light as it passes from one medium into another.

Prisms separate light into colors by the process of refraction. As sunlight passes through the air and enters a glass prism, the light slows down. The light also bends and shows the spectrum of colors. Each color of light has a different wavelength. So each color bends a little differently. Refraction also happens in a rainbow. Sunlight passes through raindrops and bends into the different colors of the visible spectrum.

The colors in the visible spectrum are in order by their wavelengths. The color red has the longest wavelength. The colors after red are orange, yellow, green, blue, indigo, and violet. Violet has the shortest wavelength. You can remember the order of the colors by thinking of the first letter of each color. The first letters spell out the name *Roy G. Biv.*

A prism bends light to show the color spectrum.

rainbow

them. They *absorb*, or soak in, some wavelengths of light. The other wavelengths of light are reflected off the object.

The color that you see is determined by which colors are reflected and which are absorbed. You see the reflected wavelengths as the color of that object. A red book reflects the color red. All the other colors of light are absorbed. When all the colors of light are reflected, you see white. You see black when all the colors of light are absorbed.

Why are darker-colored clothes usually warmer? Darker colors absorb more of the light energy from the sun. The sun's energy makes the molecules in the clothing move faster. The temperature of the clothing rises and keeps the person warmer.

Refraction is one way that light changes its direction. When light passes through transparent (trans PARE unt) or translucent (trans LOO sunt) things, it slows down and bends. *Transparent* objects let all light pass through them. Only some light can pass through *translucent* objects, though.

Light can also change direction by reflection. **Reflection** (rih FLEK shun) happens when light bounces off an object. **Opaque** (oh PAYK) objects do not let any light pass through them.

Science and the BIBLE

Light that reflects off an object must come from another source. An object that is reflecting light is not the source of that light. It simply reflects light that came from somewhere else. In the same way, a Christian reflects Christ to a dark and sinful world. A Christian's light is only a reflection of Jesus, the Light of the World.

Combining Colors

An amazing variety of color is all around you. From a beautiful blue sky to a bright yellow flower, the world is full of color. However, all of these colors are made by combining just three colors. The three colors that can be used to make all other colors are called **primary colors**. Primary colors cannot be made from other colors.

The primary colors of light are red, blue, and green. All the colors of light are formed by different combinations of these primary colors. If red light, blue light, and green light are mixed together in equal amounts, they make white light.

Most colored televisions and computer monitors use this property of light to produce colors on their screens. Little groups of red, blue, and green lights combine to make all the other colors that you see on the screen.

When equal amounts of two primary colors of light are mixed, secondary colors are made. For example, equal amounts of red light and green light combine to make *yellow* light. Mixing green light and blue light makes *cyan*. *Magenta* is an equal mix of red light and blue light. A lemon appears yellow because it absorbs blue light and reflects equal amounts of red light and green light. The red light and green light combine to form the color yellow. Our eyes see the reflected light, so we see yellow.

You may have learned in art that the primary colors are red, blue, and yellow. Actually these colors are the secondary colors of light: magenta, cyan, and yellow. Each of the primary colors in art is an equal mix of two of the primary colors of light.

Colors of Light

Art tools, such as paints and crayons, contain pigments. Pigments are opaque substances used to color other materials. Paint and crayon colors cannot give off light. They can only reflect it. Red paint looks red because it reflects red. Blue paint reflects the color blue.

Like the primary colors of light, the primary colors of art can be combined to make other colors. But mixing all the primary colors of art does not make white, as the primary colors of light do. Instead, mixing the primary colors of art makes a black color. Each color absorbs the wavelengths of the other colors. Because the wavelengths are not reflected, they cannot be seen.

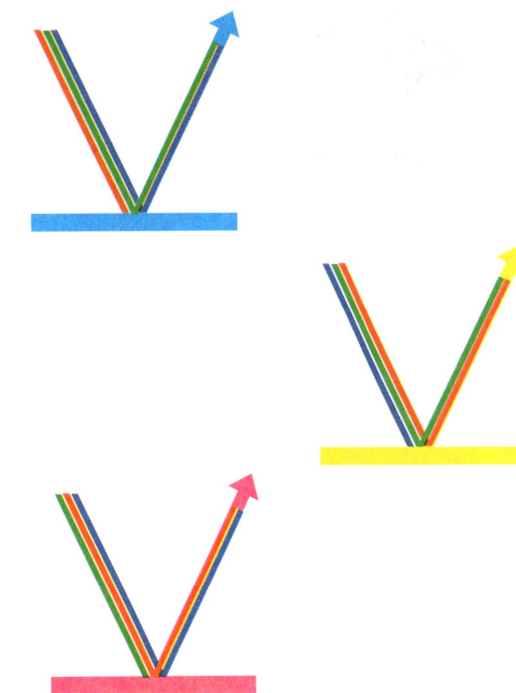

Light reflects from a surface and combines to form the colors we see.

Color is a wonderful gift from God. When He said in Genesis, "Let there be light," He had already planned for His earth to be beautiful with color. He created the pigments and light to work together. He knew that a wide variety of colors would bring pleasure to man.

Many books and papers are printed by a four-color printing process. The printers use combinations of cyan, yellow, magenta, and black ink to produce all the colors you see in a book. Use a magnifying glass to look at a colored comic strip in a newspaper. Do you see all the individual dots of color? The dots are so close together that your eyes blend them together. This makes the color and shading that you see in the picture.

QUICK CHECK

1. How is reflection different from refraction?
2. What determines the color of an object?
3. What are the primary colors of light?

Fog Vision

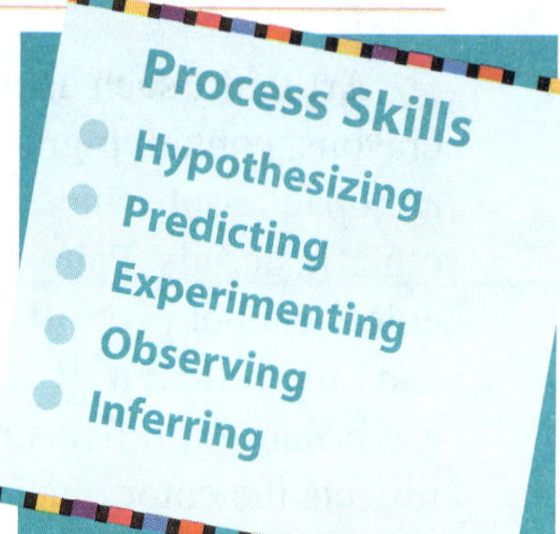

Have you ever noticed how hard it can be to see through fog? Fog can make it hard for people to see the lights of the other cars around them. This can cause car accidents. To help prevent these accidents, vehicles have colored lights. Brake lights are usually red. Police cars often have red and blue lights. Construction vehicles may have yellow or orange lights. Colored lights like these help other drivers see the vehicles, even when the visibility is not good.

In this activity, you will test different colors of light to determine which color is best to use in foggy situations.

Materials:

- 5 plastic sandwich bags
- broad-tipped overhead markers (red, blue, green, yellow, and purple)
- small flashlight
- rubber band
- white wall (or a similar white surface)
- 15 translucent white plastic cups, 3 oz
- Activity Manual

Problem

Which color of light is the easiest to see through fog?

Procedure

1. Predict which color of light you think will be the easiest to see through the fog. Complete the hypothesis in your Activity Manual.
2. Turn the plastic bags inside out. Use one of the overhead markers to color a large square on one side of one bag. On each of the other bags, color a similar square. Use a different color of marker for each bag. Wait a few minutes to let the ink dry. Turn the bags right side out.
3. Darken the room.
4. Choose one color to test first. Cover the end of the flashlight with the colored area of the bag. Use a rubber band to hold the bag on the flashlight.

5. Turn on the flashlight and aim it at a white wall or another white surface. Hold it about 45 cm (18 in.) away from the surface.
6. Place one translucent plastic cup over the flashlight. The plastic cups represent the fog. Continue adding one cup at a time until you can no longer see the beam of light on the wall.
7. Count how many cups the colored light passes through before disappearing. Record that number in your Activity Manual.
8. Repeat steps 5–7 for each of the other colored bags. Remember to record the number of cups used for each color.

Conclusions

- Which light was the easiest to see through the "fog"?
- Was your hypothesis correct?

Follow-up

- Put five cups on the flashlight. Use a light meter to measure how much light from each color can be seen through the "fog."

Mirrors

Have you ever bounced a ball against a wall? Light reflects off different surfaces in much the same way that a ball bounces. When light shines at an angle onto a smooth surface, the light bounces off at the same angle but in the opposite direction. Mirrors reflect light in this way.

When light shines on a rough or bumpy surface, the reflected light goes in many different directions. Some surfaces, such as paper, look smooth. However, if you use a microscope to look at a piece of paper, you will see that its surface is rough. So light that reflects off the paper will go in many directions.

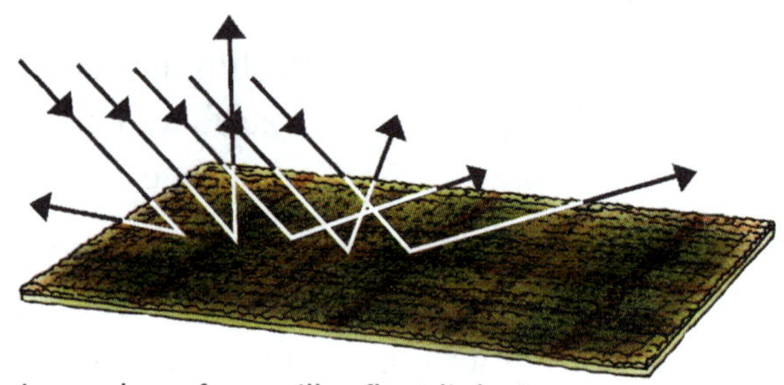

A rough surface will reflect light in many directions.

Rough surfaces, such as paper and snow, reflect light. But they do not make good mirrors. Mirror surfaces are shiny and smooth. A **mirror** is any surface that can reflect light to form an image, or picture, of an object.

Most mirrors have a flat surface. These mirrors are called **plane mirrors**. Bathroom mirrors and the rearview mirrors inside cars are usually plane mirrors. A plane mirror shows an image that looks exactly like the real object. The only difference is that the image appears backwards.

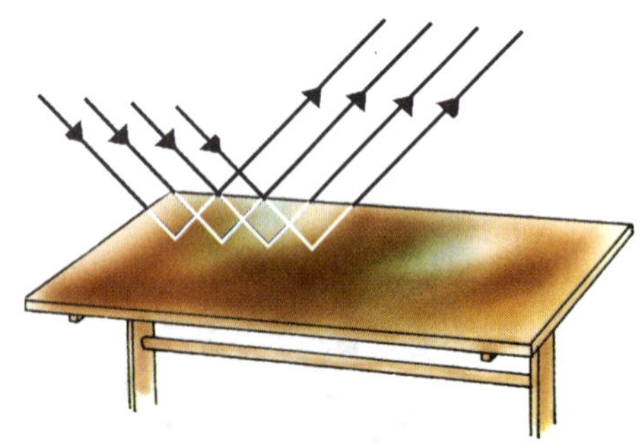

A smooth surface will reflect light at the same angle but in the opposite direction.

Science and the BIBLE

Mirrors today are usually made of glass that has a silver coating on one side. In Bible times, mirrors were sometimes made from metals, such as silver or bronze. The metals were polished until they shone.

Exodus 38:8 tells us that the brass laver in the tabernacle was made from looking glasses, or mirrors. The Israelite women willingly gave their mirrors to be used in the tabernacle.

The word *ambulance* is written backwards so it can be read correctly in a mirror.

You may have noticed that the front of an ambulance has the word *ambulance* written backwards. This is so a person driving a car in front of an ambulance can then look in the rearview mirror and read the word clearly. This lets the person quickly know to get out of the way.

Some mirrors are curved. Curved mirrors change the way an image looks. They can make the image look larger or smaller than the object really is. You may have seen curved mirrors at a fair or an amusement park.

The amount of curve can vary. Some mirrors curve a lot. Others have a curve so small that it may not even be noticeable.

Mirrors that curve inward are called **concave (kon KAYV) mirrors**. These mirrors reflect light inward. If you stand close to a concave mirror, your image is *magnified*, or made larger. Dentists use concave mirrors to see people's teeth better. Many ladies use concave mirrors when they put on makeup. Some telescopes use concave mirrors.These mirrors help faraway objects look bigger.

Mirrors that curve outward are called **convex (KON VEKS) mirrors**. These mirrors reflect light outward. Images seen in a convex mirror always look smaller than the objects really are. You can use a convex mirror to help you see a large area. Many stores use convex mirrors to watch for shoplifters. An automobile's side mirrors are convex mirrors.

A concave mirror curves inward toward the person looking at it.

A convex mirror curves outward away from the person looking at it.

Light and Technology

What do some telescopes, lasers, and cameras have in common? They use mirrors and lenses to change the direction of light. A **lens** is a piece of glass or other transparent object that refracts light and produces an image.

Telescopes help people see things that are far away, such as planets and stars. Some telescopes are small. Others are huge. The Subaru telescope located in Hawaii weighs 555 tons. That is more than the total weight of 56 buses! Regardless of size, however, all telescopes use mirrors or lenses or both to collect and bring the light to a point, or focus.

A *reflecting telescope* uses a concave mirror to gather and focus light. The light is reflected to the eyepiece lens, which magnifies the object. A *refracting telescope* uses two convex lenses. One lens gathers the light. The other magnifies the image.

Cameras also use mirrors and lenses. There are many kinds of cameras, though. And each works in a slightly different way. A single-lens reflex camera uses a mirror, a lens, and a prism.

reflecting telescope

Many 35mm cameras are single-lens reflex cameras.

Science and HISTORY

Early cameras could not produce lasting images. They were mainly used to help artists sketch their pictures. In 1826, Joseph Niepce took the first true photograph. He coated a metal plate with a light-sensitive chemical and placed it inside a camera for several hours. The photo showed the view from his window.

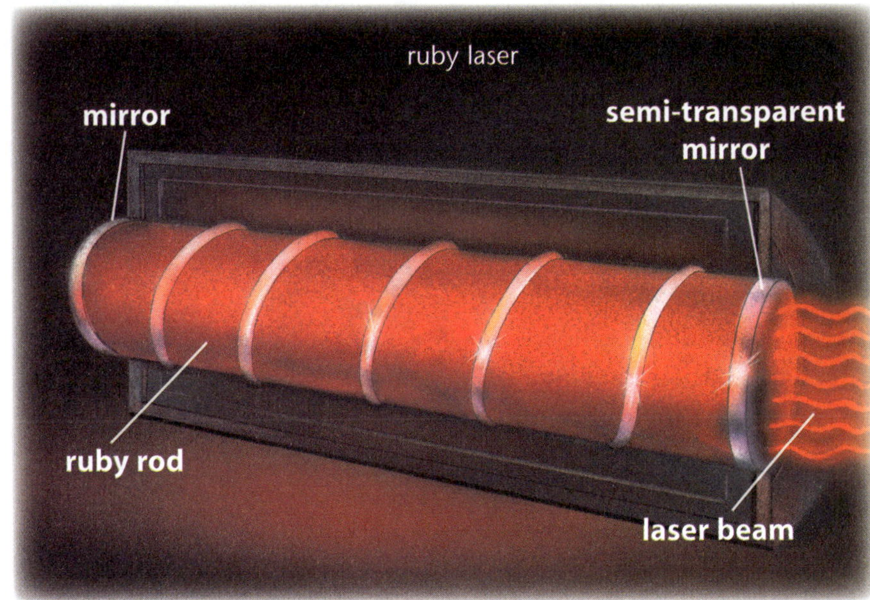

The color of the laser depends on the type of medium that is used. Ruby lasers have a solid ruby rod inside the laser. These lasers give off red light. Other lasers with red light may use a gas instead of a ruby. Different gases can cause lasers to give off blue light or green light.

Lasers can be found almost anywhere. DVD players and CD players use lasers to read the content of a disc. Checkout scanners in many stores use lasers to read bar codes. Doctors sometimes use lasers to perform delicate surgeries or to look inside a patient's body. Some lasers cut cheese into fancy shapes. Others are powerful enough to cut through steel.

Lasers use mirrors to produce a thin beam of light that is very powerful. This beam of light is only one color. Inside a laser tube is a medium for the light to travel through. This medium can be a gas, a liquid, or a solid.

At each end of the tube is a mirror. As light travels back and forth through the medium, it is reflected from the mirrors. One of the mirrors in the laser is semi-transparent. It reflects some light and lets some light pass through it. Some of the light "leaks" out of the tube through the mirror and produces the beam of light.

QUICK CHECK

1. What are three types of mirrors?
2. Which kind of mirror magnifies an object?
3. How is a refracting telescope different from a reflecting telescope?

Angles of Reflection

Have you ever used a mirror or a glass to change the direction of light? If a ray of light hits a mirror at an angle other than 90°, the light will reflect away from the mirror in a different direction. The angle at which light hits a mirror is called the *angle of incidence* (IN sih duns). The angle at which light is reflected is called the *angle of reflection*. In this activity, you will be measuring the angle of reflection.

Process Skills
- Predicting
- Measuring and using numbers
- Observing
- Inferring
- Defining operationally

Purpose

Compare the angle of reflection with the angle of incidence.

Materials:
- *Protractor* page
- centimeter ruler
- colored pencils (red, blue, green, and orange)
- rectangular mirror with a flat surface
- rubber band
- small flashlight
- black paper or folder, optional
- Activity Manual

Procedure

1. On the *Protractor* page, use a ruler and a blue colored pencil to trace one of the lines that marks 30°. Use red for one of the 50° lines, green for one of the 70° lines, and orange for the 90° line. These colored lines are the angles of incidence that you will use.
2. Set the *Protractor* page in front of you so that the straight edge of the protractor is at the bottom.
3. Wrap the rubber band around the center of the mirror. Have a partner stand the mirror along the straight edge of the protractor. The rubber band should touch the center point of the protractor. Hold the mirror perpendicular to the page. Be sure the mirror does not move.
4. Darken your work area.
5. Turn the flashlight on and shine the light straight down the red line to the rubber band. Look for the angle of reflection. If needed, hold the black paper around the

curve of the protractor. *Hint: The shadow of the rubber band is the angle of reflection.*

6. With the red colored pencil, circle the degree on the protractor where you see the angle of reflection. Record the number in your Activity Manual.

7. Repeat steps 5–6 for the blue, green, and orange lines. Make sure that your circles match the colors of the lines.

Conclusions

- How does the angle of incidence compare with its angle of reflection?
- What was different about the angle of reflection for 90°?

Follow-up

- Use the mirror and the light to reflect light to specific places around the room.
- Use the mirror and the light to send coded messages to a friend.

Electromagnetic Spectrum

Even though we can see light waves, there are many kinds of waves that we cannot see. Like light, these waves are electromagnetic waves, but light is the only type that is visible to the human eye. Electromagnetic waves come from the sun and other sources.

All electromagnetic waves travel at the same speed, but they have different wavelengths and frequencies. Electromagnetic waves can be arranged in order of their wavelengths. This arrangement is called the **electromagnetic spectrum**.

Light waves have a specific wavelength and frequency. Some other electromagnetic waves have shorter wavelengths and higher frequencies. Waves that have longer wavelengths than that of a light wave have lower frequencies.

Electromagnetic Spectrum

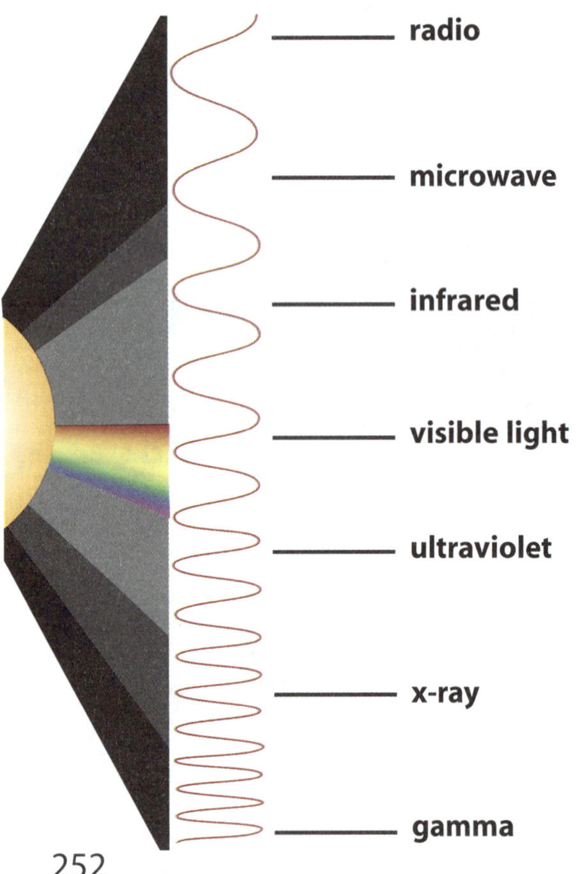

Longer than Light

Radio waves are the longest kind of electromagnetic wave. Radio waves carry energy that is used for radio and television broadcasting. Sound information is added to radio waves by changing either the frequency or the amplitude of the wave.

Radio waves do not come out of the radio. Antennas pick them up from the air and send them through wires to the radio. The radio then changes the radio waves into sound.

Radio waves are not used just for radios, though. Garage-door openers and baby monitors also use radio waves. Even wildlife-tracking collars use them. The waves help track the location of wild animals.

A remote car key uses radio waves.

Microwave towers are used by cellular phones.

Microwaves have a shorter wavelength than radio waves do. Microwave ovens use microwaves to cook and reheat food. Cellular phones also use microwaves.

Radar uses microwaves to detect the speed and location of objects. A police officer "shoots" microwaves from a radar gun. When a car passes, the waves reflect off it and return to the radar gun. The rate at which the waves return helps the police officer know how fast the car was going. Radar is also used to direct airplanes, to locate ships at sea, and to track weather systems.

On the electromagnetic spectrum, *infrared (IN fruh RED) waves* are next to visible light. The heat that you feel from the sun or a fire is infrared waves. This heat is also called radiant heat.

Most objects give off at least some infrared waves. Warmer things, such as people or animals, give off more infrared waves than cooler things, such as buildings, do. Our eyes cannot see infrared waves, but some equipment can detect them. Police officers can use this equipment to track criminals at night.

Equipment that uses infrared waves can show a person in a dark parking lot.

You also use infrared waves each time you use a remote control. You do not see the infrared waves that go between the remote control and the television, but they are there. Each time you press a button, the remote sends an infrared wave that the television picks up.

Some binoculars and cameras can change infrared waves into light that you can see. Satellites and telescopes may use infrared cameras. Pictures from these cameras help scientists see things even when there is no visible light.

Shorter than Light

Other waves in the electromagnetic spectrum have wavelengths that are shorter than that of light. Because the waves are shorter, their frequencies are higher. These waves are also invisible to humans.

The wavelengths of *ultraviolet (UL truh VY uh lit) rays* are just a little shorter than those of violet light. Ultraviolet rays cause some materials to glow. Some things, such as glow-in-the-dark balls, can absorb the rays and give off visible light. In normal light, we do not see the glowing colors of the ball, but in the darkness, the ball glows.

Ultraviolet rays can help keep people healthy. Some kinds of bacteria are harmful if found in water or food. Ultraviolet light can detect some kinds of bacteria. So the light is used to test for bacteria in food areas. The rays can even kill some kinds of bacteria. Some hospitals use the rays to sterilize their equipment.

Although humans cannot see ultraviolet light, many insects can. In 1910, Karl von Frisch, an Austrian scientist, tested the eyesight of bees. He found that honeybees see fewer colors of visible light than humans do. But, unlike humans, the bees can see ultraviolet light. The ultraviolet light helps them find nectar. Flowers reflect ultraviolet light in certain patterns. These patterns act like a map and lead the bee to the nectar.

Small amounts of ultraviolet rays help your skin cells produce Vitamin D. But too much of these rays can cause sunburn, skin damage, skin cancer, or wrinkles. You should always be careful when outside. Rays from the sun can reach the earth even on cloudy days. Using a sunscreen lotion with a high SPF (sun protection factor) can protect you from getting too much ultraviolet light.

This ultraviolet light is being used to check money.

X-rays have very short wavelengths. They carry a lot of energy and can pass through many different materials. Many things in space, such as stars and comets, give off x-rays.

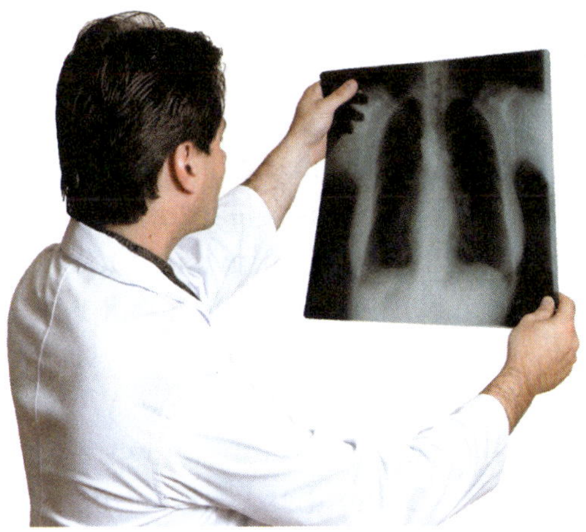

This doctor is examining an x-ray of a person's lungs.

Doctors use x-rays to see the bones inside someone's body. X-rays can pass through skin and muscles but are absorbed by bones. The places where the x-rays were absorbed the most show up as bright spots on the x-ray film.

Too much exposure to x-rays can cause cancer. That is why dentists and doctors use special coverings to protect the parts of the body that are not being x-rayed.

For a long time, x-rays have been used on pieces of art. Historians can use x-rays to see whether a painting was painted on top of an earlier one. Sometimes an old canvas was reused in order to save money. At other times, the painting on top might be a forgery, a painting made to look as though someone else painted it.

The Visit of the Queen of Sheba to Solomon (detail), Jacopo Robusti, called Il Tintoretto, from the Bob Jones University Collection.

X-ray detail from *The Visit of the Queen of Sheba to Solomon* by Jacopo Robusti, called Il Tintoretto from the Bob Jones University Collection.

X-rays can also be used in industry and engineering. Engineers can x-ray structures made of steel or concrete. The x-rays show if there are any tiny cracks. Airports also use x-rays for security and to check baggage.

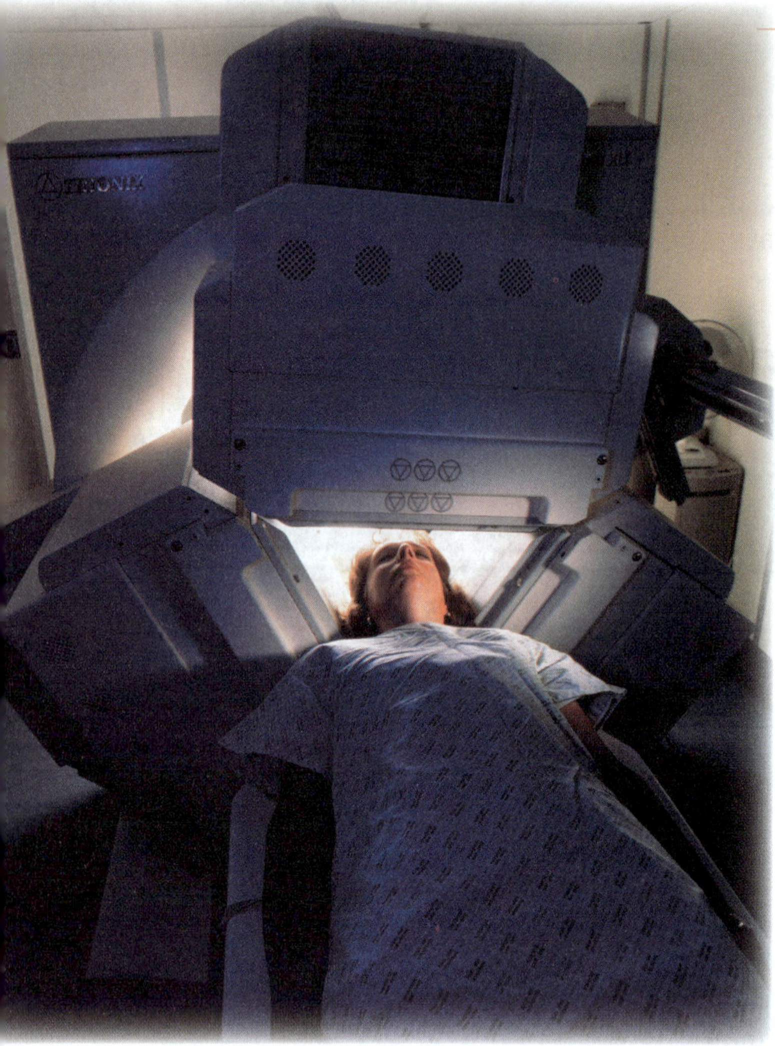

Gamma rays are used to treat medical conditions such as cancer.

The shortest waves in the electromagnetic spectrum are called *gamma rays*. The sun and other stars produce gamma rays. Most of these waves are absorbed by the ozone layer of the atmosphere.

Gamma rays are very powerful and can cause serious illnesses. When used in a controlled situation, though, gamma rays can be very helpful. They can treat some kinds of cancer. The rays can also kill bacteria in some foods. This process, called irradiation (ih RAY dee AY shun), helps the food stay fresh longer. Gamma rays can also be used to sterilize bandages and other medical equipment.

Most electromagnetic waves are invisible to us. We know little about how these waves of energy work. Yet our God, Who created them, knows all about them. His wisdom and power are much greater than ours. As we use and study what He has created, we should remember the One Who has created all things, both the visible and the invisible.

1. What is the only electromagnetic wave that we can see?
2. Which kind of electromagnetic wave is the longest? Which is the shortest?
3. What are some ways in which x-rays are used?

Explorations Light at Work

We know that we need light to see. But many kinds of technology also use light. Some types of telephone cables use light to carry the sound waves from one telephone to another. The lasers in CD players use light to play music. Cameras use light to capture images. Reflected light is used to measure far distances, such as that from the earth to the moon.

In this exploration, you will search for information about products that use light. The products may include things such as photocopiers and telescopes. Photocopiers use light to copy documents. Telescopes gather and focus light. You will need to search carefully. Sometimes it will not be obvious that a product uses light.

optical fiber cables

What to do

1. Look through advertisements, magazines, and newspapers. Cut out at least 12 examples of different products that use light for a specific purpose. Include any product information given.
2. Make a collage or notebook of your examples. With each example, include a brief description of how the product uses light.
3. Present your collection.

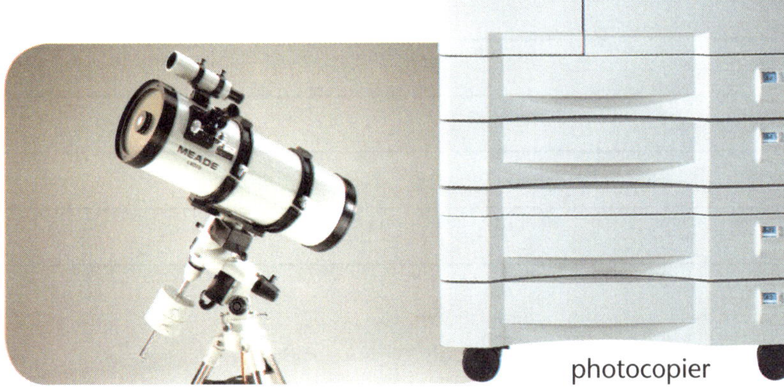

photocopier

telescope

Answer the Questions

1. What are some properties that are characteristic of all waves?

____

____

____

2. Why are the side mirrors on cars convex mirrors?

____

____

____

3. What are the primary colors of light?

____

____

____

Solve the Problem

You are planning to hike with some friends on Saturday. Two of your shirts are alike except that one is white and the other is black. You cannot decide which to wear. The weather forecast for Saturday predicts a hot, sunny day. Which shirt would be the better choice? Why?

____

____

____

____

____

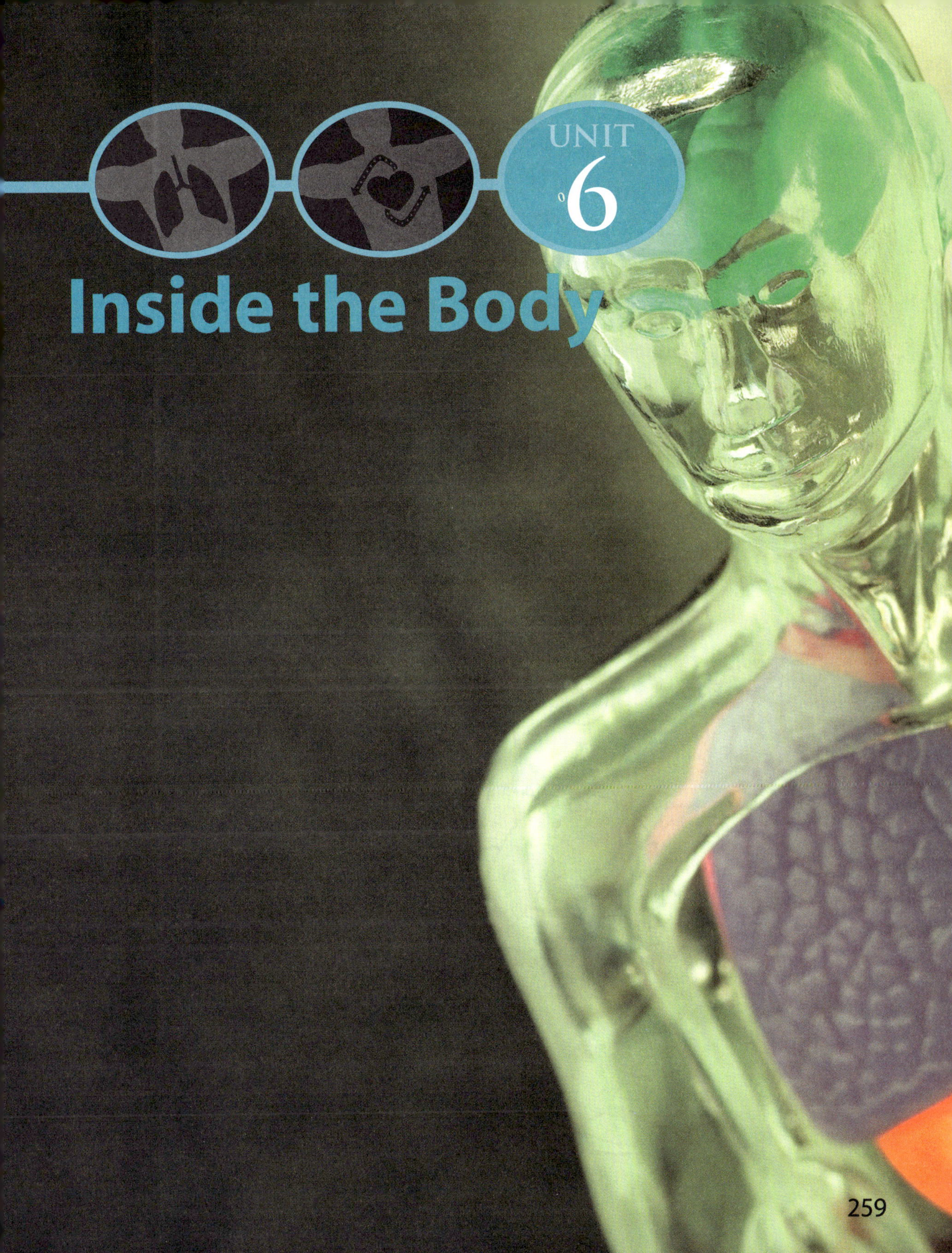

UNIT 6

Inside the Body

Inside your body is a very important "cage." In Chapter 11, you will learn what this cage is made of and what it does.

The Bible speaks often of blood. Chapter 12 tells why the Old Testament sacrifices for sin required the shedding of blood.

Find out in Chapter 11 about what funny noise can occur when air cannot flow freely though the back of the mouth and the nose.

Respiratory System

11

REMEMBER *now* thy CREATOR

God put tiny hairlike structures called cilia inside our bodies. The cilia move unwanted material, such as dust, out of our respiratory system. Each little hairlike structure can move the material only a small distance. However, all of the cilia work together. This way, they can move the material to where the body can get rid of it.

Engineers are working on a new technology that imitates cilia. The plan is to use electricity to power different parts of tiny cilialike devices. Each part moves only when it receives electricity. The part can move an object only a little. But together, the parts can move an object to a specific location. Small satellites on a spacecraft may one day be positioned in this way. This is yet another example of how man's designs only mimic God's.

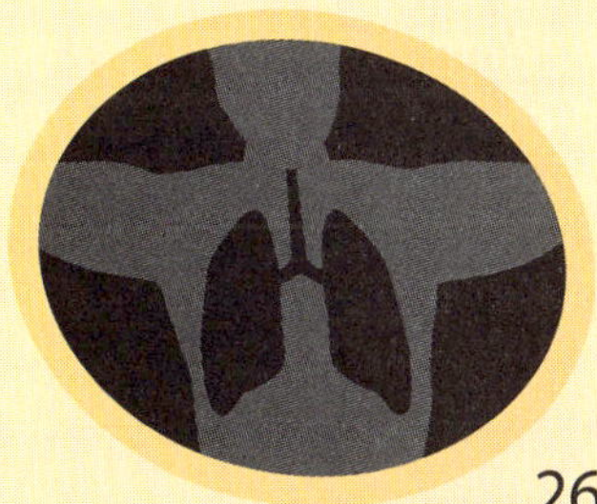

Breathing

You need to breathe in order to stay alive. Most of the time, you do not think about breathing, though. If you did, you would not be able to do anything else. Imagine how hard it would be to talk, work, or play if you had to stop every few seconds and remind yourself to take a breath. Even when at rest, most fifth graders breathe between 15 and 25 times each minute.

In fact, you breathe in more than 14,000 L (3,698 gal) of air each day. During your life, you will breathe enough air to fill up millions of balloons.

Genesis 2:7 tells us that God created man and breathed into him the breath of life. With this breath, man became a living soul. Breathing is a gift of God. The human **respiratory (RES pur uh TOR ee) system**, or breathing system, is one of His amazing designs.

Why You Breathe

Every cell in your body needs oxygen in order to live and function. Without oxygen, you would not have any energy. You would not be able to think, digest food, pump blood, or move.

When you **inhale**, or breathe in, you take in air. Your blood takes the oxygen from the air to every cell in your body. The cells use the oxygen and produce carbon dioxide. Too much carbon dioxide in your body, though, can be harmful. So the carbon dioxide is sent out of your body when you **exhale**, or breathe out.

A person needs more oxygen when he exercises or participates in activities such as baseball.

How You Breathe

The brain controls how you breathe. Most of the time, you do not have to think about it. Your brain does it automatically. This automatic breathing is called **involuntary (in VOL un TARE ee) breathing**. You breathe involuntarily when you are unconscious, asleep, or simply not thinking about breathing.

God made us able to control our breaths at times, though. **Voluntary breathing** takes place when you think about breathing and control it. Your brain can tell your body to stop breathing for a short amount of time. Without this control, you would not be able to hold your breath when swimming. You also could not do things like play wind or brass instruments.

The brain also controls how fast and how deeply you breathe. When your brain registers that there is too much carbon dioxide, it sends a signal for you to breathe more deeply. For example, when you exercise, a signal is sent to the brain that more oxygen is needed by the cells. This causes you to breathe faster.

Science and HISTORY

History records many examples of people free-diving, or diving while holding one's breath. In some cultures free-divers search for sponges or pearls. This is not always the case, though. One free-diver searched for something very interesting an anchor!

In 1911, an Italian ship lost its anchor in a storm. So the ship's captain hired a Greek sponge diver, Yorgos Haggi Statti, to get the anchor back. Statti claimed that he could hold his breath for up to seven minutes. He tied a stone to himself and dove 77 m (252 ft) into the deep Aegean Sea to try to recover the anchor. On his third try, he ran a rope through the anchor's eye. The ship's crew was then able to pull up the anchor.

Breathing Muscles

Two special sets of muscles work with your brain to help you breathe. These muscles, your diaphragm (DIE uh FRAM) and your chest muscles, change the space and pressure inside your body to allow you to breathe. The **diaphragm** is a strong, curved muscle attached below the lungs to the lower ribs and backbone. It separates the chest from the abdomen.

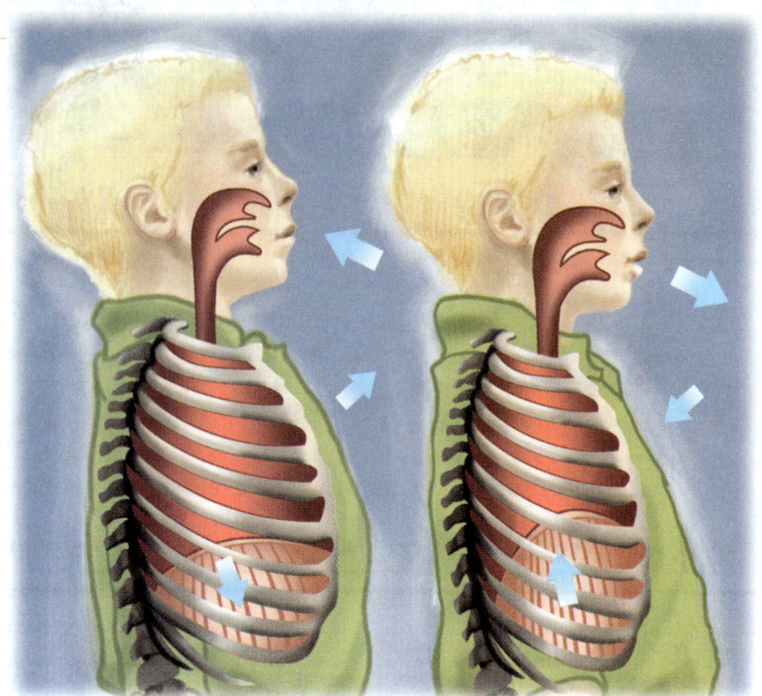

When a person inhales, the diaphragm moves downward and the rib cage moves up. When a person exhales, the diaphragm pushes upward and the rib cage moves inward.

When you inhale, your diaphragm tightens and moves downward. At the same time, your chest muscles, which are located behind and between your ribs, lift your rib cage up and out of the way. This provides more space for your lungs. More space means the volume of your lungs expands. This, in turn, causes the air pressure inside them to decrease. The air pressure inside your lungs becomes less than the pressure outside your body. To equalize the pressure, air is sucked into your lungs.

When you exhale, the process is reversed. Your diaphragm and chest muscles relax. As your diaphragm relaxes, it pushes up. As your chest muscles relax, they push in. These actions decrease the amount of space in your chest and increase the air pressure. This forces the air in your lungs out of your body, releasing the carbon dioxide and other gases back into the air.

QUICK CHECK

1. What is your breathing system called?
2. Which gas does every cell in your body need?
3. Which muscles help you breathe?

Breathe In, Breathe Out

Take a deep breath of air. Could you feel your muscles move? In this activity, you will make a model of part of your respiratory system.

Process skills
- Making and using models
- Inferring
- Defining operationally

Purpose

Make a model of part of the respiratory system.

Procedure

Materials:
- drinking straw
- small balloon
- rubber band
- 20 oz clear plastic bottle, cut in half
- clay
- large balloon
- Activity Manual

1. Slide the straw into the small balloon and secure them together with a rubber band.
2. Place the balloon and straw inside the bottle. The balloon should hang inside and most of the straw should stick out of the top.
3. Press clay around the straw to hold it in place and to seal the bottle top.
4. Cut the neck off a large balloon. Stretch the large piece of balloon over the cut end of the bottle.

5. Pull down gently on the bottom of the large balloon. Record your observations of the small balloon in your Activity Manual.

Conclusions

- What happened to the balloon inside the bottle?
- How is this model similar to your respiratory system?

Follow-up

- Use two small balloons inside the bottle to represent both lungs.

The Path of Air

Your Nose

Most of the air you breathe comes in through your nose. Your nose has two openings that are separated by a wall of cartilage and bone. These openings are called *nostrils*. Air enters through your nostrils and passes into your nasal cavity. The *nasal cavity* is a large air space located behind your nostrils. The open spaces from the front of the nose to the beginning of the throat are called the *nasal passages*.

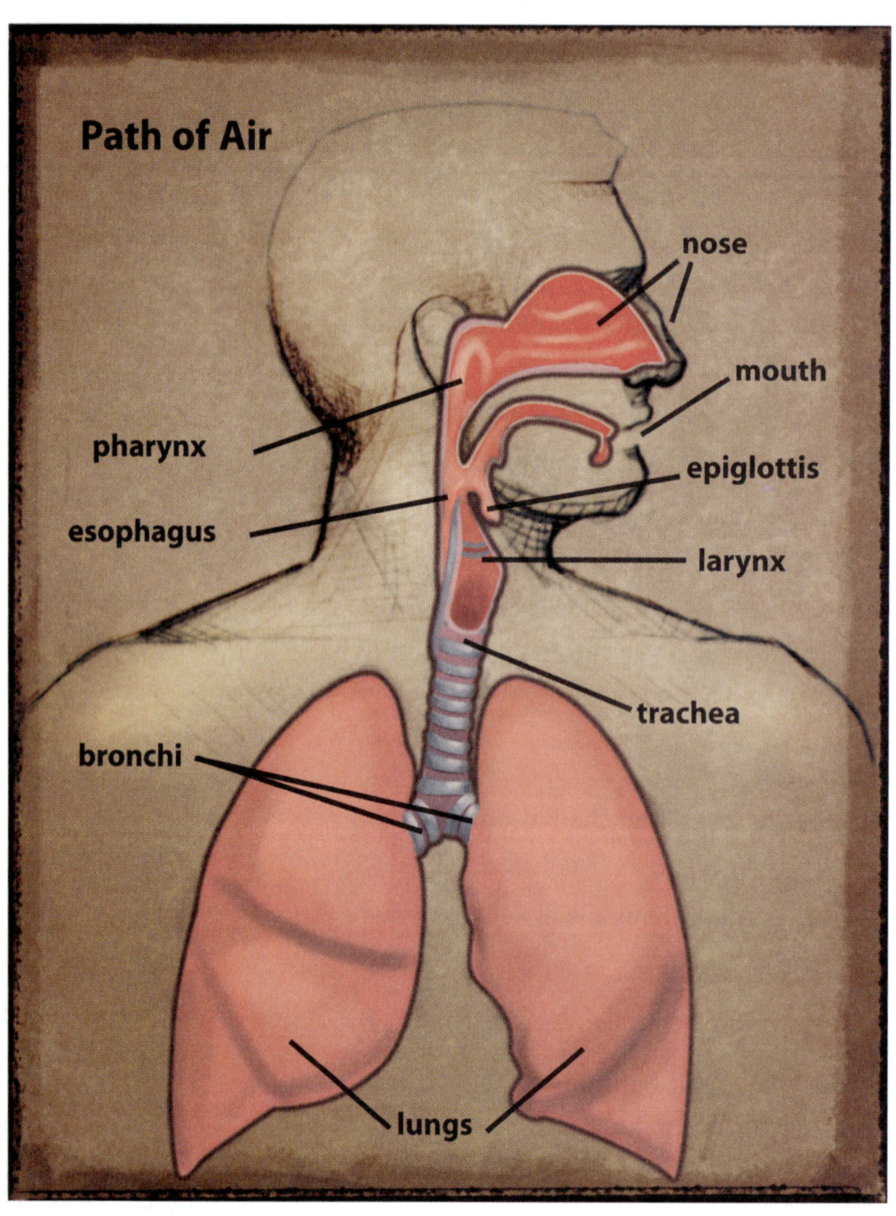

The air you breathe in is filtered through tiny hairs in your nose called **cilia** (SIL ee uh). Special cells in your nose produce *mucus* (MYOO kus), a sticky substance that moistens the air. The cilia and mucus trap dust, dirt, and other particles. This helps keep your respiratory system clean.

The cilia sweep the trapped particles toward your throat, and you swallow them. There, the acid in your stomach destroys the particles. Sometimes, though, the particles do not reach your stomach. Instead, they may irritate the lining of your nose or throat and cause you to sneeze or cough.

Air can also enter your body through your mouth. However, your mouth cannot protect your respiratory system as the cilia in your nose can. For this reason, it is best to breathe through your nose. At times, though, you may have to breathe through your mouth. When you have a cold, for instance, your nasal passage may become blocked. In this case, the only way to get air is through your mouth. You also tend to breathe through your mouth when you do strenuous exercise.

Fantastic FACTS

Have you ever wondered why your voice sometimes sounds different when you have a bad cold? The answer is that your sinuses are blocked up. Your sinuses are the empty spaces in the bones around your nose. Like the nose, each sinus is lined with a mucus membrane. Because sinuses are empty air spaces, they help reduce the weight of the skull. They also amplify sound. When you are sick and the sinuses get blocked with extra mucus, the air cannot circulate freely through the nasal passages. This makes your voice sound different.

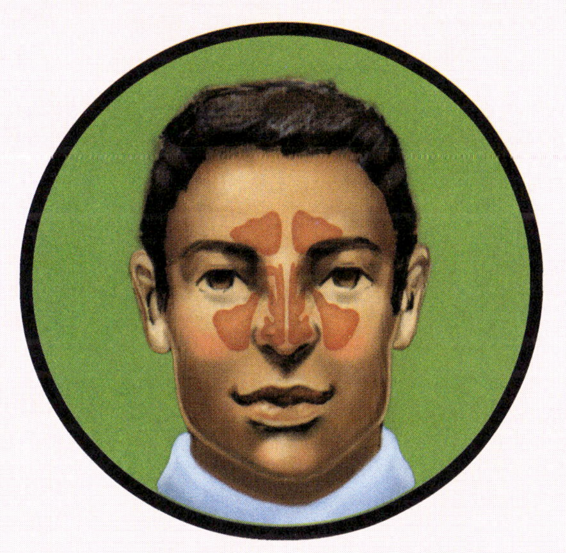

Upper Respiratory System

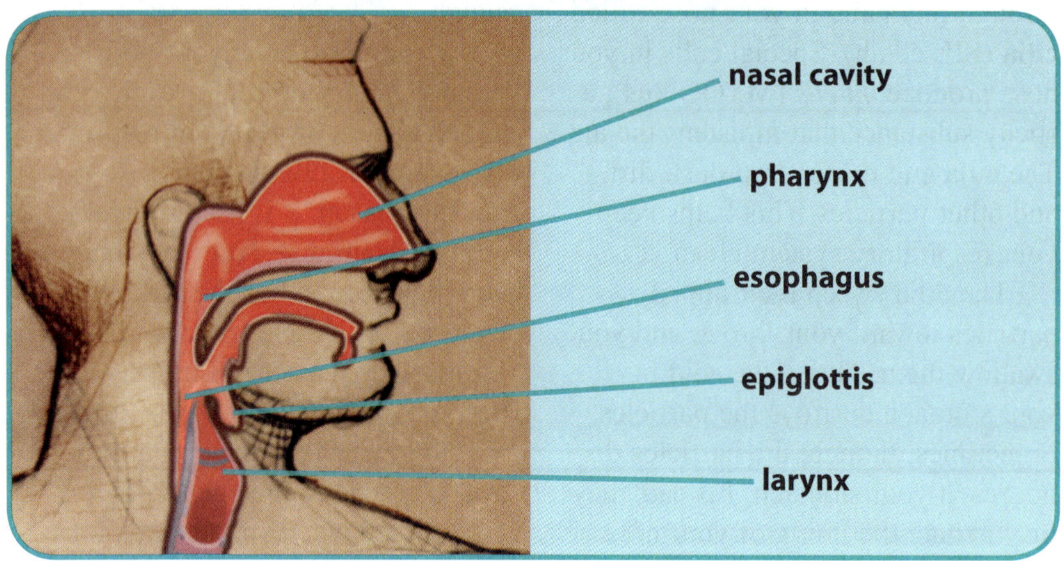

Your Throat

The air moves from your nose or mouth into your throat, or **pharynx** (FAIR ingks). At the end of your pharynx are two separate tubes, each with a different purpose. One tube leads to your stomach and is called your **esophagus** (ih SOF uh gus), or food pipe. The other tube is your **trachea** (TRAY kee uh), or windpipe. It leads to your lungs.

When you swallow your food, a flap of tissue called the **epiglottis** (EP ih GLOT iss) closes automatically over your trachea. The epiglottis keeps food from going down the trachea to your lungs. When you are breathing, the epiglottis stays open. This allows the air to enter your lungs instead of going to your stomach.

Talking or laughing with food in your mouth may cause your epiglottis to work improperly. It may stay open because you are talking though it needs to close so you can swallow your food. Instead of the food going down your esophagus, the food may accidentally go down your trachea and cause you to choke. Choking occurs when an object, such as a piece of food, goes down the wrong "pipe."

Your Larynx

At the top of your trachea is your **larynx** (LARE ingks), or voice box. It is made up of nine pieces of cartilage and many small muscles. Two small bands of elastic tissue stretch across the inside of the larynx. These soft bands are called your **vocal cords**.

Vocal Cords

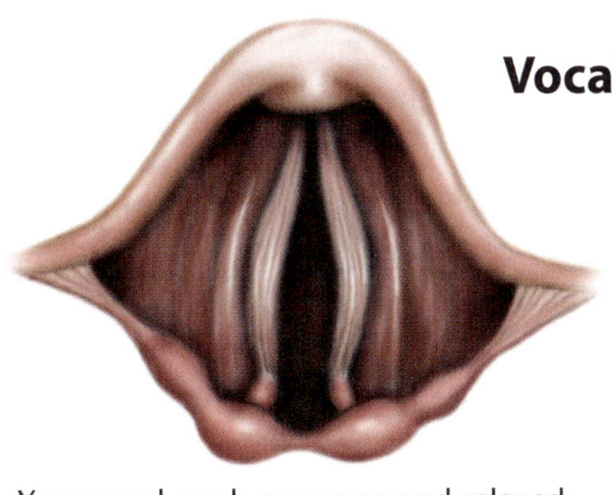

Your vocal cords are open and relaxed when you breathe.

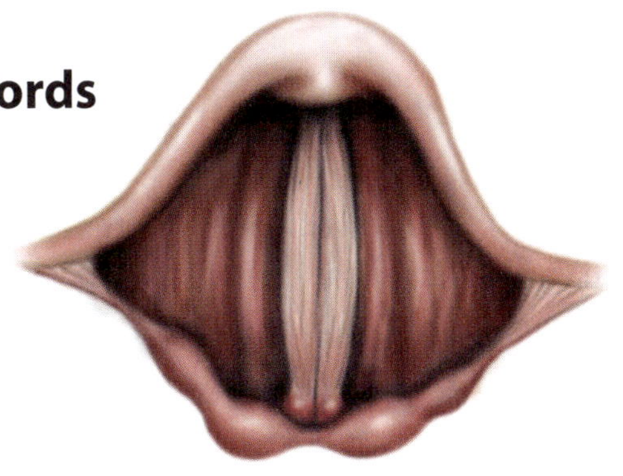

Your vocal cords tighten and narrow when you talk or sing.

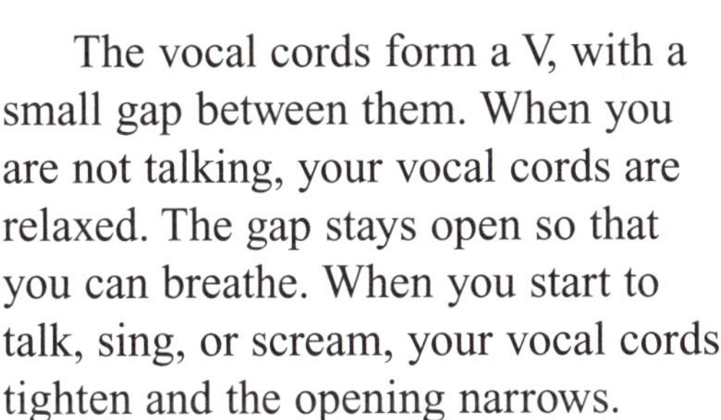

The vocal cords form a V, with a small gap between them. When you are not talking, your vocal cords are relaxed. The gap stays open so that you can breathe. When you start to talk, sing, or scream, your vocal cords tighten and the opening narrows.

Speech happens when air is exhaled. As you exhale, the air moves upward from your lungs and goes into your trachea. The air pushes through the closed vocal cords and makes them vibrate. This creates sound waves. Your throat, mouth, nose, sinus cavities, teeth, tongue, lips, jaw, and cheeks then work together to shape the sound into understandable speech.

The pitch of the sound depends on the thickness and length of the vocal cords. Long, thick vocal cords vibrate slowly and produce a deep sound. Short, thin vocal cords vibrate faster and produce a higher-pitched sound. Men have thicker vocal cords than women do. This is why men's voices are usually deeper than women's voices are.

TRY IT Yourself

Your larynx changes the pitch of sound by changing the thickness and the length of the vocal cords. You can model this with a balloon. Inflate a balloon and let the air escape. While the air is escaping, stretch open the mouth of the balloon. This will change the length and thickness of the opening. Try this several times. Predict whether the sound will be higher or lower as the size of the opening changes.

QUICK CHECK

1. Why is it better to breathe through your nose?
2. What is the name of the flap of tissue that keeps food out of your trachea?
3. What is another name for your voice box?

Your Trachea and Bronchi

Your respiratory system is divided into two parts. The nose, throat, and larynx make up the *upper respiratory system*. Below the larynx, from the trachea into the lungs, is the *lower respiratory system*.

The trachea stretches from the larynx into the upper chest. It is about 10–11 cm (4 in.) long in most adults. The trachea branches off into two tubes called the **bronchi** (BRONG KIE). One tube goes to the left lung. The other tube enters the right lung.

Both your trachea and your bronchi have C-shaped rings of cartilage on the outside of them. The rings keep them from collapsing and allow them to move as your neck and chest move. If a piece of food gets past your epiglottis, the muscles in your trachea walls react. The muscles can squeeze the rings together to try to keep the food from going into your lungs.

Just like in your nasal passages, the lining inside your trachea and bronchi has mucus and cilia. The mucus and cilia trap particles of dust and dirt. The particles are pushed back up to your throat. There, you usually swallow them down your esophagus. If you have ever coughed to clear your throat, you have experienced those particles moving out of your trachea.

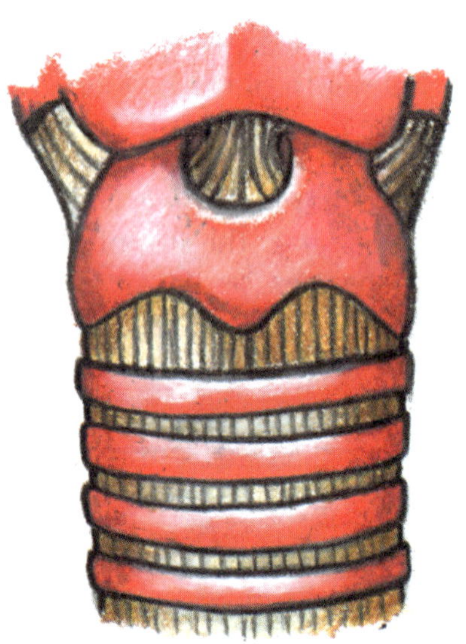

The rings of cartilage on the trachea and bronchi help keep the airways open.

Cilia line the inside of the nasal passages, the trachea, and the bronchi.

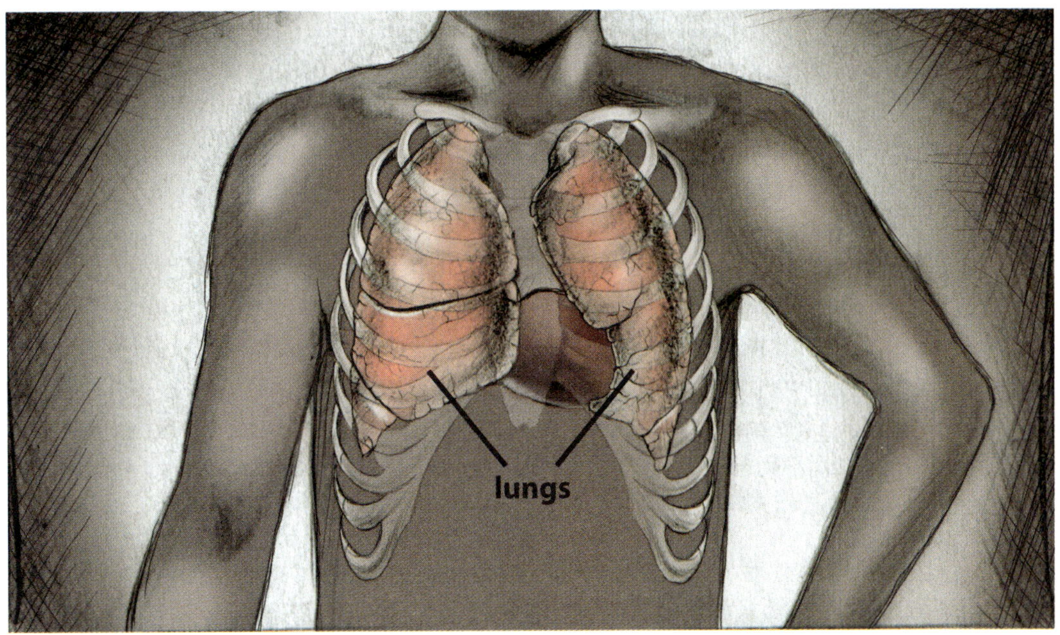

Your Lungs

Your **lungs** are two saclike organs that replace the carbon dioxide in your blood with oxygen. A flexible "cage" of bones protects your lungs. This cage is formed by your ribs, breastbone, and backbone. The top of your lungs reaches above your shoulder bones and is behind your collarbone. The base of your lungs rests on the diaphragm.

Healthy lungs are a pinkish-gray color. Each lung is about the size of a football. Your left lung is slightly smaller than your right lung. That is because your left lung has a space next to it for your heart. Your heart and main blood vessels are located between your lungs.

Lungs do not have any muscles of their own. Instead, your diaphragm and chest muscles control how your lungs move. When you breathe in, your lungs stretch and fill with air. When you breathe out, air is pushed out of your lungs, and they return to their smaller size.

The amount of air that can be taken into the lungs with one breath is called *lung capacity*. A normal breath for an average man is about half a liter of air. Lungs can hold more air if necessary, though. When a man breathes in as much air as possible, his lungs can hold about 6 L (6.4 qt) of air. A woman's lungs can hold about 4.2 L (4.5 qt) of air.

Bronchial tubes

Inside your lungs, your bronchi branch off into many smaller *bronchial tubes*. These tubes get smaller and smaller as they spread to all the parts of your lungs. Many of these tubes are less than 1 mm wide. Some are thinner than human hairs. All of the bronchial tubes, though, have muscles and rings of cartilage to keep them open wide. The smallest tubes are called *bronchioles* (BRONG kee OLES).

Alveoli

The bronchioles end in tiny air sacs called **alveoli** (al VEE uh LIE). The alveoli look like bunches of grapes. Each lung has about 300 million alveoli. They are surrounded by a network of tiny blood vessels called *capillaries*. The walls of the alveoli and the capillaries are very thin. In some places, they are only one cell thick.

It is in the alveoli that the exchange of gases takes place. The air you inhale contains oxygen. The oxygen passes through the walls of the alveoli into the blood in the capillaries. The blood then carries it to all the parts of your body. At the same time, carbon dioxide passes from the blood in the capillaries into the alveoli. There, the carbon dioxide can be exhaled from your body. This exchange of gases is called breathing, or respiration.

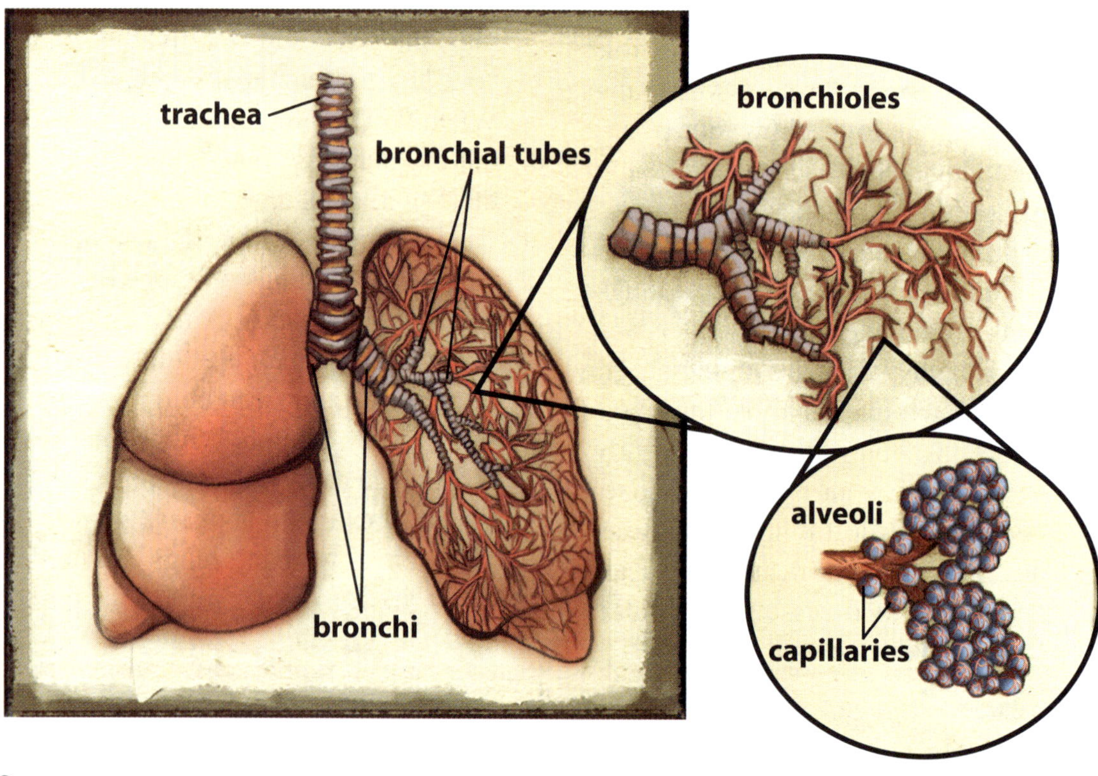

Respiratory Sounds

Coughs and Sneezes

Coughs and sneezes are caused whenever something irritates the lining of the airways. The force of the cough or sneeze moves the offending particles out of the respiratory system. When you cough, your diaphragm relaxes while your other muscles contract. This violently pushes air out through your mouth. A sneeze happens in much the same way, except that the air rushes out through your nose.

Hiccups

Hiccups are caused by involuntary movements of the diaphragm that disrupt normal breathing. When you have the hiccups, your diaphragm muscle contracts quickly and causes you to take quick, short breaths of air. The epiglottis closes suddenly while the diaphragm is contracting. This causes the hiccup noise.

Many times there is no obvious cause for hiccups. Some people may get hiccups when they are full or when they eat a spicy food. Strong emotions, such as fear or anger, can also cause them. Hiccups can be noisy or quiet, but they cannot be controlled.

Snoring

A person snores whenever air cannot flow freely through the back of the mouth and the nose. The snoring sound is caused when parts of the mouth and throat vibrate and hit together. There are many reasons why a person snores. The person may have an allergy or a cold. If the wall of cartilage that separates a person's nostrils is crooked, he may snore. A person may also snore if he is overweight, sleeps on his back, or has swollen tonsils.

sneezing

QUICK CHECK

1. What is the name of the two air tubes that branch off the trachea?
2. What are alveoli?
3. What causes the hiccup noise?

How Much Air Is in Your Lungs?

Process skills
- Hypothesizing
- Measuring and using numbers
- Collecting, recording, and interpreting data

The amount of air in the lungs, or *lung volume*, is different for each person. Your age, gender, size, and physical fitness determine how much air your lungs can hold.

Doctors measure different things about your lung volume. Sometimes they measure your lung volume during normal, quiet breathing. Other times they may measure the maximum amount of air that you can exhale after a deep breath. This is called your *vital lung capacity*.

In this activity, you will use a balloon to measure your vital lung capacity.

Materials:
- round balloon, 12 in.
- meter stick
- centimeter ruler
- calculator
- Activity Manual

Problem

How much air can you exhale in one breath?

Procedure

1. Complete the hypothesis in your Activity Manual.
2. Stretch a large round balloon, and then blow into it several times, letting the air out of the balloon after each time.
3. Take a deep breath. Exhale as much air as possible into the balloon. Be sure that you are exhaling only once.
4. Twist the end of the balloon, and pinch it closed with your fingers. Do not let air escape from the balloon.
5. Have your partner hold the meter stick in a vertical position. The end of the meter stick should rest on a desk or table. Place the balloon on its side against the meter stick. Rest the centimeter ruler across the top of the balloon. Do not push down on the balloon.

6. Use the ruler to measure the width of the balloon that you blew into. The place on the meter stick that the centimeter ruler points to is the diameter of the balloon. Record the diameter of the balloon that you blew into.
7. Repeat steps 3–6 two more times. Record the diameter each time.
8. Calculate and record the average diameter of the balloon.
9. Exchange places with your partner. Repeat steps 1–8 for your partner. Make sure that your partner uses a different balloon.
10. Look at the graph on your Activity Manual page. Use the average diameter to find out how many liters of air you exhaled and record the amount.

Conclusions

- Was your hypothesis correct?
- Did the diameter of the balloon change the second and third times that you blew into the balloon? If so, why do you think it changed?

Follow-up

- Compare the lung volumes of boys and girls.
- Compare the vital lung capacity of students who play a wind or brass instrument with those who do not.

Respiratory Problems

The respiratory system involves many parts. When all the parts are working properly, you hardly notice any of them. However, if one part stops working well, you usually notice very quickly. The problem may be merely an annoyance, such as a stuffy head or a runny nose. Or it could be a life-threatening problem, such as when the body is not able to get the air that it needs.

Respiratory problems vary a lot. Some affect only one part of the respiratory system. Others, however, cause trouble for many parts of the respiratory system. Some are sicknesses that come and go. Others may last a person's whole life.

Diseases

Many diseases can affect the body's ability to breathe properly. The most common respiratory disease is a cold. Cold viruses usually affect the nose and throat, causing the cells in the nose and throat to swell. The cells start producing more mucus than normal, and the person may have trouble breathing through his nose. Colds can also affect the sinuses, ears, and bronchi.

Influenza (IN floo EN zuh), or the flu, is also caused by a virus. Flu viruses are similar to cold viruses. They often have some of the same symptoms. Flu viruses, though, usually also cause fevers, headaches, and muscle aches. The viruses may lead to a more serious illness or infection.

Both colds and the flu are very *contagious*, or easy to spread to other people. Colds and the flu are usually spread through the air when a sick person coughs or sneezes. When another person inhales, he breathes in the virus. That particular virus may or may not make him sick. Sometimes a person may get sick by touching his

Colds and the flu can spread when a person coughs or sneezes.

mouth or nose after he has touched something that a sick person has coughed or sneezed on. Frequent hand washing can help keep viruses from spreading.

Some problems affect another part of the respiratory system, the throat. Many different things cause sore throats. Sometimes dust or smoke in the air can irritate the throat and cause it to be sore. The extra mucus produced because of a cold or flu may also irritate the lining in the throat. The throat usually has a coating that helps keep it moist. Sometimes extreme coughing will dry out the throat and cause it to hurt.

Occasionally a virus or bacteria may infect the throat or larynx. Strep throat is a type of infection that is caused by bacteria. A person with strep throat will usually have a high fever for several days. A doctor can test to see if a sore throat is strep throat. If it is, the doctor can prescribe medicine to help the body get rid of the bacteria.

Sometimes a cold or the flu can turn into bronchitis (bron KY tiss). This disease causes the bronchi to become infected and swollen. A germ, such as a virus, irritates the lining of the bronchi. This often causes the cilia to stop moving. They cannot trap or remove particles. The air passages become blocked, and more mucus is produced. The extra mucus in the bronchi makes it harder for the air to pass in and out of the lungs. This is why a person with bronchitis often sounds raspy. He may also cough a lot. Coughing is the body's way to try to remove the extra mucus.

Pneumonia (neh MON yuh) is a lung infection. It is caused by viruses or bacteria and may develop from another illness. The infection causes the lungs to fill with fluid. The fluid keeps the lungs from being able to properly fill with air. Oxygen cannot reach all areas of the lungs. This makes it hard for oxygen to get from the alveoli to the bloodstream.

Streptococcus bacteria can cause strep throat.

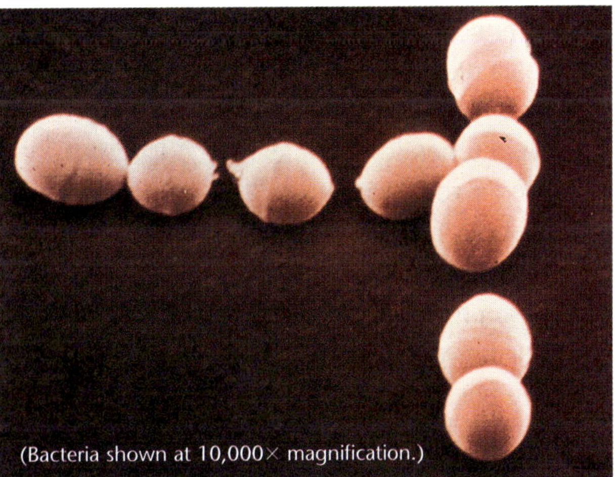

(Bacteria shown at 10,000× magnification.)

Allergies

Sneezing does not always mean that you have a cold. It may mean that you are having an allergic reaction to something in the air. The air that we inhale usually contains particles such as dust and pollen. For some people, this dust or pollen may cause breathing problems. Their bodies react to things in the air that other people never even notice.

People with respiratory allergies often sneeze. They may also have runny noses, itchy eyes, or breathing problems. Allergies often come and go with the seasons. For example, pollen comes out the most in the spring and the fall. A person may be fine in the winter but react as soon as the spring pollen arrives. An allergy is not contagious. It cannot be spread like a cold or the flu can.

Asthma

Asthma (AZ muh) is a disorder that causes the small bronchial tubes to become narrow from time to time. This can make it hard for the person to breathe. Asthma can vary a lot from person to person. Some people with asthma have very few problems. Others have a lot more.

Allergies and air pollution are two things that may cause someone to have an asthma attack. During an attack, the muscles around the bronchial tubes tighten more than normal. This makes the bronchial tubes smaller. The airways are often swollen and irritated. This makes it difficult for the person to breathe. The person may cough and wheeze as they breathe.

Someone with asthma may use an inhaler. The inhaler contains medicine that can be breathed in. It can help prevent an asthma attack from starting or getting worse. Asthma is not contagious. Most people with asthma are able to keep it under control. This way, they can still participate in sports and other activities.

Some people need regular treatments for asthma.

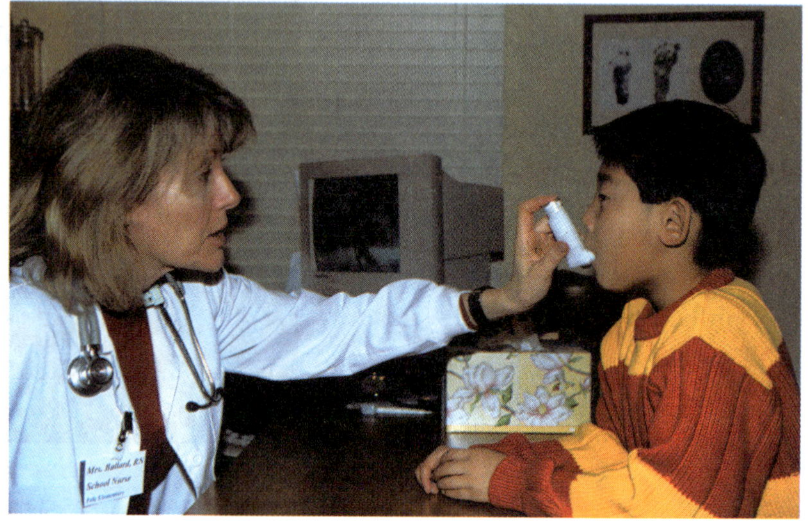

Smoking

healthy lung

smoker's lung

Smoking is harmful to your health. Cigarette smoke contains poisonous chemicals that harm the lungs and other parts of the body. Most of the smoke particles are very small. They cannot be trapped by the cilia and mucus in the airways. These poisonous chemicals then get into the lungs. As the smoke particles cool, they form a sticky tar that stays in the lungs. The tar makes the cilia clump together so that they cannot work properly. When this happens, dust, dirt, and smoke stay in the lungs. This sticky tar may cause diseases such as *lung cancer*.

Another deadly disease caused by cigarette smoking is *emphysema* (EM fih SEE muh). Sometimes cigarette smoke causes the alveoli to stop working properly. This keeps the lungs from being able to transfer oxygen and carbon dioxide between the air and the blood. Once the alveoli are damaged, they cannot be repaired. People with emphysema have difficulty breathing. They also get tired a lot. This is because they do not get enough oxygen into their bloodstream. For them, even blowing out a match can be difficult to do.

The human body is one of God's marvelous designs. He created all the parts of our body to work together. The respiratory system works with other systems in our body to keep us alive. We should say with the psalmist in Psalm 139, "I will praise thee; for I am fearfully and wonderfully made: marvelous are thy works." Our bodies were made by God and belong to Him. Taking care of our bodies brings glory to Him.

1. What is the most common respiratory disease?
2. If a person has pneumonia, which part of the respiratory system is infected?
3. What respiratory disorder causes the bronchial tubes to narrow?
4. What are two lung diseases that are often caused by smoking?

Answer the Questions

1. Why is it incorrect to call the lung a muscle?

____

____

____

2. How do the cilia in the nose, trachea, and bronchi help protect the respiratory system?

____

____

____

3. What gases are exchanged in the alveoli?

____

____

____

Solve the Problem

While playing you get hit very hard in the stomach area with a basketball. The next day you are still sore, and it hurts to breathe. Why would being hit in the stomach area affect your breathing?

____

____

____

____

____

Circulatory System

12

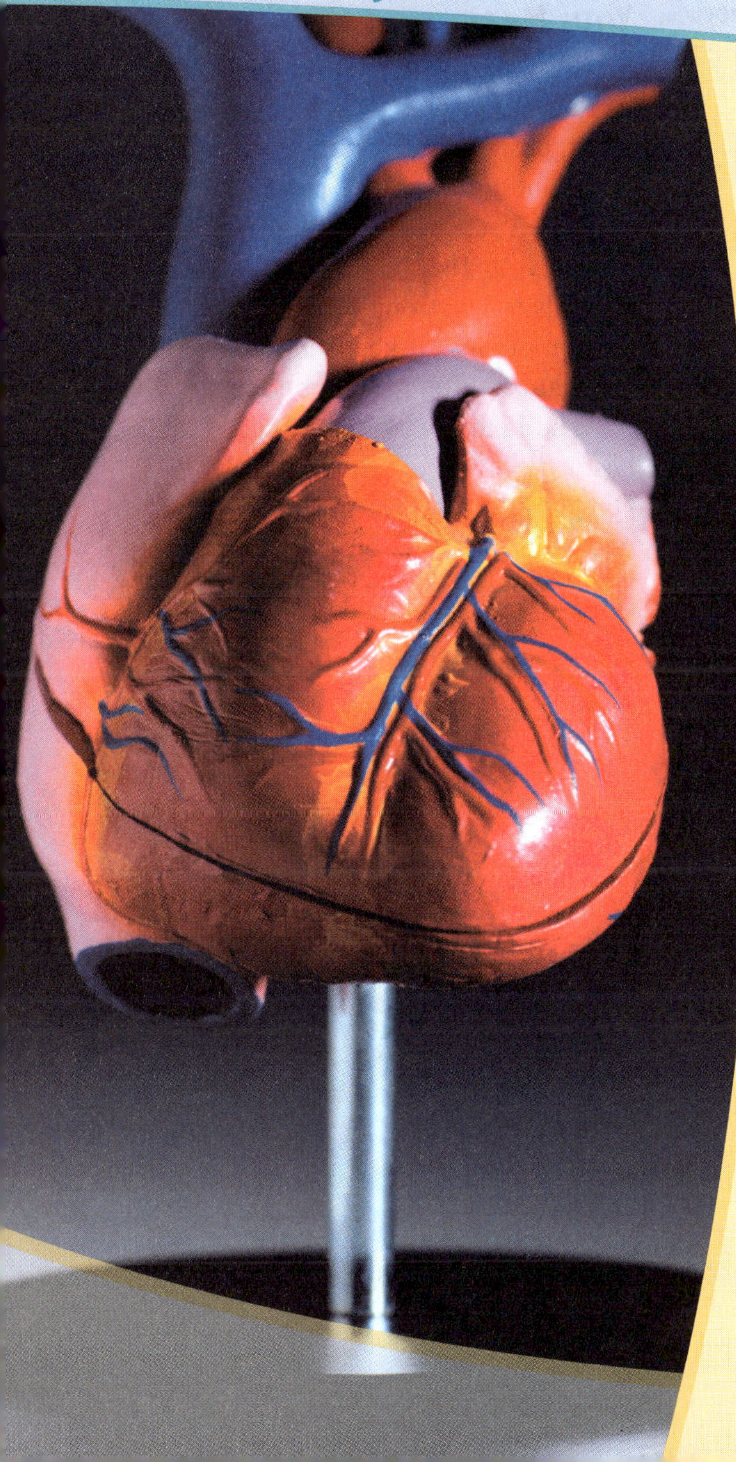

REMEMBER *now* thy **CREATOR**

People once thought that man's spirit resided in his physical heart. Now we know that the physical heart is an organ that pumps blood through the body. Like other parts of the body, the heart can be damaged. But doctors can do many things to help the heart work properly. They sometimes repair or replace damaged parts of man's physical heart.

Although man's spirit does not reside in the physical heart, sometimes his spirit affects his physical heart. His spiritual heart may become weak and damaged. Psalm 31:24 says, "Be of good courage, and he shall strengthen your heart, all ye that hope in the Lord." Not trusting in God can cause us to be angry, worried, or fearful. These emotions cause stress to our bodies. This stress, in turn, can cause damage to our physical hearts. So putting our hope in God helps both our spiritual and physical hearts.

Circulating Your Blood

Have you ever traveled on interstate highways? These roads connect many cities in the United States. But some cities and towns are not near an interstate. In those places, smaller roads merge into a main road that connects to the interstate. This network of roads allows you to travel almost anywhere in the United States.

The circulatory (SUR kyuh luh TORE ee) system is also a transportation system. It does not transfer people, though. It transfers blood. In this way, God designed your body so that the oxygen and nutrients in your blood can reach every part of your body. Without the oxygen and nutrients, your cells would die. The circulatory system consists of the heart, blood vessels, and blood.

Your Heart

The heart is the main organ of the circulatory system. It is located in the chest, between the lungs. Both the lungs and the heart are protected by the ribs. Your heart is only about the size of your fist, but it is very strong. It needs to be strong because it never stops pumping. It keeps blood always circulating through your body.

The **heart** is a hollow organ that has walls made of strong muscle. A slippery sac of tissue around the heart protects it from rubbing against the lungs or the ribs.

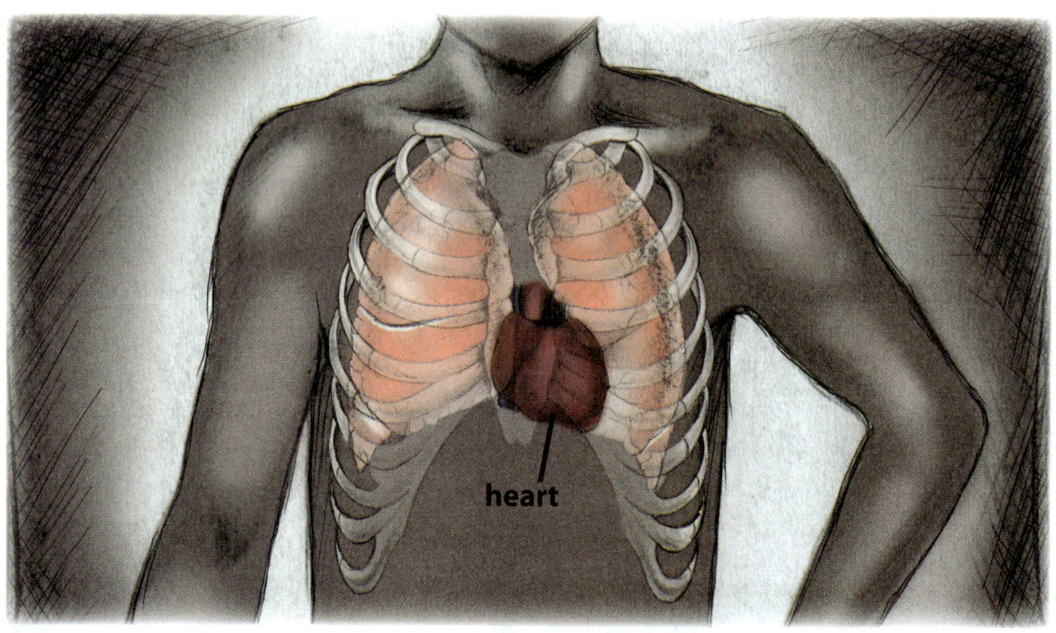

Inside the heart are four empty chambers, or sections. These chambers are "stacked," two on the top and two on the bottom. The upper chamber on each side is called an **atrium** (AY tree um). The lower chamber on each side is called a **ventricle** (VENT trih kull). The left and right sides of the heart are divided by a thick wall of muscle called the *septum* (SEP tum). The right side of the heart pumps blood to the lungs. The left side of the heart pumps blood to the rest of the body.

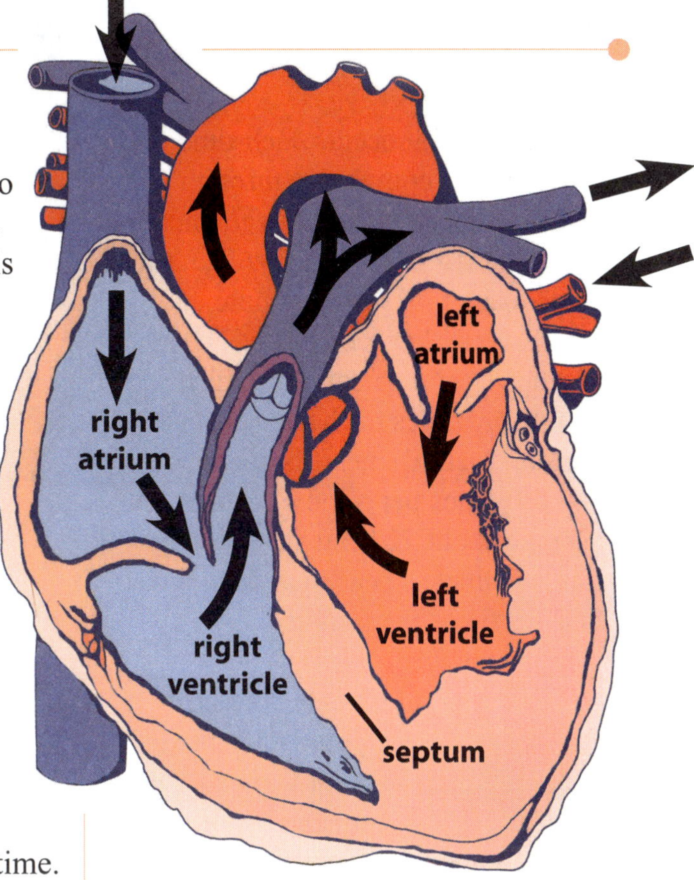

All four chambers of the heart work together to constantly pump blood. The upper chambers contract, or squeeze, at the same time. As they contract, they force the blood into the ventricles below them. Then both ventricles contract to push blood out into the blood vessels. While this is happening, each atrium relaxes and fills with blood.

The blood flows in only one direction. Blood enters the heart through the right atrium. When the right atrium contracts, it pushes the blood into the right ventricle. The blood goes through a small flap of tissue called a *valve*. The valve opens to let the blood through. Then the valve closes to prevent the blood from flowing backwards. The heart has valves between the atrium and ventricle on each side and where the blood vessels leave the ventricles.

The right ventricle of the heart contracts to send the blood to the lungs. In the lungs, the blood releases carbon dioxide and picks up oxygen. The blood flows from the lungs back to the heart and enters the left atrium.

Then the left atrium contracts. Its valve opens, and the blood flows down into the left ventricle. The left ventricle contracts and pumps the blood out into a large blood vessel that branches into smaller blood vessels that carry the blood throughout the rest of the body. This whole process occurs very quickly.

Heartbeats

A heartbeat occurs each time the blood moves completely through the heart. With each heartbeat, the heart pushes blood into the body. The heart beats many times each minute and can rest only between beats. The age and health of a person will affect how many times his heart beats per minute. A child's heart beats about 90–120 times per minute. Adults average about 72 beats per minute. A trained athlete's heart may beat fewer than 60 times per minute.

The number of times your heart beats in a minute is called your *heart rate*. You can find your heart rate by counting the times that you can feel your pulse. Your **pulse** is the push of blood through the blood vessels. It occurs each time your heart beats. You can feel your pulse on several places on your body. The easiest places to check your pulse are probably on your wrist or on your neck.

The heart slows down while a person sleeps.

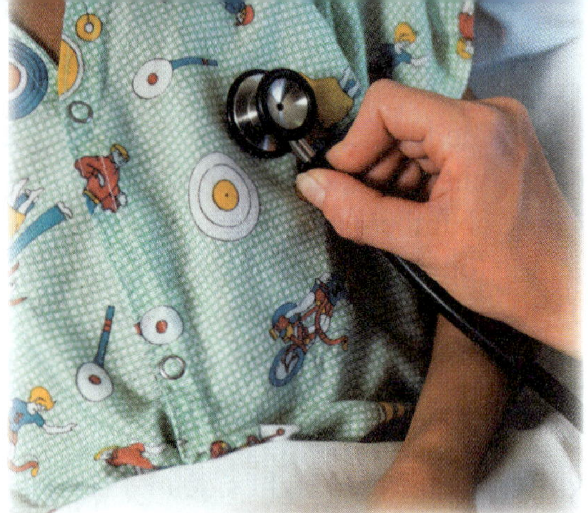

A doctor uses a stethoscope to listen to a person's heart.

Your heartbeat makes a "lubb-dubb" sound. This is the sound that the valves in your heart make as they close. A doctor can tell much about how your heart is functioning by listening to the sounds it makes. He uses a device called a *stethoscope* to hear your heart beating. If the sound is not normal, a problem may exist. The doctor may do more tests to check it out.

Although your heart is always beating, it does not always beat at the same rate. When you are active, it beats quickly. When you are sitting still, it beats more slowly. Your heart beats even slower yet when you are sleeping. Getting enough sleep can provide more rest for your hard-working heart!

Exercise is important, too. The heart muscle needs to be exercised in order to be strong. Hearts that are healthy and strong do not have to beat as often.

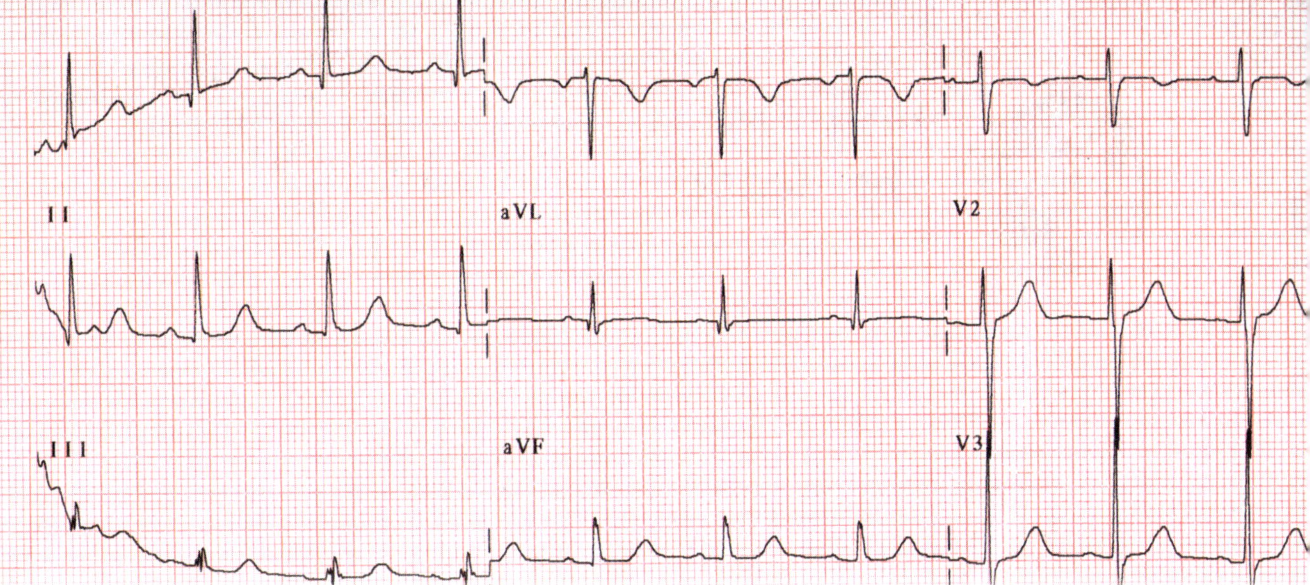

An EKG printout shows the electrical changes in a person's heart.

One part of your heart acts as a "control center." This control center, called a **pacemaker**, is a small group of cells that makes sure your heart beats at a steady pace. Your pacemaker cells send electric currents to your heart muscle. Each electric current causes your heart to contract. These cells set the pace, or the number of times, that your heart beats.

Your body gets oxygen from the blood that your heart pumps around your body. Your pacemaker constantly receives messages from your body about how much oxygen your body needs. Your pacemaker then adjusts your heart rate to match the amount of oxygen you need. For example, when you exercise, your body uses more oxygen. So your pacemaker makes your heart beat faster. This pumps blood around your body more quickly.

The electrical signals made by your pacemaker can be read by a special machine. This machine is called an *electrocardiograph* (ih LEC tro KAR dee uh GRAF), or EKG. This machine records the electrical changes that happen during the heartbeat cycle. Doctors can use this information to detect heart problems.

QUICK CHECK

1. What are the lower chambers of the heart called?
2. What keeps the blood from flowing backwards through the heart?
3. What causes the "lubb-dubb" sound of the heartbeat?
4. What is the function, or job, of the pacemaker?

How Fast Is the Beat?

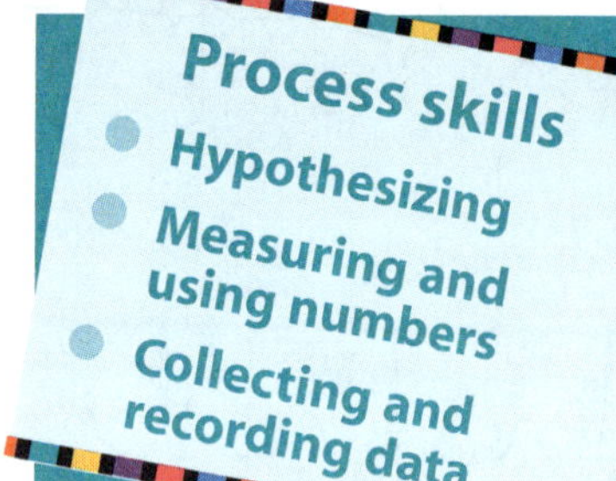

When you check your pulse, you are measuring how fast your heart is beating. You can feel your pulse in the arteries that are closest to your skin. The easiest places to check your pulse are probably on your wrist or on the side of your neck. You might also be able to feel your pulse behind your knee or on the inside of your elbow.

In this activity, you will test to see how quickly your heart rate returns to normal after exercising.

Problem

How long will it take for your heart rate to return to normal after exercising for two minutes?

Materials:
stopwatch
Activity Manual

Procedure

1. Complete the hypothesis in your Activity Manual. Then sit quietly for 1 minute.
2. Find your normal heart rate. Use two fingers to find your pulse on the underside of your wrist or on the side of your neck. Count how many times you feel your pulse in 15 seconds. Record that number in the Pulse column. Calculate and record your Normal Heart Rate.
3. Stand up and run in place for 2 minutes.
4. Find your pulse. Count how many times you feel it in 15 seconds. Have your partner record that number in your chart.
5. Keep your fingers on your pulse. For the next 5 minutes, check your pulse every 30 seconds. Check for 15 seconds, then rest for 15 seconds. Have your partner record the numbers. Stop checking your pulse when it matches your normal pulse.

6. Switch places with your partner. Repeat steps 2–5 for your partner. Record his numbers in his Activity Manual.
7. Calculate your heart rate for each number that was recorded.
8. Make a line graph in your Activity Manual to show how your heart rate changed.

Conclusions

- Was your hypothesis correct?
- How long did it take your heart rate to return to normal?

Follow-up

- Use a different physical activity for exercising.
- Change the amount of time that you spend exercising.

Your Blood Vessels

Blood vessels are the "pipes" that carry blood around your body. There are billions of them. In fact, if all the blood vessels in your body were laid end to end, they would be long enough to wrap around the earth at least two and a half times!

All your blood vessels are linked together. This provides the "transport system" for your blood. It is very effective. It takes only about one minute for your blood to travel through your circulatory system.

Blood vessels are classified by where they carry blood. **Arteries** (ARE tuh rees) carry blood from the heart to all the parts of the body. **Veins** carry the blood back to the heart. **Capillaries** (KAP uh LER ees) are the small blood vessels that connect the arteries and veins.

Every cell in the body, even those that make up the heart, needs blood. A network of arteries, capillaries, and veins supplies the heart with blood. The arteries and veins that provide blood for the heart are called *coronary (KOR uh NAIR ee) arteries* and *coronary veins*. *Coronary* is a word that means "heart."

Arteries and veins are often named by where they are located in the body. *Pulmonary* (PULL muh NAIR ee) is a word that means "relating to the lungs." The artery that goes to the lungs is called the *pulmonary artery*. The *pulmonary veins* come from the lungs back to the heart.

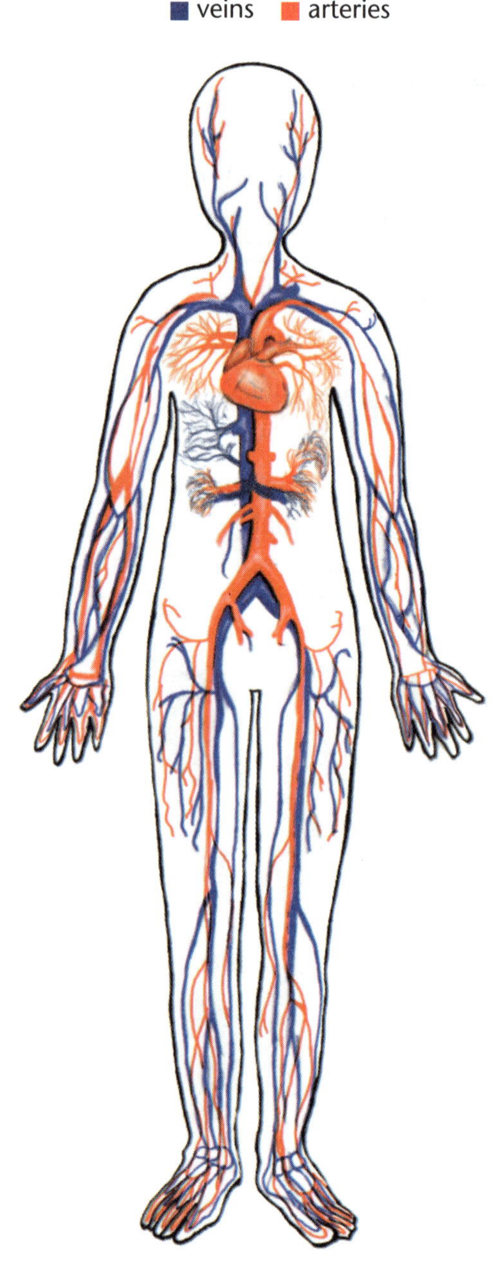

Arteries

Arteries have thick, muscular walls. The artery walls can expand and relax as the heart pumps blood through them. The heart contracts and pushes blood into the arteries. This makes the artery walls expand, or stretch out. When the heart relaxes, the walls spring back into place. This causes the arteries to become smaller. The blood is pushed forward. When you feel your pulse, you are feeling the artery wall expand and then relax.

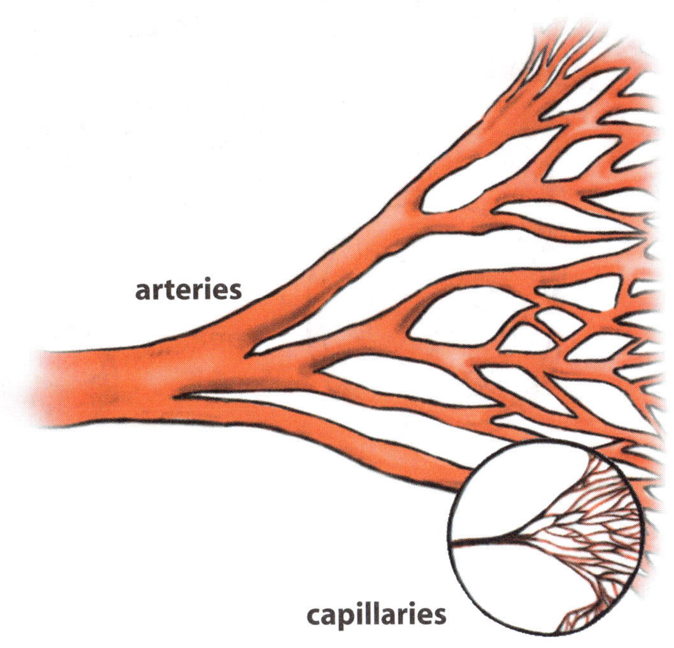

The **aorta** (ay OR tuh) is the largest artery in the body. It is about the diameter of a garden hose. The aorta is attached to the left ventricle of the heart and carries blood away from the heart. Arteries branch off the aorta and form smaller arteries. The smallest arteries are called *arterioles* (are TIER ee OLS).

Capillaries

Capillaries are the smallest blood vessels. They are so small, in fact, that they can be seen only with a microscope. It takes about 10 capillaries to equal the thickness of one human hair!

Capillaries spread out from the arterioles in a web of blood vessels. The body has many of these webs. Every cell in the body is close to a capillary.

Even though they are small, capillaries have a very important job. Capillaries have thin walls. As the blood in the capillaries flows past other cells, oxygen and nutrients in the blood pass through the capillary walls into surrounding cells. At the same time, carbon dioxide and other wastes from the cells pass into the capillaries and are carried away by the blood. This keeps the cells healthy.

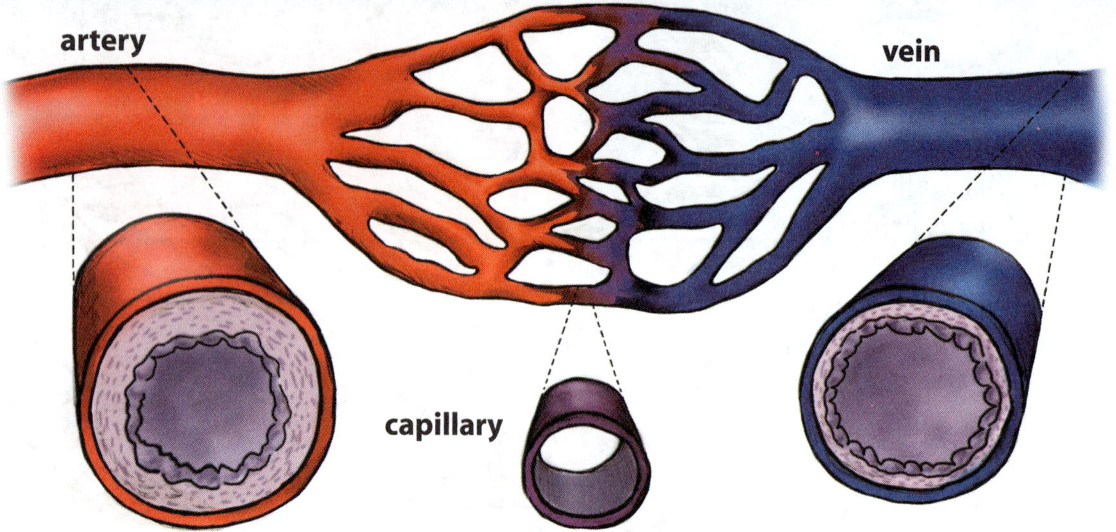

Veins

Capillaries link the smallest arteries with the smallest veins, which are called *venules* (VEN yools). These venules eventually become the larger blood vessels called veins. Veins return the blood to the heart.

Vein walls are thinner than artery walls are. The muscle fibers in veins are also not as strong as the muscle fibers in arteries are. Muscles in your body help push blood through your veins and back to your heart. Like the heart, veins have valves that keep the blood from flowing backwards.

All the veins in the body flow into two large veins called the vena cavae (VEE-nuh KAY-vee). The **vena cavae** are the largest veins in the body. The *superior vena cava* carries blood going back to the heart from the upper body. The *inferior vena cava* carries blood going back to the heart from the lower body. Each of these veins is about 2.5 cm (1 in.) in diameter.

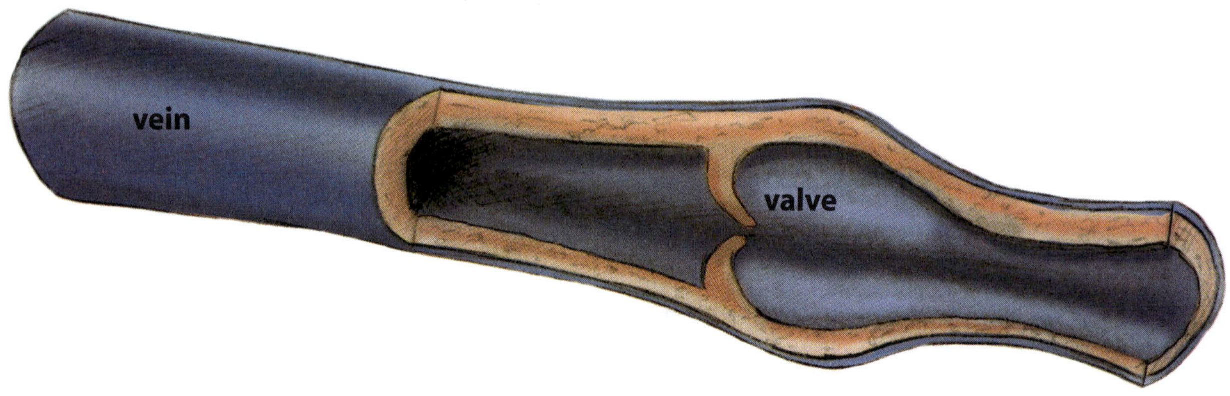

William Harvey

William Harvey

People used to think that air, not blood, flowed through arteries and veins. Later, people thought that arteries came out of the heart and veins came out of the liver. They thought that food was changed into blood by the liver and that the blood was consumed by the body. Most people in the 1500s and 1600s thought that the lungs moved blood through the body.

William Harvey, an English doctor born in 1578, was the first to realize how the circulatory system really works. By dissecting animals and studying people, Harvey knew that the theories of his day were wrong. He discovered that the arteries, veins, heart, and lungs are all part of one big circulatory system.

In 1628, Harvey published a book based on his research. He was the first to say that the heart is a pump that moves blood through the body. He explained how the blood is circulated through the body and then returns to the heart. His book had many critics at first. People said he was crazy. As man's technology improved, though, Harvey's ideas were shown to be true. His ideas became the basis for all modern research on the heart and blood vessels.

✓ QUICK CHECK

1. Which blood vessels carry blood away from the heart?
2. Which blood vessels carry blood to the heart?
3. Which blood vessels are the smallest?

Contents of a Drop of Blood

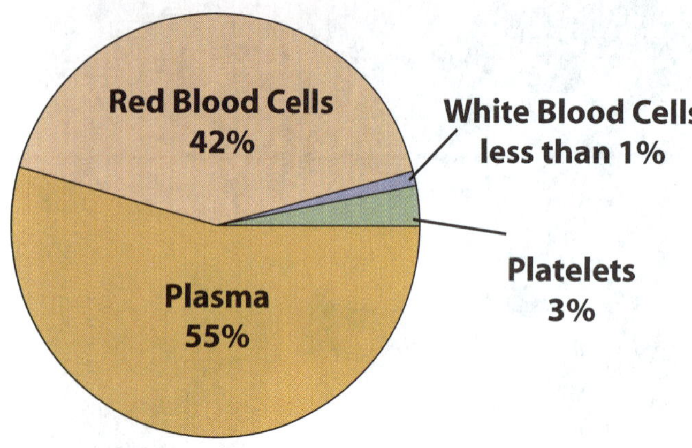

Your Blood

An adult usually has about 4.7 L (5 qt) of blood flowing through his body. The blood has three very important jobs. Blood transports substances around the body. As the blood circulates, it helps keep the body's temperature at about 37°C (98.6°F). Blood also helps to defend the body against infections and diseases.

Blood is made up of plasma, red blood cells, white blood cells, and platelets. **Plasma** (PLAZ muh) is the liquid part of blood. It is a clear, yellowish liquid that is mostly water. The plasma can dissolve many substances, such as proteins, sugars, and nutrients. The blood then carries these substances to all the parts of the body. The red blood cells, white blood cells, and platelets float in the plasma. One tiny drop of blood contains at least 5 million red blood cells, 8 thousand white blood cells, and 250 thousand platelets.

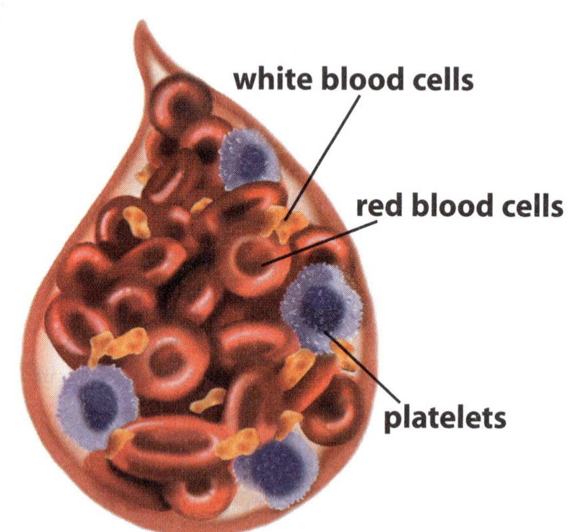

Science and the BIBLE

Long before man understood the importance of blood, the Bible said, "the life of the flesh is in the blood" (Leviticus 17:11). In the Old Testament, atonement for sins could occur only when blood was shed. These sacrifices were a sign of a sacrifice to come. They pointed to the great sacrifice that Jesus Christ made for man's sins. Hebrews 9:22 says that "without shedding of blood is no remission." Only when Christ shed His precious blood could man's sins be forgiven.

Red blood cells

Red blood cells are tiny blood cells that carry oxygen to all parts of the body. Each red blood cell is concave on both sides. This shape helps them squeeze through small capillaries without bursting.

Each red blood cell is like a bus traveling on a route through the body. At the different "stops," the red blood cell "bus" lets oxygen out and picks up some carbon dioxide. When the "bus" travels through the lungs, it lets out the carbon dioxide and picks up oxygen.

Red blood cells are made in the bone marrow inside the bones. About 100 million of them are produced every minute. If the body does not produce enough red blood cells, a person might become *anemic* (uh NEE mik). People with anemia are often very tired and may feel dizzy at times. These symptoms are caused by a lack of oxygen. With fewer red blood cells, not as much oxygen can be carried by the blood.

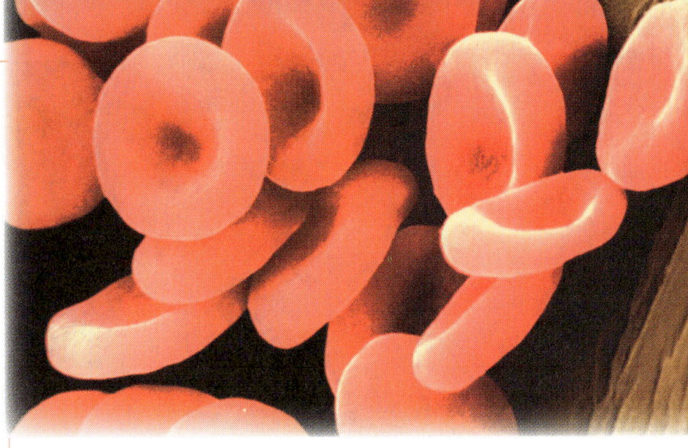

Red blood cells have a biconcave shape.

Each red blood cell lives about 120 days. As red blood cells get older, they lose their shape and become fragile. They shrink in size and are carried to the spleen or the liver. There they are destroyed. Most parts of the old red blood cells are recycled by the body and used to make new cells.

Inside each red blood cell is a protein called *hemoglobin*. Oxygen from the lungs attaches itself to the hemoglobin molecule. In this way, oxygen is carried to each part of the body. Together, the hemoglobin and oxygen give blood its bright red color. Each red blood cell has about 250 million hemoglobin molecules. Each of these molecules can carry four molecules of oxygen. So each red blood cell carries about 1 billion oxygen molecules!

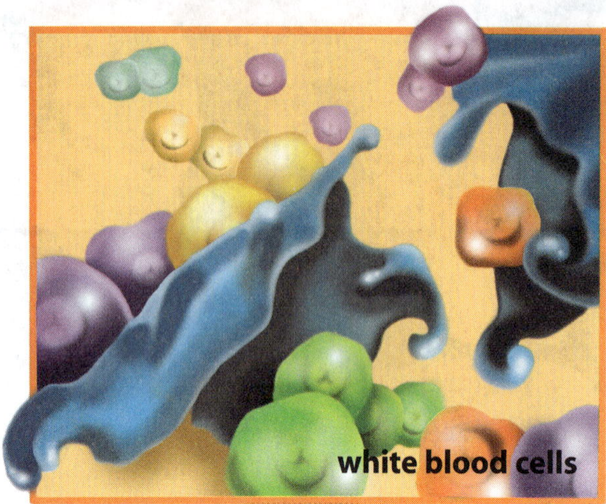

White blood cells

White blood cells help the body fight diseases and infections. The body has many types of white blood cells. Some recognize and identify germs such as bacteria or viruses. Others make chemicals that fight the invading germs. Yet another type of white blood cell surrounds and kills the invaders. White blood cells can move to wherever they are needed to fight the invading germs.

Your body has fewer white blood cells than it has red blood cells. However, your body can make more white blood cells when they are needed. For example, when you are sick, your body makes more white blood cells to fight the infection or disease. A person whose body does not produce many white blood cells gets sick easily. His body cannot protect him from invading germs.

Platelets

Platelets are small fragments of cells. These fragments help form blood clots. A blood clot is a jellylike mass of blood cells that stops the flow of blood from an injury. If the skin is injured, the platelets help plug the broken blood vessels. A scab forms on the skin. Underneath the scab, the body begins repairing the damaged tissues. The scab makes a barrier to keep out germs until the skin grows back. The scab falls off when the tissues have healed.

Platelets also make sure that blood vessels do not leak. They can stick to torn blood vessels and form a patch

that slows any blood loss. A platelet is less than half the size of a red blood cell. Each usually wears out in about nine days. However, new platelets are always being formed in the bone marrow.

Blood types

For many years, people tried to transfer the blood from a healthy person to an injured person. Sometimes this transfer of blood, called a **blood transfusion**, helped the patients. Many times, however, the patients did not get better. Instead they got worse or even died. It was not until 1901 that Karl Landsteiner, an Austrian physician, discovered why. He found that blood is not all the same. Instead, there are different types. Today we know that there are four main types of blood. We also know that some types cannot be successfully mixed with certain other types.

The blood types are called A, B, AB, and O. These names identify the special proteins found in the red blood cells. Some people have only the A protein or only the B protein. Other people have both proteins, and some have neither.

If a person with type A blood receives type B blood, the white blood cells in the A blood identify the B proteins as enemies. In trying to get rid of the enemy, the white blood cells cause the red blood cells to clump together. This clogs the blood vessels.

Since type O blood does not have either type of protein, it can safely mix with any other type of blood. Type O blood is called the *universal donor*. Type AB blood is called the *universal receiver*. It has both A and B proteins, so it can safely receive any other type of blood.

BLOOD TYPES

Blood Type	Special Protein	Can Give Blood To	Can Receive Blood From
A	A	A and AB	A and O
B	B	B and AB	B and O
AB	A and B	AB	Anyone
O	Neither	Anyone	O

Blood donation

Blood transfusions have saved many lives. Blood is often needed for people who have been in accidents or who are having surgery. If other healthy people did not donate some of their blood, these blood transfusions would not be possible.

Usually, to donate blood, a person must be at least 17 years old. He must be healthy and weigh at least 110 lb. When a person donates blood, his body makes more blood cells to replace the ones he has given.

After the blood is donated, it is tested to determine the blood type. It is also checked for diseases. The blood is often separated into its parts: plasma, red blood cells, white blood cells, and platelets. This way several patients can use different parts of the same unit of donated blood. The blood is stored in a blood bank until someone needs it. Most donated blood can be stored for only a short time before it is no longer useful. That is why **blood donors**, people who donate their blood, are always needed.

1. What is the liquid part of the blood?
2. Which blood cells carry oxygen to all parts of the body?
3. Which blood cells help fight disease?
4. What are the four main blood types?

Meet the SCIENTIST Charles DREW

Charles Drew (1904–1950) was an African American surgeon in the early twentieth century. At that time, blood could not be stored for very long. After a few days, it would no longer be good. Drew, however, found a way to separate the plasma from the red blood cells. This way, the blood could be stored for much longer and then later mixed and used. He also discovered that plasma by itself can be used with blood of any type. This means that people who could not receive a certain type of whole blood could still receive plasma from that type of blood.

During World War II, Drew helped establish blood banks. He also found ways to preserve plasma so that it could be shipped over great distances. Many wounded soldiers were saved because of Drew's discoveries. He also created "bloodmobiles." These refrigerated trucks could safely carry donated blood to where it was needed. Bloodmobiles are still used today by organizations such as the Red Cross.

Explorations Inside of Me

You know the names of several important organs in your body, such as the heart, liver, and lungs. You also know some of the functions, or jobs, of each of these organs. But do you know where these organs are located inside of you? In this exploration, you will make a map of the inside of your body.

What to do

1. On a large sheet of paper, have a partner trace an outline of your body. Use illustrations in a reference book to help cut out shapes to represent your lungs and heart. Use red construction paper for the heart and tan paper for the lungs.
2. Attach the lungs and heart to the appropriate places on the outline of your body. Use illustrations in a reference book to help you know where to place the organs. You may choose to add other organs, such as the liver, kidneys, and stomach.
3. With a red marker or a red colored pencil, draw and label the aorta and pulmonary artery. You may choose to add coronary arteries and other main arteries, such as the hepatic artery, carotid artery, subclavian artery, and femoral artery.
4. With a blue marker or a blue colored pencil, draw several of the main veins. Include and label the superior vena cava, inferior vena cava, and pulmonary veins. You may choose to add coronary veins and other major veins, such as the hepatic vein, jugular vein, subclavian vein, and femoral vein as well.
5. Add other features, such as hair and eyes, if desired. Display the map of your body.

Pump and Pour

Can you work as fast as your heart does? Every time your heart beats, it pushes about 60 mL of blood into your arteries. In just about one minute, your blood has been circulated throughout your entire body!

In this activity, the water represents the blood in your body. The plastic cup represents the amount of blood that your heart pumps with each beat. See if you can transfer water as efficiently as your heart pumps blood.

Process skills
- Predicting
- Measuring and using numbers
- Making and using models
- Collecting and recording data
- Defining operationally

Problem

How many cups of water can you transfer in one minute?

Materials:
2 buckets
5 L water
plastic cup, 3 oz
stopwatch
Activity Manual

Procedures

1. You will need at least two people for this activity—one person to time and to count and one person to transfer the water.
2. Complete the hypothesis in your Activity Manual.
3. Place the two buckets next to each other. Fill one bucket with 5 L of water.
4. Have one person start timing. Have the other person use the plastic cup to scoop water out of the bucket. The cup should be completely full. Pour the water into the other bucket without spilling any. The timer should count the number of cups of water that are transferred.
5. Stop the timing at one minute. Record the number of cups transferred.
6. Refill the first bucket with 5 L of water.

 7. Repeat steps 4–6 for each person in your group.

 8. Record the number of cups each member of the group transferred. Graph them in your Activity Manual.

Conclusions

- Was your hypothesis correct?
- How does the amount of water that you transferred compare to the amount of blood that your heart pumps in one minute?
- How did your amount compare to those of others in your group?

Follow-up

- Time how long it takes to transfer all 5 L of water to the other bucket.

Cleaning Your Blood

The circulatory system carries oxygen and nutrients to every cell in your body. As your cells use the oxygen and nutrients, they produce waste products. These wastes include carbon dioxide and unwanted minerals. If the wastes stayed inside of you, your cells could not work as they should. Your body would get poisoned. You might even die.

So God gave you organs that "clean" your body. These organs work with your circulatory system to remove waste products from your body. Some of these organs are your skin, lungs, and kidneys. These organs are always at work to help remove wastes from your body.

Your Skin

Some wastes are released from the body as sweat. A mixture of water, salts, and other wastes are moved out of the blood into sweat glands. When your body temperature rises, the fluid, or sweat, is released from your sweat glands. It travels to the surface of your skin through a tube and exits your body through the pores in your skin.

Your Lungs

Other wastes, such as carbon dioxide, are removed by the lungs during respiration. When you inhale, you breathe in the mixture of gases that are in the air. In your lungs, the red blood cells pick up oxygen from the air. The red blood cells also release the carbon dioxide that your body produces. Your lungs then exhale the carbon dioxide and the unused gases out of your body.

Your Skin

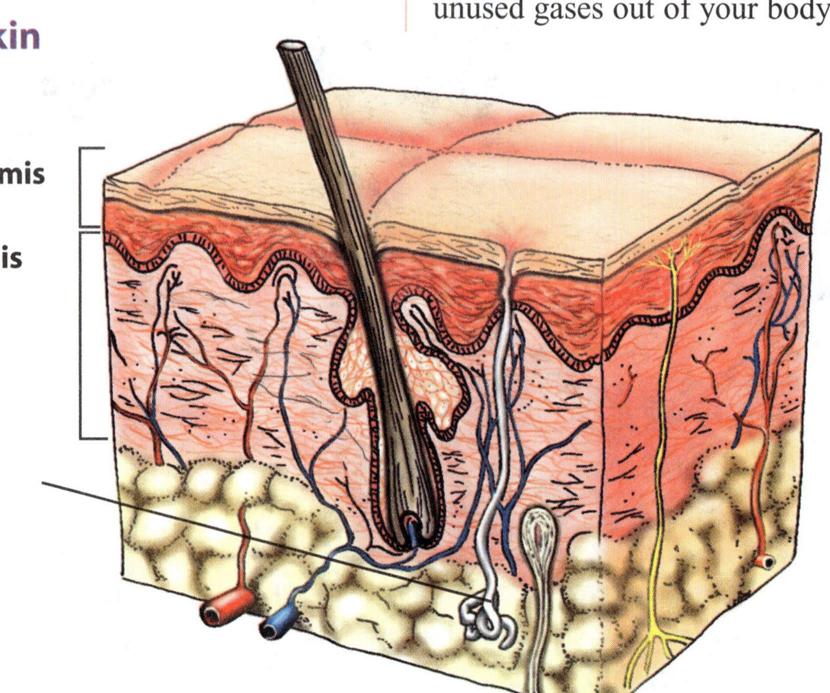

Your Kidneys

Most people have two kidneys. These bean-shaped organs are located on either side of your spine, just under your bottom rib. Each of your kidneys is about the size of your fist. Your kidneys have many functions, but their most important job is cleaning your blood. They remove wastes and excess water from your blood.

Blood flows into the kidneys from the *renal artery*. Inside each kidney, there are tiny filters, called *nephrons* (NEF rons). Each kidney has more than one million nephrons. They clean the blood by removing waste material. Once the blood is cleaned, it flows out of the kidneys and back to the heart. The wastes that have been cleaned out of the blood are combined with water to make *urine*. These wastes are sent to the bladder and stored there until they are eliminated from the body.

Your Kidneys

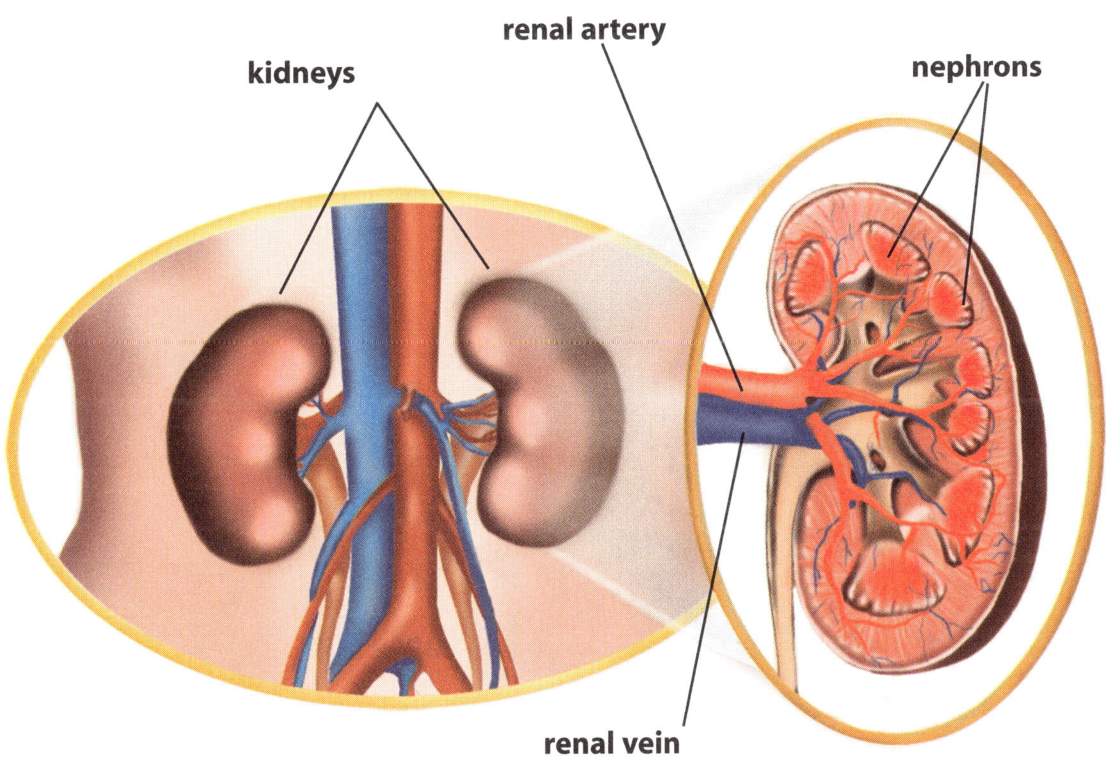

Protecting Your Heart

"Stay active." "Get plenty of exercise." "Eat your vegetables." "Visit the doctor for regular checkups." You have probably heard this kind of advice many times. And this advice can help your heart stay healthy.

Some heart-related problems and diseases are inherited. Others are the result of habits and choices. How you live your life can affect the health of your heart. Wise choices and healthy living habits can help you avoid some heart problems and diseases.

Eating the right kind of food is one of the best ways to keep your heart healthy. Doctors usually suggest that people eat a variety of foods from each food group. Eating food that is good for you can help prevent many health problems.

Some problems can develop from poor eating habits. For example, a person who often eats high-fat foods, such as fried food and potato chips, can damage his arteries. The fatty materials build up inside the arteries. Over time, the arteries can become clogged. This can be very dangerous. The blocked blood vessels do not allow blood to get through. This can prevent the oxygen and nutrients in the blood from getting to organs and other areas of the body. Surgery may need to be done so that the blood flow is restored.

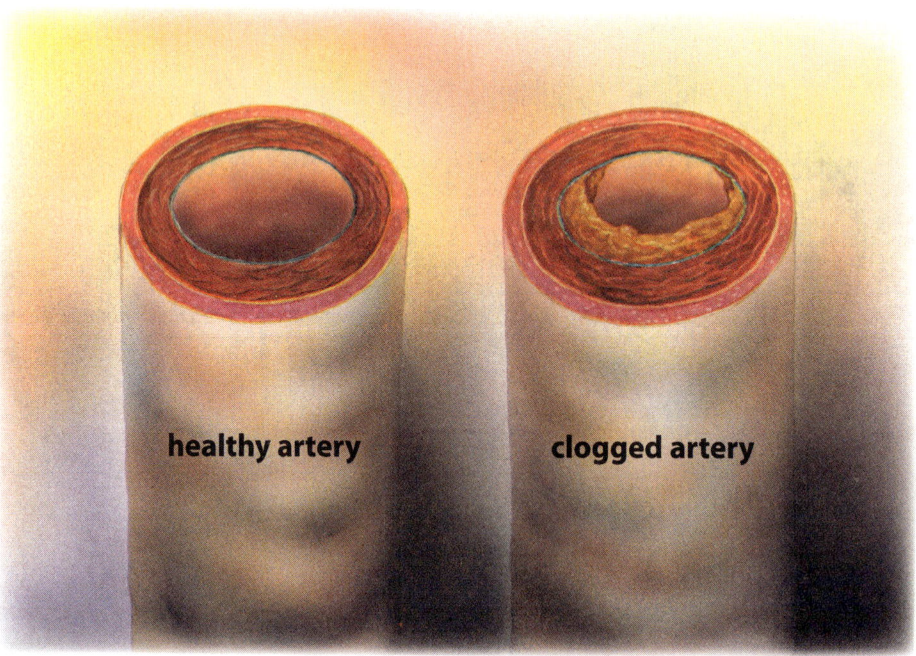

Exercise helps keep the heart healthy.

Another way to keep your heart healthy is to exercise. Just like other muscles, the heart muscle needs to be exercised. Walking, running, swimming, bike riding, and jumping rope are good exercises. They all will strengthen your heart.

You can help prevent many kinds of health problems simply by not smoking. Smoking leads to many heart problems. It damages the heart and blood vessels. This makes them work harder. Smoking also reduces the amount of oxygen in the blood. A person who smokes is more likely to develop heart disease or other problems.

Remembering Our Creator

God is the perfect Creator. In His wisdom, He has given man an amazing transportation system. The heart pumps blood. The blood vessels carry blood to every cell in the body. Each cell receives the oxygen and nutrients that it needs. This system keeps the body alive. No man-made transportation system could ever be as efficient.

God allows man to discover and imitate many of His designs. Man's technology has improved health care, has made life easier, and has made us aware of things that cannot be seen. But none of this would be possible without God. He holds all things in place. As Colossians 1:16–17 reminds us, "all things were created by him, and for him: And he is before all things, and by him all things consist."

1. What are three organs that help the body "clean" itself?
2. How do the kidneys help remove wastes?
3. What are some ways to keep your heart healthy?

Answer the Questions

1. What causes a person's heart rate to adjust when he exercises?

___

___

___

2. What are the three main types of blood vessels, and what is the basic job of each type of blood vessel?

___

___

___

3. What are three organs that help the body remove wastes from the circulatory system?

___

___

___

Solve the Problem

The college that your older sister attends is having a blood drive. Your sister has type O blood. One of her friends says that your sister would be an especially good donor because of her blood type. Why would that be true? What requirements must she meet in order to give blood?

___

___

___

___

___

Glossary

A

acoustics The science of sound.

adaptation Any special characteristic or skill that helps a living thing survive in its environment.

air A mixture of nitrogen, oxygen, carbon dioxide, and other gases in the atmosphere.

air mass A large body of air that has about the same temperature and moisture.

air pressure The pressure caused by the weight of the gases in the air.

altitude A measurement of the distance above sea level.

alveoli The tiny air sacs in the lungs where the exchange of carbon dioxide and oxygen takes place.

amber The sap from a plant that has hardened into a yellow gemlike substance.

amplitude A measurement that shows the amount of energy in a wave. In a transverse wave, such as light, amplitude is measured by the height of the wave. In a sound wave, amplitude is the intensity of the sound.

anemia A disorder that occurs when a person's body does not have enough red blood cells or hemoglobin, thus limiting the amount of oxygen available to the body.

anemometer An instrument that measures the speed of wind.

aorta The largest artery in the body, attached to the left ventricle of the heart.

arteriole One of the smallest arteries in the body.

artery A blood vessel that carries blood from the heart to the rest of the body.

asthma A respiratory disorder that causes the bronchial tubes to become narrow from time to time.

atmosphere A thin blanket of gases and dust particles that surrounds the earth.

atom The smallest particle that makes up matter.

atrium One of the top chambers on each side of the heart.

B

barometer An instrument that measures air pressure.

biodiversity A term that refers to how many species of plants and animals are found in a specific area.

biome A large area of the earth with plants and animals that share similar environmental conditions.

biosphere All of the different areas on the earth where life can exist and the living organisms that live there.

blizzard A snowstorm with strong, freezing winds and blowing snow.

blood donor A person who donates blood.

blood transfusion The transfer of blood from one person to another.

bronchi The two respiratory tubes inside the lungs that branch off the trachea.

bronchial tube One of the smaller air passages that branches off the bronchi.

bronchiole One of the smallest air passages; connects the bronchial tubes and the alveoli.

C

calorie The amount of thermal energy needed to raise the temperature of one gram of water one degree Celsius.

capillary One of the smallest blood vessels; connects arteries and veins.

carbon dating A dating method that measures the amount of carbon 14 in a fossil to try to determine when the fossilized organism lived.

carbon film A fossil formed when leaves decay underneath the weight of sediment and leave an outline of themselves on a rock.

carnivore A consumer that eats other consumers instead of eating plants.

cast A perfect replica of the shape of an organism formed by sediment that has been pressed into a mold.

chemical change A change to matter that occurs when two or more pure substances combine chemically and lose their individual properties.

cilia The tiny, hairlike projections found in the nasal passages, trachea, and bronchi, as well as in other parts of the body.

cirrus cloud A high, thin, curly-looking cloud.

cleavage The breaking of a mineral along smooth, straight lines or into flat sheets.

climate The typical weather of a region over a long period of time.

cloud A mass of water droplets or ice crystals that is suspended in the air.

cold front A type of front that occurs when a cool air mass pushes itself under a weaker warm air mass.

color The color of the mineral that you see.

commensalism A type of symbiotic relationship in which one partner is benefited and the other partner is neither helped nor harmed.

community All the different species, both plant and animal, that live in a particular ecosystem.

competition Two or more organisms trying to use the same resources.

compound A kind of matter that is formed by combining atoms from different elements.

compression The part of a sound wave or other longitudinal wave in which the particles of matter are pushed together.

concave mirror A mirror that curves inward.

concentration The measurement of the amount of a solute dissolved in a solvent.

condensation The process of a substance changing from a gas to a liquid.

conduction The heat that occurs when the particles of a substance bump into each other.

conductor A substance that allows heat to move easily through it.

conifer A type of tree whose seeds develop in cones.

consumer An organism that depends on producers for food. Consumers cannot get energy directly from the sun.

convection The heat that occurs as the particles of a liquid or a gas move from one place to another in a circular motion.

convex mirror A mirror that curves outward.

core The center of the earth.

coronary artery One of the arteries located in the heart.

coronary vein One of the veins located in the heart.

crest The highest point of a transverse wave.

crust The outer layer of the earth.

crystal The structure that results from the orderly arrangement of mineral particles.

cumulus cloud A large, fluffy cloud with a flat base.

cycle A regular pattern of change.

D

decibel A unit for the measurement of the intensity of a sound.

deciduous tree A tree that loses its leaves in the winter.

decomposer An organism that helps break down dead things and wastes, returning minerals and nutrients to the environment.

decomposition The process of decaying, or rotting away.

density The mass of a certain amount of matter in a certain space.

diaphragm A strong, curved muscle below the lungs attached to the lower ribs and backbone.

drought A stress that occurs when the amount of rainfall in an ecosystem is less than what is considered normal for that area.

E

echo A sound wave that reflects back toward its source and is heard again.

echolocation The ability to "see" by using sound waves.

ecologist A scientist who studies how living things interact with their environment.

ecosystem The combination of all the living organisms and their environment in a certain section of the earth.

electrocardiograph (EKG) A machine that records the electrical changes that happen during the heartbeat cycle.

electromagnetic spectrum All the electromagnetic waves arranged in order of their wavelengths or frequencies.

electromagnetic wave A wave that can move through matter and through space.

element Matter that is made up of only one kind of atom.

endangered species A species whose population is so small that it is in danger of becoming extinct.

energy The ability to do work.

environment The nonliving part of an ecosystem.

epiglottis The small flap of tissue covering the trachea that closes when eating and opens when breathing.

erosion The movement of sediment and other materials from one place to another.

esophagus The food pipe; the passage that leads to the stomach.

evaporation A form of vaporization that occurs when the temperature of a liquid is below its boiling point.

evolution A theory stating that life on earth developed through a series of gradual changes over a period of millions of years.

evolved To have gradually developed.

excavation The process of removing fossils from the surrounding rock.

exhale To breathe out.

extinct Describes a species that no longer exists.

extinction The condition of being extinct.

F

fog A stratus cloud that lies on the surface of the earth.

food chain The transfer of energy and nutrients through a community.

food web Several food chains linked together.

fossil Any part or trace of a living organism that is naturally preserved after it dies.

fossil fuel A fuel formed when the remains of plants and animals are buried quickly.

freezing The process of a liquid changing to a solid.

frequency The number of waves that pass a point in one second.

front The boundary formed when two unlike air masses meet.

fuel A substance that releases energy when burned.

G

gamma ray A powerful and invisible electromagnetic wave used to treat some kinds of cancer; the shortest wave in the electromagnetic spectrum.

gas The state of matter that does not have a definite shape or a definite volume.

gemstone A mineral that can be cut and polished for use.

geologic ages The long periods of time during which evolutionists believe that life on earth developed gradually.

geologist A scientist who studies the nonliving parts of the earth.

global winds Winds that move in large circular belts around the earth.

ground water Precipitation that has soaked into the ground and is stored there.

H

habitat The place where an organism lives.

habitat destruction The destruction of plant and animal habitats.

hail Frozen precipitation that usually falls during warm weather.

hardness The ability of a mineral to resist scratching.

heart A hollow organ with muscular walls that pumps blood throughout the body.

heart rate The number of times that the heart beats in one minute.

heat The transfer, or movement, of thermal energy from one substance to another.

heat wave A period of time with higher-than-average temperatures.

herbivore A consumer that eats only plants.

hertz A unit for the measurement of the frequency of a wave.

hibernation The deep sleep experienced by some animals during the winter months.

host The plant or animal that a parasite lives on.

humidity Water vapor in the atmosphere.

hurricane A storm with spiraling winds that forms over the Atlantic Ocean or the eastern Pacific Ocean.

I

igneous rock A rock that has formed from volcanic magma or lava.

individual One member of a certain population.

inferior vena cava The vein that carries blood back to the heart from the lower body.

infrared wave An invisible electromagnetic wave that transmits heat from objects.

inhale To breathe in.

inorganic Describes a substance made of things that have never been alive.

instinct The basic knowledge and skills needed for survival that are inherited by each member of a population.

insulator A substance that does not allow heat to move easily through it.

invasive species A species that is not native to a certain area and either is causing harm or could cause harm to native populations.

involuntary breathing The automatic breathing controlled by the brain.

K

kidney One of two bean-shaped organs located on either side of the spine; removes wastes and excess water from the blood.

kinetic energy The energy that an object or substance has because of its motion.

L

lapidary A skilled craftsman who cuts gemstones in order to reveal their beauty.

larynx The area of the trachea containing the vocal cords; used in breathing, swallowing, and talking.

learned behavior A behavior that cannot be inherited but must be learned.

lens A piece of glass or other transparent object that refracts light and produces an image.

light A form of wave energy; an electromagnetic wave that can be seen.

lightning A type of static electricity that moves between clouds or between clouds and the earth.

liquid The state of matter that has a definite volume but no definite shape.

local wind A wind that is influenced by temperature changes in a small area or place.

longitudinal wave A wave in which the particles of a medium vibrate back and forth along the same path that the wave is moving; also called a compressional wave.

lung capacity The amount of air that can be taken into the lungs with one normal breath.

lungs The two saclike organs that remove carbon dioxide from the blood and replace the carbon dioxide with oxygen.

lung volume The amount of air in the lungs at one time.

luster The quality and intensity of light reflected from a mineral's surface.

M

magma The hot, melted rock found in the mantle.

mantle The middle layer of the earth.

marine biome Another name for a saltwater biome, such as the ocean.

mass The amount of material in a substance.

matter A substance that has both volume and mass.

mechanical wave A wave that must have a medium to travel through.

medium The matter through which a wave travels.

melting The process of a solid changing to a liquid.

metamorphic rock Rock that forms by heat and pressure deep below the earth's crust.

meteorologist A scientist who studies the atmosphere and the weather.

microwave An invisible electromagnetic wave used by radar, cellular phones, and microwave ovens.

migration The movement of a population from one ecosystem to another.

mineral An inorganic substance found naturally in the earth.

mineralogist A scientist who studies minerals.

mirror Any surface that can reflect light to form an image, or picture, of an object.

mixture Matter that consists of two or more substances that are physically combined.

mold The imprint of an organism that has been pressed into a rock

molecule A particle formed when atoms join with other atoms. The atoms that make up molecules can be from the same element or from different elements.

monsoon A wind that changes direction with the seasons.

mucus A sticky, moist substance produced by special cells in the nose and other parts of the body.

mutualism A type of symbiotic relationship in which both partners are benefited by the interaction.

N

nasal cavity A large air space located behind the nostrils; divided into two passages by a wall of bone and cartilage.

nasal passage One of the two passages of the nasal cavity; extends from the nostrils to the beginning of the throat.

native species Any plant or animal species that is originally living in an ecosystem.

nephrons Tiny filters inside the kidneys that remove waste material from the blood.

niche An organism's specific function, or job, in an ecosystem. This includes where it eats, what it eats, how it gets shelter, how it reproduces, and how it raises its young.

nimbus A term that describes clouds that produce precipitation.

nocturnal Describes organisms that are active at night and sleep during the day.

noise A sound that is harsh, unwanted, or surprising.

nonrenewable resource A resource that is being used faster than it is forming.

nostril One of the two openings in the nose.

O

omnivore A consumer that eats both plants and other animals.

opaque A term used to describe an object that does not let light pass through it.

ore A type of rock containing a minable amount of minerals.

organic Describes any particles that were once part of a living thing.

oscilloscope A machine that changes mechanical sound waves into electrical pictures that can be seen on a graph.

P

pacemaker The small group of cells that send an electric current to the heart, controlling the number of times that the heart beats.

paleontologist A person who studies fossils.

paleontology The scientific study of fossils.

parasite An organism that lives on or in another organism and takes nourishment from that organism.

parasitism A type of symbiotic relationship in which the interaction helps one partner but harms the other partner.

peat Dense layers of partially decayed plant material; usually found in bogs.

permafrost The permanently frozen soil found on the tundra.

petrified fossil A fossil formed when part of a living organism decays and is replaced by minerals that harden into rock.

pharynx Another name for the throat.

photosynthesis The process by which plants use energy from the sun, carbon dioxide, and water to make food. Sugar molecules are formed, and oxygen is released.

physical change A change in matter that does not form a new substance.

physical property A characteristic of a substance that can be observed without changing the identity of the substance.

pigment An opaque substance used to color other materials.

pitch The highness or lowness of a sound.

plane mirror A mirror that has a flat surface.

plasma The liquid part of blood in which the blood cells and platelets are suspended; contains dissolved proteins, nutrients, and sugars.

platelet A small cell fragment that helps form blood clots.

pollution Anything that makes the water, air, or land dirty.

population All the organisms of a species that live in an ecosystem.

potential energy The energy that an object or substance has because of its position or condition.

precious stone A gemstone that is beautiful and rare.

precipitation Any type of moisture that falls through the atmosphere to the earth; includes rain, snow, sleet, and hail.

predator An animal that hunts and eats other animals.

prey The animals that a predator hunts.

primary colors The basic colors that can be used to make other colors.

producer An organism, such as a plant, that makes its own food. Producers get their energy directly from the sun.

pulmonary artery The artery that goes from the heart to the lungs.

pulmonary vein Any of the veins that go from the lungs to the heart.

pulse The push of blood through the arteries.

R

radiation Heat transmitted through air or empty space in the form of electromagnetic waves.

radio wave An invisible electromagnetic wave that carries energy used for radio and television broadcasting; the longest wave in the electromagnetic spectrum.

rain Precipitation formed when water droplets in the clouds join together to form larger drops and fall to the earth.

red blood cell A biconcave-shaped blood cell that carries oxygen to all parts of the body.

reflection The bouncing of a wave, such as a light wave or a sound wave, off an object.

refraction The bending of light as it passes from one medium into another.

relative humidity The amount of water vapor in the air compared to the amount that the air could hold at that temperature.

renewable resource A resource, such as trees, that can be replaced.

resource Any available material that can meet a need of a living organism.

respiration **1.** The process through which living organisms use sugar and oxygen for energy. Carbon dioxide is released. **2.** The process of breathing.

respiratory system Another name for the breathing system.

rock A hard, natural substance made of one or more minerals.

S

salinity The amount of dissolved salt in a certain amount of water.

saturation The point at which a solvent cannot dissolve any more of a solute.

scavenger An animal that eats things that have already died.

season A regular division of the year.

sediment Weathered particles of rock.

sedimentary rock Rock that forms when layers of weathered rock, minerals, and organisms harden.

semi-precious stone A gemstone that is less valuable than a precious stone.

sleet Precipitation that occurs when liquid raindrops fall through air that is below freezing.

smelting One process used to separate ore from rock.

snow Precipitation that forms when ice crystals in the clouds join together and fall toward the earth.

soil The loose material on the surface of the earth formed from bits of weathered rock and other materials.

solid The state of matter that has a definite volume and a definite shape.

solubility The ability of a solvent to dissolve a certain amount of a solute.

solute A substance that is dissolved in a solution.

solution A type of mixture in which all the substances are spread evenly throughout; also called a homogeneous mixture.

solvent The substance that dissolves the solute in a solution.

sound A vibration that can be heard.

speed The distance that one wave travels in one second.

speed of sound The measurement of how fast sound travels through the air under specific atmospheric conditions.

states of matter The physical properties of being in the form of a solid, liquid, or gas.

stationary front A type of front that occurs when air masses push against each other but do not move.

stomata The tiny pores in the leaves of plants that allow air and water to move in and out of the plant.

stratus cloud A low, flat cloud.

streak The color of the mark made when a sample of a mineral is rubbed on a harder surface.

stress Any physical hazard to life caused by having too much or too little of things needed for life.

succession A series of gradual changes in the populations of organisms in an ecosystem.

succulent A plant that has the ability to store water in its stem or leaves.

superior vena cava The vein that carries blood back to the heart from the upper body.

symbiosis An interaction between two species over a long period of time.

synthetic Describes an object or a substance that is manmade.

T

taiga The biome located just below the tundra; also called the coniferous forest.

temperature The measure of the average kinetic energy of the particles in a substance.

thermal energy The total kinetic energy of the particles in an object or a substance.

thermal expansion The property of a substance in which its kinetic energy increases without changing the state of the substance.

thermometer An instrument that measures temperature.

threatened species A species whose population could become endangered in the near future.

thunder Vibrations in the air produced by the rapid change of air temperature after a bolt of lightning occurs.

thunderstorm A type of storm that occurs when a large, swift-moving warm front meets a cold air mass.

timbre The quality of a sound that distinguishes the sound from others of the same pitch and volume.

tornado A funnel-shaped windstorm on land; has strong winds.

trace fossil A fossil that is not an actual part of an organism but is of something that a plant or animal left behind.

trachea The windpipe; the air passage that leads to the lungs.

translucent A term used to describe an object that allows most light waves to pass through it.

transparent A term used to describe a clear object that allows all light waves to pass through it.

transpiration The process through which plants release water vapor into the air.

transverse wave A wave that moves perpendicular to the way that its medium is moving.

troposphere The layer of the atmosphere that is closest to the earth.

trough The lowest point of a transverse wave.

typhoon A storm with spiraling winds that forms over the western Pacific Ocean.

U

ultraviolet ray An invisible electromagnetic wave that causes some materials to glow.

V

valve A small flap of tissue found in the heart and veins that opens and closes to allow blood to flow in only one direction.

vaporization The process of a liquid changing to a gas.

vegetation The plant life found in a certain area.

vein **1.** A pocket or strip of a mineral within the earth. **2.** A blood vessel that carries blood back to the heart.

vena cavae The largest veins in the body.

ventricle One of the lower chambers of the heart.

venule One of the smallest veins in the body.

vibration A rapid back-and-forth movement.

visible spectrum The colors of visible light arranged in order by their wavelengths or frequencies.

vital lung capacity The maximum amount of air that a person can exhale after a deep breath.

vocal cords The two small bands of elastic tissue that stretch across the inside of the larynx.

volume **1.** The amount of space taken up by an object. **2.** The loudness of sound.

voluntary breathing The breathing that is controlled by thinking about the actual action.

W

warm front A type of front that results when a warm air mass moves over a slower cool air mass.

wave A disturbance that moves energy from place to place.

wavelength The distance from one point on a wave to the same point on the next wave.

wave speed The distance that one wave travels in one second.

weather The condition of the atmosphere at any moment in time.

weather forecast A prediction of future weather conditions.

weathering The wearing away of rocks.

weather warning A warning issued by the National Weather Service that a storm has begun.

weather watch A warning issued by the National Weather Service to alert people that a storm may occur.

weight The measure of the amount of force that gravity places on an object.

wetland Land that is almost always wet; usually classified as a marsh, swamp, or bog.

white blood cell A blood cell that helps the body fight diseases and infections.

wind Moving air.

wind vane An instrument that shows the direction from which the wind is blowing.

X

x-ray An invisible electromagnetic wave used in medicine, art, industry, and engineering.

Index

A

acoustics, 230
adaptation, 182–85
air, 112
air mass, 117–18
air pressure, 113
allergies, 278
alloy, 75
altitude, 113
alveoli, 272
amber, 32
amplitude, 238
anemometer, 121
Anning, Mary, 45
aorta, 289
aquatic biome, 158–61
arterioles, 289
artery, 288–89
asthma, 278
atmosphere, 112, 114–15
atrium, 283

B

barometer, 113
biodiversity, 154, 159
Biome, 140–41
  aquatic, 158–61
  coniferous forest, 144–45
  deciduous forest, 146–47
  desert, 150–51
  grassland, 148–49
  mountain, 156
  rainforest, 154–55
  tundra, 142–43
biosphere, 140
blizzard, 131
blood, 292–96
blood donor, 296
blood transfusion, 295
blood types, 295
bog, 145, 163
bronchi, 270
bronchial tubes, 272
bronchioles, 272
bronchitis, 277

C

calorie, 92–93
capillary, 272, 288–89
carbon cycle, 194–95, 199
carbon dating, 40–41
carbon film, 31
carnivore, 173
carnivorous plants, 183
cast, 31, 36–37
chemical change, 67
cilia, 267
circulatory system, 282–303
cirrus cloud, 127–28
cleavage, 13
climate, 140, 156
cloud types, 127–28
community, 171
competition, 179
compound, 66
compression, 217
concave mirror, 247
concentration, 76
condensation, 65, 124, 198
conduction, 94–95
conductor, 95
coniferous forest, 144–45
conifers, 145
consumer, 172–73
convection, 96
convection current, 96
convex mirror, 247
coral reef, 159
Creation, 33–35, 40–41
crest, 238

crystal structure, 8–9
cumulonimbus cloud, 127, 129
cumulus cloud, 127, 129
Cycle, 192
carbon, 194–95, 199
nitrogen, 196–97, 199
seasons, 192–93, 199
water, 124, 198–99

D

decibels, 224
deciduous forest, 146–47
decomposer, 173
density, 59
desert, 150–51
dew, 126
diaphragm, 264
dinosaurs, 44–51
Drew, Charles, 296
drought, 204

E

Earth layers
core, 4–5
crust, 4–6, 8, 20, 22
mantle, 4–5
echo, 226
echolocation, 227
ecologist, 181
ecosystem, 170–73, 176–77
electrocardiograph, 285
electromagnetic spectrum, 240–49, 252–56
electromagnetic waves, 236–37, 252–56
element, 66
endangered species, 211
Energy, 84
kinetic, 84–85
potential, 84
thermal, 85
energy pyramid, 178
environment, 170, 202, 204
epiglottis, 268
erosion, 6, 24
esophagus, 268
evaporation, 65, 124, 198
evolution, 33–35, 40–41
excavation, 38–39
exhale, 262
extinction, 32, 50–51
extinct species, 211

F

fire, 202–3
flood, 203
fog, 127
food chain, 176
food web, 176–77
fossil, 30–35, 38–49
fossil fuel, 100
fracture, 13
freezing, 64
frequency, 218, 239
freshwater biomes, 160–61
Frisch, Karl von, 254
front (weather), 118
frost, 126
fuel, 100–101

G

Galilei, Galileo, 236
gamma rays, 256
gas, 62
gemstone, 16–17, 20
geologist, 4
grassland, 148–49
ground water, 198
Gutenberg, Beno, 5

H

habitat, 171
habitat destruction, 171, 208–9
hail, 125
Harvey, William, 291
heart, 282–83
heart rate, 284
heat, 94–106
heat wave, 131
hemoglobin, 293

herbivore, 172
hertz, 218
hibernation, 147, 185
host, 186
Howard, Luke, 127
humidity, 126
hurricane, 131

I

igneous rock, 22–23
individual, 171
infrared waves, 253
inhale, 262
instinct, 188–89
insulator, 95
invasive species, 210
involuntary breathing, 263

K

Kelvin, Lord, 87
kidneys, 301
kinetic energy, 84–85

L

Landsteiner, Karl, 295
lapidary, 20
larynx, 268–69
laser, 249
learned behavior, 189
lens, 248
light, 236–57
lightning, 130
liquid, 56, 61
longitudinal wave, 237
lung capacity, 271
lungs, 271–72
lung volume, 274
luster, 11

M

magma, 4–5, 20, 22
marine biome, 158–59
marsh, 162
mass, 58
matter, 56
mechanical wave, 216, 237
medium, 231, 240
melting, 63
metamorphic rock, 25
meteorologist, 134
Michelson, Albert, 236
microwaves, 253
migration, 147, 184–85
mineral, 8–13, 16–21
mineralogist, 8
Minerals, characteristics of
  cleavage, 13
  color, 10
  crystal structure, 8–9
  fracture, 13
  hardness, 12
  luster, 11
  streak, 10
mirror, 246–47
mixture, 70–75
Mohs scale, 12
mold, 31, 36–37
molecule, 66–67
monsoon, 193
montane forest, 156
mountains, 156

N

nasal cavity, 266
nasal passages, 266–67
National Weather Service, 132
native species, 210
Newton, Sir Isaac, 240
niche, 171
Niepce, Joseph, 248
nimbostratus cloud, 127–28
nimbus cloud, 127
nitrogen cycle, 196–97
nocturnal, 151
noise, 226
nostrils, 266

O
ocean, 158–59
omnivore, 172
opaque, 241
ore, 18, 101
organic, 7
oscilloscope, 218
Owen, Sir Richard, 44
ozone, 115

P
pacemaker, 285
paleontology, 38
parasite, 186
peat, 163
permafrost, 142
petrified fossil, 31
pharynx, 268
photosynthesis, 172, 182–83, 194
physical change, 63
physical property, 60
pigments, 243
pitch, 222–23
plane mirror, 246
plasma, 292
platelets, 294
Plot, Robert, 48
pneumonia, 277
pollution, 209
population, 171
potential energy, 84
prairie, 148
precipitation, 124–25, 127, 198–99
predator, 176
prey, 176
primary colors, 242–43
producer, 172, 176, 178
pulse, 284

R
radiation, 97
radio waves, 252
rain, 124
rainforest, 154–55
red blood cells, 293
reflecting telescope, 248
reflection, 241, 246–47
refracting telescope, 248
refraction, 240–41
respiration (breathing), 272
respiration (cellular), 194
respiratory system, 262–79
rock, 22–27

S
salinity, 158
saturation, 76
savanna, 149
scavenger, 173
seasons, 192–93
sediment, 6, 24
sedimentary rock, 24
septum (heart), 283
sleet, 125
smelting, 18
smoking, 279, 303
snow, 125
soil, 7
solid, 61
solubility, 77
solute, 74
solution, 74–77
solvent, 74
sonar, 227
sound, 216–33
speed of sound, 218–19
states of matter, 60–65
stethoscope, 231, 284
stomata, 152, 182, 198
stratus cloud, 127–28
streak, 10
stress, 202–11
succession, 205
succulent, 151
swamp, 162

Symbiosis, 186–87
commensalism, 187
mutualism, 187
parasitism, 186–87

T

taiga, 144–45
temperature, 86–87
thermal energy, 85
thermal expansion, 91
thermometer, 86–87
Thomson, William, 87
threatened species, 211
thunder, 130
thunderstorm, 130
timbre, 225
topsoil, 7
tornado, 131
trace fossil, 31
trachea, 268–70
translucent, 241
transparent, 241
transpiration, 198
transverse wave, 237–39
trough, 238
tundra, 142–43
typhoon, 131

U

ultrasound, 227
ultraviolet rays, 254

V

valve, 283, 290
vaporization, 64–65
vegetation, 148
vein (blood), 290
vein (mineral), 20
vena cavae, 290
ventricle, 283
venules, 290
vibration, 216–17
visible light, 240–49
visible spectrum, 240–43
vocal cords, 269
volume (matter), 56–57
volume (sound), 224–25
voluntary breathing, 263

W

water cycle, 124, 198
Wave, 216
electromagnetic, 237, 252–56
light, 236–57
longitudinal, 237
mechanical, 217, 237
properties, 238–39
sound, 216–33
transverse, 237–39
wavelength, 218, 238
weather, 115–21, 124–32, 134–35
weather forecast, 134–35
weathering, 6, 23–24
weather warning, 132
weather watch, 132
weight, 58
wetland, 162–63
white blood cells, 294
Wind, 116
global winds, 119
land and sea breezes, 120
local winds, 120
mountain and valley winds, 121
polar easterlies, 119
prevailing westerlies, 119
trade winds, 119
wind vane, 121

X

x-rays, 255

Photograph Credits

The following agencies and individuals have furnished materials to meet the photographic needs of this textbook. We wish to express our gratitude to them for their important contribution.

American Geological Institute
Art Resource
David Aubrey
Jack Ballard
Nick Baker
Bob Jones University Museum & Gallery
Patty Brdar
Dr. Richard Busch
William M. Ciesla
Brandon Cole
Albert Copley
Corbis
COREL Corporation
Gerald & Buff Corsi
Dr. Custer
Jeff J. Daly
Alain Darbellay
DeBeers
Aaron Dickey
Harold Dickey
Reinhard Dirscherl
Wally Eberhart
Patrick J. Endres
Petty Officer 1st Class Wes Eplen
Fabre Minerals
Federal Emergency Management Agency (FEMA)
The Field Museum
Floridanature.org
Megan Foreman
Forest Health Management International
Forestry Images
Joyce Garland
Geolite
Getty Images
GGGems.com
Arthur Glauberman
Beth Hamel
Harbor Branch Oceanographic Institution
Hemera Technologies, Inc.
Abi Howe
Irocks.com
iStock International, Inc.
Brian D. Johnson
JupiterImages Corporation
Karen Wattenmaker Photography
Breck Kent
James King-Holmes
Ted Kinsman
Roger Klocek
C. Knight
Dr. Dennis Kunkel
Joyce Landis
Library of Congress
M. Long
Gil Lopez-Espina
Ken Lucas
Tim McCabe
Joe McDonald
Meade
Howard Miller
Gene E. Moore
National Air and Space Administration (NASA)
National Center for Atmospheric Research
National Oceanic and Atmospheric Administration (NOAA)
David Newman
Joseph O'Brien
Ohaus
Jim Peaco
Susan Perry
PhotoDisc
Photo Researchers, Inc.
John Reade
Kjell B. Sandved
Tobias Schwoerer
Science Photo Library (SPL)
John Sohlden
Doug Sokell
Ron Spomer
Stem Labs, Inc.
Sarah Strawhorn
Simon Taylor
Tom Uhlman
United States Department of Agriculture Forest Service (USDA Forest Service)
United States Department of Agriculture Natural Resources Service (USDA Natural Resources Service)
United States Fish and Wildlife Service (USFWS)
United States Mint (US Mint)
United States Navy (US Navy)
Unusual Films
Visuals Unlimited
Tom Walker
John Weinstein
Pfc. Mary Rose Zenikakis

Cover

Aaron Dickey (hamster)

Unit 1 Opener

© 2005 iStock International, Inc. All Rights Reserved 1

Chapter 1

© 2005 iStock International, Inc. All Rights Reserved 3, 6 (bottom), 19 (middle), 21; PhotoDisc/Getty Images 6 (top, middle), 25 (middle); www.irocks.com/photo by Megan Foreman 8, 10 (top all), 11 (bottom right), 12 (diamond); © Wally Eberhart/Visuals Unlimited 10 (bottom); Unusual Films—Collection of Dr. Custer 11 (top left), 12 (gypsum, apatite); Unusual Films 11 (top right), 12 (quartz, glass), 15, 19 (top left), 22 (both), 26; © Dr. Richard Busch/ www.earthscience.org 11 (bottom left), 12 (talc, topaz), 13 (top, middle), 24 (middle); Fabre Minerals/ www.faberminerals.com 12 (calcite, fluorite, orthoclase), 19 (inset, top right, bottom right); Image by Alain Darbellay courtesy of GGGems.com 12 (corundum); Aaron Dickey 12 (finger, pocket knife), 18; US Mint 12 (penny); © Albert Copley/Visuals Unlimited 13 (bottom); Art Resource, NY 16; photo provided by Geolite,www.geolite.com 17 (bottom); DeBeers 17 (top); © Doug Sokell/Visuals Unlimited 23 (left); ©pattybrdarphoto.com 23 (top right); Joyce Landis 23 (bottom right); © Abi Howe, American Geological Institute/www.earthscience.org 24 (top); Corbis 24 (bottom); © M. Long/Visuals Unlimited 25 (top); Getty Images/Hemera/Thinkstock 25 (bottom)

Chapter 2
Brian D. Johnson 29, 30 (both), 31 (all); © Jeff Daly/Visuals Unlimited 32; Unusual Films 35, 37; © John Reade/Photo Researchers, Inc. 38; Simon Taylor 40; The Field Museum, GN89671_53c, photographer John Weinstein 41; © Ken Lucas/ Visuals Unlimited 47

Unit 2 Opener
PhotoDisc/Getty Images 53

Chapter 3
© 2005 JUPITERIMAGES/ photos.com All Rights Reserved 55; © 2005 Hemera Technologies, Inc. All Rights Reserved 56, 61 (both), 62, 67, 71 (bottom right); Aaron Dickey 57 (both), 64 (top), 70, 71 (bottom left), 73 (bottom); Ohaus 58; © 2005 iStock International, Inc. All Rights Reserved 60 (both), 75 (right); Unusual Films 64 (bottom), 65, 69, 71 (bottom left, top right), 72 (top both), 74 (both), 76 (both), 77 (both), 78, 81; © Dr. Richard Busch/www.earthscienceworld.com 71 (top left); Sarah Strawhorn 75 (left)

Chapter 4
© 2005 JupiterImages Corporation 83; Unusual Films 84, 89, 99; © 2005 iStock International, Inc. All Rights Reserved 87, 97, 100 (middle); © Tom Uhlman/ Visuals Unlimited 91; Aaron Dickey 92; Army photo by Pfc. Mary Rose Zenikakis, 22nd Mobile Public Affairs Detachment 100 (top); © John Sohlden/Visuals Unlimited 100 (bottom left); © 2005 Hemera Technologies, Inc. All rights reserved 100 (bottom right); PhotoDisc/Getty Images 101 (both), 105; Susan Perry 102; Harold Dickey 103; NASA 104 (both)

Unit 3 Opener
© 2005 iStock International, Inc. All Rights Reserved 109

Chapter 5
NASA 111; Unusual Films 113, 137; Library of Congress 117; © 2005 iStock International, Inc. All Rights Reserved 121 (both), 124, 126 (both); Joseph O'Brien, USDA Forest Service, www.forestryimages.org 125 (top); Beth Hamel 125 (middle); C. Knight, National Center for Atmospheric Research 125 (bottom); © 2005 Hemera Technologies, Inc. All Rights Reserved 128 (top); © 2005 JUPITERIMAGES/photos.com. All rights Reserved 128 (left, right); PhotoDisc/Getty Images 129 (both); COREL Corporation 130 (left); NOAA 130 (right), 131 (right), 134 (both); Gene E. Moore—Clearwater, KS tornado of 1991 131 (left)

Chapter 6
PhotoDisc/Getty Images 139, 143 (top left), 151, 159 (left), 160 (bottom), 163; © Patrick J. Endres/Visuals Unlimited 142; Tobias Schwoerer 143 (top right); © 2005 JUPITERIMAGES/photos.com. All Rights Reserved 143 (bottom), 145, 148; Breck Kent 144; COREL Corporation 146; USFWS 147 (left), 162 (both); © Gerald & Buff Corsi/Visuals Unlimited 149 (top); William M. Ciesla, Forest Health Management International, www.forestryimages.org 149 (bottom); © David Newman/Visuals Unlimited 150; Unusual Films 153, 156, 157, 165; © Kjell B. Sandved/ Visuals Unlimited 155 (top left, bottom); Nick Baker 155 (top right); © Brandon Cole/Visuals Unlimited 158; © 2005 Harbor Branch Oceanographic Institution 159 (right); NASA 160 (top)

Unit 4 Opener
© 2005 iStock International, Inc. All Rights Reserved 167

Chapter 7
© 2005 Hemera Technologies, Inc. All Rights Reserved 169; Unusual Films 175, 181; © Ron Spomer/Visuals Unlimited 179 (top); Joe McDonald/Visuals Unlimited 179 (bottom), 183 (bottom); © 2005 iStock International, Inc. All Rights Reserved 183 (top), 187 (bottom right); PhotoDisc/Getty Images 184, 187 (middle); © Tom Walker/ Visuals Unlimited 185 (top); Breck Kent 185 (bottom); © 2005 JUPITERIMAGES/ photos.com. All rights Reserved. 186 (left); © Roger Klocek/Visuals Unlimited 186 (right); © Gil Lopez-Espina/Visuals Unlimited 187 (top); © Reinhard Dirscherl/ Visuals Unlimited 187 (bottom left)

Chapter 8
© Karen Wattenmaker Photography 191; © 2005 Hemera Technologies, Inc. All Rights Reserved 192 (left); PhotoDisc/Getty Images 192 (right), 193 (left); Breck Kent 193 (right), 208, 209 (top); © Wally Eberhart/Visuals Unlimited 196; Unusual Films 201, 207; Jim Peaco 202 (top); Joyce Garland 202 (bottom); FEMA 203; Photo by Tim McCabe, USDA Natural Resources Conservation Service 204; USFWS 209 (bottom), 210 (left); © David Aubrey/SPL/ Photo Researchers, Inc. 210 (right); floridanature.org 210 (bottom)

Unit 5 Opener
© 2005 iStock International, Inc. All Rights Reserved 213

Chapter 9
Aaron Dickey 215; Unusual Films 218, 221, 224 (both), 233; courtesy of Howard Miller 222; © 2005 iStock International, Inc. All Rights Reserved 223, 225, 227; PhotoDisc/Getty Images 229 (top); © 2005 Hemera Technologies, Inc. All Rights Reserved 229 (bottom); COREL Corporation 230

Chapter 10
© 2005 iStock International, Inc. All Rights Reserved 235, 252, 253 (left), 255 (left), 257 (bottom right); US Navy photo by Petty Officer 1st Class Wes Eplen 241; Unusual Films 245, 251; PhotoDisc/Getty Images 247; © 2005 Hemera Technologies, Inc. All Rights Reserved 248 (both), 257 (top); © Ted Kinsman/Photo Researchers, Inc. 253 (right); © Jeff J. Daly/Visuals Unlimited 254 (left); © Edward Kinsman/ Photo Researchers, Inc. 254 (right); Bob Jones University Museum & Gallery 255 (inset, top right); © James King-Holmes/Photo Researchers, Inc. 256; Meade 257 (bottom left);

Unit 6 Opener
© 2005 JUPITERIMAGES/ photos.com. All Rights Reserved 259

Chapter 11
© 2005 iStock International, Inc. All Rights Reserved 261, 273, 276; Corbis 263; Unusual Films 265, 275; Stem Labs, Inc. 277; © Jack Ballard/Visuals Unlimited 278; © Arthur Glauberman/ Photo Researchers, Inc. 279

Chapter 12
PhotoDisc/Getty Images 281, 284 (top), 303; © 2005 iStock International, Inc. All Rights Reserved 284 (bottom), 285; Unusual Films 287, 299; © Dr. Dennis Kunkel/Visuals Unlimited 293